Unbroken

About the Author

Katarina Johnson-Thompson is an English athlete. A multi-eventer, she is primarily known as both a heptathlete and an indoor pentathlete. In the heptathlon, she is a double world champion and double Commonwealth Games champion. Representing Great Britain, Johnson-Thompson won the heptathlon gold medal at the 2019 World Championships, breaking the British record with a score of 6,981 points, which ranks her at No. 6 on the all-time lists. Her heptathlon results include finishing fourteenth at the 2012 London Olympics, fifth at the 2013 World Championships, sixth at the 2016 Rio Olympics and fifth at the 2017 World Championships. She won the gold medal in the heptathlon at the 2018 Commonwealth Games before claiming silver at the 2018 European Championships, and retained her title at the 2022 Commonwealth Games. She also holds the British indoor pentathlon record of 5,000 points and won gold in that event at the 2018 World Indoor Championships, as well as the 2015 and 2019 European Indoor Championships. Johnson-Thompson has also occasionally represented Great Britain in her two strongest individual disciplines: the high jump and long jump. In the long jump, she was the 2012 World Junior champion and the 2014 World Indoor silver medallist. She won a silver medal in the heptathlon at the Olympic Games in Paris in 2024.

Unbroken

My Journey from Despair to Glory

Katarina Johnson-Thompson

with Sarah Shephard

MACMILLAN

First published 2024 by Macmillan
an imprint of Pan Macmillan
The Smithson, 6 Briset Street, London EC1M 5NR
EU representative: Macmillan Publishers Ireland Ltd, 1st Floor,
The Liffey Trust Centre, 117–126 Sheriff Street Upper,
Dublin 1, D01 YC43
Associated companies throughout the world
www.panmacmillan.com

ISBN 978-1-0350-5517-3 HB
ISBN 978-1-0350-5518-0 TPB

Copyright © Katarina Johnson-Thompson 2024

The right of Katarina Johnson-Thompson to be identified as the author of this work has been asserted by her in accordance with the Copyright, Designs and Patents Act 1988.

The picture credits on pp. 385–6 constitute an extension of this copyright page.

All rights reserved. No part of this publication may be reproduced, stored in a retrieval system, or transmitted, in any form, or by any means (electronic, mechanical, photocopying, recording or otherwise) without the prior written permission of the publisher.

Pan Macmillan does not have any control over, or any responsibility for, any author or third-party websites referred to in or on this book.

1 3 5 7 9 8 6 4 2

A CIP catalogue record for this book is available from the British Library.

Typeset by Palimpsest Book Production Ltd, Falkirk, Stirlingshire
Printed and bound by CPI Group (UK) Ltd, Croydon, CR0 4YY

This book is sold subject to the condition that it shall not, by way of trade or otherwise, be lent, hired out, or otherwise circulated without the publisher's prior consent in any form of binding or cover other than that in which it is published and without a similar condition including this condition being imposed on the subsequent purchaser.

Visit **www.panmacmillan.com** to read more about all our books and to buy them. You will also find features, author interviews and news of any author events, and you can sign up for e-newsletters so that you're always first to hear about our new releases.

To anyone who has ever been hit by a Blue Shell.

Contents

Prologue	1
1 Passion	5
2 Identity	24
3 Body Image	40
4 Relationships I	57
5 Manifesting	77
6 Fame	94
7 Belief	116
8 Expectation	132
9 Imposter Syndrome	158
10 Change	180
11 Grief	201
12 Relationships II	215
13 Acceptance	242
14 Race	263
15 Resilience	276
16 Despair	305
17 Unbroken	332
18 Paris	352
Acknowledgements	383
Picture Credits	385

All about me:

I'm dogs above cats, coffee above tea. I prefer sunsets to sunrise. I love sport, breaking down the lyrics to songs, books and interior design. I prefer flats to heels; wearing black to colour; staying in to going out; (good) wine over spirits; texts to calls; movies to TV shows; eating out over eating in.

I'm salty, not sweet; introverted, not extroverted. Most of the time, I'm about relaxing, not adventuring. I prefer Kendrick to Drake and baths to showers. I love quoting from films, journalling and a long, relaxed meal out with family and friends. I'm jeans over dresses, biscuits over cake (sorry, Mum), hair down over hair up and millennial socks over Gen Z.

But that's all superficial. Those are all things that I've said in interviews over the years; things you can google and find out, if you really want to.

This book is the real me. It's my experiences, my triumphs and my turmoils. It's the me that no camera can ever see – the me inside my head and the reality behind the headlines . . .

Prologue

I KNEW SOMETHING BAD WAS ABOUT TO HAPPEN.

I only had one option: get into my blocks, wait for the gun and then explode out of them as powerfully as I could. No matter the consequences.

Seven months, three weeks and five days.

Seven months, three weeks and five days of pain, sacrifice and unyielding hard work. After everything I'd been through – fighting with my injury, with no time to dwell on frustration or doubt, spending countless hours with a team of incredible people entirely dedicated to helping me get fit enough to compete at the Olympic Games in Tokyo – there was no chance I was going to walk away. Zero.

'Go hard or go home' is the saying, and I was going hard. It was time for the fourth event of the heptathlon: the 200m.

On your marks.

Set.

Katarina Johnson-Thompson

BANG!

Eleven seconds later, I was lying on the track, gripping my right leg to try to stop the searing pain I could feel flooding through my entire body. But there was no way of stemming it. Not on that day in Tokyo, nor during the many dark months that lay ahead of me. The worst was yet to come.

Before 2021, I thought I knew what pain felt like. I thought I knew what it was like to suffer, to feel low, to experience hard times. As it turned out, I knew nothing. In the aftermath of the Tokyo Olympics, I discovered what it really felt like to be completely and utterly b r o k e n.

Those Games were supposed to be My Games; the Olympics every athlete dreams of, when your confidence is at its highest, matched only by your form and fitness. Nine months before it was due to start, I was crowned a world (outdoor) champion for the first time in my career, having beaten the reigning Olympic champion, Nafi Thiam, by 300 points in Doha. All I needed to do was ride that wave through the winter of 2019 and all the way to Tokyo the following summer.

It should have been simple. Hard work, no doubt . . . but simple.

But then came Covid, which put the whole world on pause and postponed the Tokyo Olympics for an entire year. It was a sliding-doors moment for me; one that would change everything. For some athletes – those coming back from injury or in the very early stages of their career – the delay had a positive impact, giving them an extra twelve months to become a better athlete. For others, like me, it was an unmitigated disaster.

In December 2020, just as my Olympic preparations were (re)starting at a training camp on the beautiful French-governed island of Réunion, I ruptured the Achilles tendon on my take-off leg. The Achilles is the tendon that allows you to move your foot and ankle; it transfers the force needed to help you run faster and jump higher. It's an essential part of the athletic puzzle, especially when you're an athlete whose spring is your superpower.

Eight months before the Olympic Games, I lost my superpower.

Worse than that, it had somehow become my kryptonite.

In my head, I had no choice other than to try to get back on form in time to be on the start line in Tokyo. No matter the Covid restrictions, no matter the condensed time frame for rehabilitation and rebuilding, no matter the sacrifice – if it was possible, which I was told it was, then I would do it.

And I did. But it took everything from me. Every ounce of resolve. Every drop of resilience. When you push yourself to the absolute limit, mentally and physically, over a prolonged period of time – seven months, three weeks and five days, in my case – there is always a price to be paid.

After the knockout blow came in Tokyo, my debts caught up with me. The wave I'd been riding as a newly crowned world champion had crashed into the rocks and sent me sinking into the depths of utter despair.

I'd given everything I had to make the start line in Tokyo and I felt like it had all been in vain. I felt that I'd failed not only myself but everyone in my team, who had worked so tirelessly to help me.

At that point, I stopped caring. I had no capacity left for trying. I was an empty shell. And I was done with the sport.

For a time, I hated it.

In the post-Tokyo haze, that was my mental state. I had no coach, no plan and no desire for either of those things. I didn't want to try any more. And for someone who'd spent a large part of their twenty-eight years on this planet devoting almost every waking moment to pushing herself to succeed, that was a scary place to be. If I wasn't Katarina the athlete, who even was I?

Everyone who watched me in Tokyo thought that my getting to the finish line of that 200m race was the hard part. They thought that me refusing the offer of a wheelchair to get off the track was brave, or showed some kind of great strength. In all honesty, that was the easy part.

What was hard was what came next.

How do you dig yourself out of the depths of despair? How do you put yourself back on track when you've fallen so far off it? How do you rekindle a passion for something you've come to hate?

In 2021, I didn't know any of the answers. I wasn't even asking the questions. My entire belief system – based on the idea that if you work hard, you will be rewarded – had been shattered.

It took me a long time, and a lot of work on myself, to figure it all out. I'm still learning. I'm still trying to figure out who I really am and what I need to truly thrive as a human and as an athlete. Along the way, I've learned so much. About success and failure. Acceptance. Honesty. How much I can handle. How to treat others. How to treat those closest to me.

I've learned about myself as an athlete and about myself as a person.

I've learned to be proud of my journey. Proud of the lows as well as the highs. Because they're all part of the same story. My story.

It's a story I've waited a long time to tell.

1
Passion

IT STARTED WITH A SIMPLE PHONE CALL.

'Hi, Kat . . .'

I knew the voice on the other end of the phone straight away. It was Lauren, a girl from school who I would battle with every year to be the fastest runner. She had been picked ahead of me for leg four of the relay in the Catholic School Games that year – a competition we got to take part in at the end of the summer term. I'd been so gutted about it. I loved running, and being the fastest girl in the class was something I wanted more than anything, especially in Year 6, my final year at St Mark's Primary.

The summer of 2004, Lauren and I went our separate ways, both set to join different senior schools. But she wasn't about to let her victory over me be forgotten. One day during the school holidays, she called my home landline to tell me one thing: 'I've joined the Harriers.'

Katarina Johnson-Thompson

That was it. End of conversation.

I was fuming. The Harriers was Liverpool Harriers, the athletics club next to Wavertree Park. We'd get the bus there for all our school competitions and I thought it was amazing. It was a proper track! On school competition days, the stands were full of kids from different schools around Liverpool, and there would be so much going on down on the track.

We'd always cross paths with the Harriers athletes too, who would arrive for their training sessions just as we were leaving the track. They were all so tall and impressive, dressed in proper athletics kit and carrying big bags of what I only assumed was more 'athletics stuff'.

I wanted to be just like them. I'd spend hours on the Harriers website, even during school computer lessons. The problem was, the home page used to blast out the *Chariots of Fire* theme tune, so if you didn't turn the volume down fast enough, the teacher would catch you skiving. I was fascinated by everything to do with the club.

I'd been asking my mum if I could join for ages, and now this girl had beaten me to it. She *was* one of them; she was a Harrier now and, to my mind, that basically made her a professional athlete.

I knew exactly what I had to do. I put the phone down and shouted across the living room: 'Mum, we're going to the Harriers!'

It's safe to say that a career as a professional athlete wasn't exactly what my mum, Tracey, had imagined for me.

I was still in nappies the first time she took me to a ballet class.

Dancing is Mum's passion. When she was in her teens, the

plan had been for her to go to secretarial college, but after she saw an advert for a theatre school, she knew that was what she wanted to do. Some parents might have said, 'No chance, you won't make a living out of that!' But my nan, Mary, just wanted her to be happy.

Mum spent thirteen years dancing professionally all over the world. She was nineteen years old when she first left home to become part of a world-famous group of classically trained dancers called the Bluebell Girls, travelling to South Korea and Taiwan, Italy, Scandinavia, Egypt and Japan. Later on, after she left the Bluebells to join another dance group, she lived in Puerto Rico for two years.

Then, in the summer of 1991, the chance came to move to the Bahamas and be part of a show that was popular with all the big cruise ships that stopped at the island.

Mum grew up in Liverpool, but deep down, she's an island person. She prefers nature, greenery and the calming sounds of the sea to the clamour and chaos of big cities. Bahamian life sounded perfect to her.

She hadn't been on the island for long when she met my dad, Ricardo Thompson. He'd helped to build the hotel where she was dancing, and then he got a job as a doorman when it opened. The two of them took the same bus to work along Cable Beach every night, and she discovered in him a kind soul with a passion for music that matched hers for dancing (when Mum was pregnant with me they decided that if I was a girl, Mum could name me and if I was a boy, then Dad could – and his dream was to name me after his favourite musician, Bob Marley).

On nights when Mum finished work too late to get the bus

home, Dad would give her a lift in the hotel's minibus. He was thoughtful like that, even turning up at her apartment with a huge Christmas tree and collection of poinsettia plants after she told him she was feeling homesick during her first Christmas in the Bahamas.

On their days off, he'd take her all around the island on the back of his motorbike, stopping at beautiful beaches and relaxed beachside bars.

It was a whirlwind romance, and when Mum fell pregnant with me, they were both still spinning.

She carried on dancing until she was six months pregnant, before flying home to Liverpool to have me at the beginning of January 1993. She was on her own in the delivery suite (aside from the midwife), with Dad not arriving from the Bahamas until the next day and my nan busy running the pub she and my grandad owned on the east side of Liverpool.

When people ask me where my strength comes from, I think the answer is pretty obvious.

At the end of the month my parents got married, and a few days later they flew back to the Bahamas with me in tow, leaving my nan in bits thinking she would never see her granddaughter again.

Shortly after they returned to the island, one of the dancers in Mum's show was fired and the dance captain asked if she would come back. She wasn't sure if she wanted to go back to dancing while I was so young and, even if she did, she doubted the costumes would fit.

'Just try them on,' said the captain.

To Mum's surprise, they fitted just fine (maybe not so surprising when you consider she'd been dancing, cycling and swimming for so much of her pregnancy). And the money on offer was too good to turn down, especially at a time when my parents were saving up to buy a house.

So Mum said yes. And by the end of March, not even three months after having me, she was back dancing in two shows a day while still trying to make sure I had everything I needed.

Every afternoon, she and my dad would get ready for work, make up three bottles of milk and drive me across the island to my grandmother's house (like my mum's mum, she was also called Mary – you can see why it's my middle name). Once Dad's shift on the door was finished, they'd speed back across the island to pick me up.

By then it would be around 2 a.m. and they'd come back to find me bathed and curled up in bed, with a bible placed carefully next to me (both of my grandmothers were very religious). Mum hated having to disturb me, especially when she knew that by 6 a.m. I'd be awake again.

They were long days (and nights), and Mum wasn't happy being away from me for so many hours. When she found out the show was finishing a few months after her return, she saw her opportunity to bring her dancing career to an end.

That's when the cracks in my parents' relationship started to show. Dad couldn't understand how Mum was able to walk away from such a good wage and felt the financial responsibility was all being put on him. And Mum didn't want to spend so much time away from her baby.

Sometimes their arguments would blow over quickly; other times Mum would grab my bottles and take me back to Liverpool, only to change her mind once she got there and book another flight back to the Bahamas. For me, getting on a plane became as familiar as getting on a bus. Before my first birthday, I'd crossed the Atlantic about five times.

Mum spent all her savings on flights before eventually saying enough was enough. In 1994, when I was around a year old, she took me back to Liverpool for good.

We hadn't been back for long when my grandma in the Bahamas became really ill. She had cancer and was told that she only had six months left to live. Mum knew how much she adored me and so we flew back to the island for the summer of 1994. Every day, she'd take me over to Grandma's and sit me on the bottom of her bed to try to bring some joy into her final days. We stayed until the end of the summer before coming back to Liverpool, where we lived with my nan and grandad above their pub.

One night the following January, Mum had a terrible night's sleep. I'd been writhing around my cot all night, sobbing as if I was in pain. Nothing she did would calm me down.

The very next day Dad rang to say that my grandma Mary had passed away.

Coming back to Liverpool wasn't easy for either of us. I had started to say a few words, but they came out with a Bahamian twang that my cousins loved to tease me about: 'Do you want some caaaaandy, Katarina?'

And Mum would often find herself standing in the pouring rain, with me in the pushchair, thinking, *What have I done?* The sun and sea of the Bahamas had been paradise by comparison.

But the reality is that she wasn't happy there. She wanted calm and peace of mind – not only for herself, but for me too.

When we talk about it today, sometimes she wonders how

things might have been different if she'd stayed in Nassau. How would it have impacted me? Would I still have had the same opportunities that I've had here? Would I be running races and entering Olympic Games on behalf of the Bahamian team?

I guess it's one of those sliding-doors moments that punctuate our lives. Do different paths always mean different destinations? I'm not sure. Either way, if we'd stayed in the Bahamas, I never would have had the chance to develop the same relationship with my mum's parents as I did.

When we came back to Liverpool, Mum returned to college to study 3D design and, later on, theatre costume design. For me, that meant spending my days in the college nursery, which I loved. Mum would come and get me after her morning classes, we'd have lunch together in the canteen, then she'd drop me back in for the afternoon.

But when her parents retired from running the pub, my nan Mary suggested putting me into the nursery at St Mark's school, near where they lived. That meant she could pick me up and look after me until Mum was finished at college. It was the start of a beloved routine that continued into my schooldays.

Nan was diabetic, but she always had bags of sweets in the car. And one of our favourite things to do after school was to go to McDonald's and get ice creams. For the first year of my life Mum had been so careful about what I ate, only feeding me things with no additives or preservatives. Now she was coming home to see me holding a fondant fancy in each hand – one strawberry and one chocolate. There was nothing she could say, though. Nan knew best . . .

We were really close. And we became even closer after we

moved into my nan's house when I was eleven years old. My grandad had been diagnosed with cancer and Mum was taking him to all his hospital and doctor appointments (I think he'd have ignored the situation completely if it wasn't for Mum). My nan's sister Lily also lived with them. She had Down's syndrome and, despite being a good fifty years older than me, was probably the closest thing I ever had to a sibling. We used to terrorize each other when I was growing up. If Mum ever asked Lily to mind me for an hour or so, it would end in either hysterical laughter or tears because we'd wind each other up so much.

By the time we actually moved into the house, though, Lily had been bedbound for around two years after a bad fall. Her health had deteriorated quite badly; she couldn't see, hear or eat solids, and she would have fits in the night. Mum was over there taking care of her so often that Nan suggested we just move in; I could have my own room, and Mum would share with Lily so that she could look after her in the night. It was also a financial help; the rent on our house (we'd moved into the one over the road from them a few years earlier) was not cheap.

My grandad passed away when I was fourteen, and Lily followed him about six months later. She'd reached sixty-five, which at the time was an incredible age for someone with Down's syndrome.

After that, it was just me, Mum and Nan, who was more like a second mum to me than a grandma.

When Mum got a job as a dresser at the Everyman Theatre, she sometimes had to work nights, so Nan would pick me up from school with my athletics kit, drive to the Sainsbury's car park where I'd get changed in the back of the car, and take me to training (she never actually came in to watch me train, though; she'd sit in the car and get on with her knitting instead).

Nan was incredibly proud of my athletics. She didn't understand much about the sport, but she loved coming to watch me compete, especially in the 800m. I think that started after she came to watch me at an indoor competition, where the track is only 200m (as opposed to 400m outdoors). I ran a really strong 800m race that day, and because of the shorter track I came very close to lapping someone. Nan never forgot it. She just thought it was the best thing ever.

She could be brutally honest, too. You know when people have bad days and most people try to make them feel better by saying, 'You'll do better next time'? She wasn't one of those people. I remember coming sixth in the European Juniors in 2011 and my mum and nan were sitting with some other friends in the crowd. I went over to them after the final event (the 800m) and nobody knew what to say to me. There was just silence. Until Nan piped up:

'Oh, it isn't as much fun when you don't win, is it?'

Everyone just burst out laughing. It was the perfect thing to say.

When I did win, she loved it more than anyone. In her living room, she had a glass cabinet that was filled with every single medal and trophy I'd ever won. Every time I got a new one, I knew it was going straight to Nan as soon as we got home so that she could add it to her collection.

Years later, when she was really ill with dementia and in hospital after a bad fall, she'd still be telling all the nurses:

Katarina Johnson-Thompson

'Do you know who my granddaughter is?' And when I'd go to see her, she'd be proudly showing me off to anyone and everyone who stopped to listen.

I was seven years old when the house opposite my nan and grandad's came up for rent and Mum decided that was the best option for us. My grandparents lived in Halewood, eight miles south-east of Liverpool. It wasn't far from where we'd been living in Netherley but the areas were quite different. When we were visiting my nan, I was always allowed to play out on the street with the other kids who lived there, but Mum wouldn't give me the same freedom at home. Netherley was more of a rough area and she was very cautious about letting me out alone.

I remember one occasion when I saw one of the local kids sitting on the wall overlooking our back garden. We got chatting and started to play together a bit. But then she came into the house and for some reason spat on the floor – to this day I have no idea why. I think that was the moment Mum realized that we needed to get out of Netherley. When I found out we were moving to a house right opposite my nan's, it was the best news of my life, mainly because most of my school friends lived closer to my nan. I was too young to realize it was a rough area.

My nan's is probably the first house I really remember, but I do have some very vivid memories of the Netherley house too. It's where we were living when my dad came over to visit about a year before we moved. We'd been back to the Bahamas to see him when I was about four years old, and we'd speak over the phone, but having him in Liverpool was something else.

Unbroken

I'll never forget the reaction of the other people in Netherley at seeing this Black man on the bus, and his response to it. They just stared at him and he did not give a shit. He just rolled with it and continued being 100 per cent authentically himself. The other thing I remember about his trip is the difference in how he and my mum parented. They had a pretty cool relationship overall, and would never say a bad word about each other, but when it came to raising me they had very different approaches. Maybe that's because Mum was with me – parenting me – all the time, whereas Dad only saw me every few years, and even then it was only for a few weeks at a time.

One evening when Dad was over, I ate about two bites of my dinner, put my fork down and said I wanted chocolate ice cream. Dad was having none of it: 'Absolutely not; finish your food first.'

In response he got a whole lot of sass: '*You* don't control me, *she* does,' I said, pointing at Mum.

It was a terrible attitude to have, I know, but I felt like the boss in that situation. Maybe I could sense there wasn't any flow of who was in charge. And it worked.

'She's skinny enough,' said Mum. 'Give her the ice cream – at least she's eating something.'

Me and Mum were super close. We still are – even now we speak on the phone every day, sometimes twice a day, and are always messaging each other in between. She was never really strict with me when I was a kid. I don't remember her shouting at me – ever. And I never feared her. But she had her rules and I stuck to them. One of those was that I always had to have a hobby – something outside of school that I could apply myself to. That's where the ballet came in.

Katarina Johnson-Thompson

From the moment I was born and the midwife told Mum I was a girl, she dreamed of two things: putting me in pretty dresses and getting me into dancing. Before I was old enough to protest, she was able to do both, but as I got older, that changed. I only ever wanted to wear tracksuits or football kit – a Liverpool kit, to be exact. I also demanded that my hair was tied back in two plaits so that it was out of my way when I was busy playing outside – my favourite thing to do.

I'd run around for hours with my friends and come home covered in dirt. When we played football, I was the one putting in slide tackles every chance I got. Even a game of hide and seek would end up with me burying myself deep in the bushes, determined to find the very best hiding spot.

But every Saturday morning, Mum would tie back my hair in a slick bun, lay out a leotard for me and drag me to a dance studio in town for ballet lessons. From the moment I could walk, it was a weekly occurrence; one that I disliked more and more as the years went on.

No one at school knew about the ballet. It was like a secret life. I hated the idea of anyone finding out, especially the boys at school who I spent most of my lunch breaks and playtimes with. They saw me as one of them and I knew that would change if they found out I was dressing up in a tutu and ballet shoes.

Every Saturday morning, I'd pull my hood up and sneak out of the house with Mum to get the bus to ballet – usually on the promise that if I did so, she'd take me to McDonald's afterwards. As soon as we got home, I'd run upstairs to change into my sports kit and get back outside playing football with my friends.

Unbroken

I did ballet to make Mum happy, and I could do it pretty well, but none of it felt natural. It felt forced.

I'd almost say I hated it.

I was around nine years old when I finally said: 'No more,' after my worst nightmare came true. I was midway through a ballet class when I saw the door open and two girls from my school walk in. They had come to join the dance school and were being shown around. We locked eyes and I froze to the spot. My face was suddenly burning hot. I wanted to sprint out of the door and never come back.

Somehow, I made it to the end of the class, but I knew I would never go back. My cover had been completely blown; I was someone else to them now. I cried my eyes out that day. All I could think about was going to school on Monday morning and everyone knowing my secret.

Mum and the dance teacher were both in tears about it. I was supposed to have auditions for the Royal Ballet School the following year and they had both been so excited about my future. The teacher even offered to give me private lessons – anything to keep me dancing.

But I was adamant: I was done.

Looking back, Mum always says she learned a lot of lessons from the time spent bribing me to go to ballet. Right from the start, she'd wanted me to have a hobby, but instead of giving me time to find my own, she'd forced *her* hobby onto me.

After that, I tried keyboard lessons for a year or so. Then it was football, which made sense because I loved playing it with my friends. But I don't think team sports are really my thing. I'm not sure I could live with the idea of letting other people down, and I like being in control of my own destiny (as much as you can be in elite sport, anyway).

In any case, from the moment I joined the Harriers, football quickly got forgotten.

My first visit to Liverpool Harriers (outside of school competitions) came a week or so after the phone call from Lauren. Mum and I boarded the number 78 bus for the half-hour journey to Wavertree from our home in Halewood (Mum didn't learn to drive until after I did) and walked for ten minutes through the park to get to the track. It was a journey we would repeat many, many times over the next six or seven years.

The first person to greet us was Stan Roberts, a grey-haired man with kind eyes who had been part of the club since 1951. Then in his mid-seventies, he was a Harriers legend. Whatever the weather, he would be there every day, helping young athletes at the beginning of their journeys, and doing it for nothing. He ended up being my first coach, and the one who introduced me to more than one event. He was brutally honest, caring and dedicated to his athletes and the sport. When I heard that he'd passed away in 2021 I was incredibly sad. Stan was a very special person who helped so many people at the early stages of their careers.

After greeting Mum and me on that first day, he pointed over to a group of kids who looked around my age and said, 'Go and stand by your mate . . .' I followed his gaze and saw that 'mate' was actually Lauren, my arch-enemy from school. Brilliant! I thought: now we'd get to see who really should have been picked for that relay spot.

Unlike on school competition days, the track was pretty quiet that day, with just a few groups there training. It was a much more chilled experience and I loved the feel of being surrounded by people working hard and just trying to get better. I know it ended up being the start of something special, but I don't remember that first session being anything life-changing. We did some warm-ups and some running drills and that was it; Mum and I were back on the bus home. But I already knew I'd be going back.

Within weeks, we discovered that there was a high jump training session that took place straight after my running session. And as much as I loved running, the high jump was *my* event.

I was introduced to it at my primary school, St Mark's, where I would spend every playtime running as far and as fast as I could. Sometimes I would race the sun by seeing if I could outrun the moving shadow of the clouds. Mum still has little drawings of mine from when I was five years old of grass and people running; next to them I've written: 'When it is playtime in school I run very fast on the grass with my friends.' Or my personal favourite: 'I like running in my special running shoes. I hope that I win a race on the school sports day.'

At the end of each school year, there was an athletics competition when kids in every class would be allocated an event to compete in. Because I was the tallest one in my class, I got thrown into the high jump. Right from the start, I was unbeatable. And every year, I'd get more and more excited as the end of term approached and I knew I'd get to do athletics again.

At the same Catholic School Games where I'd missed out on running the fourth leg in the relay to Lauren, I'd actually broken the Liverpool Catholic Schools' high jump record, which had stood since 1977. I cleared 1.32 metres that day, earning my first appearance in the *Liverpool Echo* newspaper.

Not bad for an eleven-year-old with no training.

I don't actually remember what happened to Lauren in the end, I just remember being so excited when I found out that I could do high jump every week at the Harriers, and that I wouldn't have to wait for my once-a-year outing to come around at the school sports day.

Soon I was at the Harriers training twice a week, on Tuesdays and Thursdays. A third day, Friday, then got added into the mix when another coach, Margy Jones, who still travels with my mum now to watch me compete, suggested I also join her long jump group. And that was the same day that Stan took a hurdles group, so I joined that one too.

It was all so fresh and new to me. I loved going to the track and trying out things every week, discovering what my body could do. There was no set structure to it, it was just about running as fast as you could and jumping as high and as far as possible. It was very authentic. Very fun. I'd finally discovered something that I really wanted to do, and that I was good at. And I just kept on adding more and more.

It was a journey of discovery for Mum, too. Athletics wasn't something she'd ever done or even watched much of, apart from my school sports competitions, so we were both following a steep learning curve. Her first lesson came pretty early on.

During my first winter of training she looked outside one afternoon and saw the trees in the garden bending sideways in the wind and the rain lashing down. I was still at school but we were supposed to be getting the bus to training straight after the final bell. Mum knew I would want to train whatever the weather. On training days, I always made sure she had my kit ready for pick-up before we left for school in the morning; it was the best part of my day.

Looking at the weather that day, Mum was sure training would be cancelled but she thought she'd call them to check, just in case.

'Cancelled?' said the person on the other end of the line, who we later discovered was the club secretary, Arwel Williams, or 'Taffy', as everyone knows him. 'What for?'

'Well, you know, the weather . . .' said Mum, hopefully.

Her question was answered by a loud burst of laughter.

'Oh no,' said the voice on the phone, when he eventually stopped laughing. 'We're always here; wind, rain or snow, we'll be open.'

Mum was thrilled.

On days when it rained, she'd give me a piggyback over the puddles on the walk from the bus stop to the track, making sure I wasn't starting my session with wet feet, even if I'd be ending it with them. And in the depths of winter, when it was pitch black by 4 p.m., we'd walk the long way around the edge of the park instead of taking the shortcut through the middle, which was badly lit and a popular hangout for local gangs.

Mum became a familiar sight to everyone at the Harriers, wrapped in a shawl (still looking glam, as she always does) for as many of my training sessions as she could get to, and present for every competition. She grew to love it just like I did, keeping detailed notes from every time I competed and following the sport more closely than some athletes. To this day, she's only ever missed one or two comps, when my nan was really ill.

No one would ever guess that when I was born she'd had

quite a different dream for what I might become. Ballet never felt like it fit, though. Or maybe it was me who didn't fit ballet. I always felt like I was being squeezed and shaped into something, or somebody, different.

With athletics, I could just be me. Everything came naturally. It made sense to me. I was always running everywhere and, even with the high jump, I found it so easy to run and jump over the bar – although Mum is convinced that the ballistics I learned from ballet helped with that.

Athletics is something that has been in me right from the very start. As a five-year-old, all I wanted to do was move my body as fast as I possibly could, and I don't feel like that has ever really changed. There's nothing else that gives me the same feeling. Nothing else that makes everything around me fade away, so that all I'm aware of is my own body and how it's moving.

Of the speed and power it can produce.

Of the way that it responds whenever I ask it for more.

Of the way it arches itself neatly over a high jump bar as it's positioned higher and higher, and higher again.

Of the way it hangs in the air over a long jump pit as I stretch my legs out as far as they will go.

Of the way it refuses to give in to exhaustion even when pushed to its very limits.

And what else can match the feeling of electricity that surges through your entire body when you reach a new height or distance, or cross the finish line faster than ever before?

There's nothing else. Nothing at all.

Ballet might equate to beauty in some people's eyes, but in mine it will always be athletics. Because it's passion that leads to beauty, not the other way around.

Unbroken

Every session I did at the Harriers felt like a chance for me to get even better. To experience those feelings even more.

And with each passing week, I felt a growing certainty that this was My Thing. I'd finally found My Thing.

I was never friends with that girl from school but, as it turns out, I owe her a lot.

2
Identity

'Stop squeezing, Katarina, you're making it worse,' whispered Mum, pulling my hand away from the giant boil on my face.

It was August 2006, and we were on a half-empty National Express coach travelling from Liverpool to Stoke for a competition I'd been looking forward to for weeks: my first ever pentathlon. It was a two-and-a-half-hour journey and I was passing the time with my head bent over my knees trying to squeeze the life out of this monstrosity I'd woken up with. Not only that, but I was also having one of my first ever periods.

It was a lot for a thirteen-year-old to be dealing with.

We'd been up since the crack of dawn too, leaving the house at around 5.30 a.m. to get a bus from Halewood, where we were living, into Liverpool city centre in time for the 6.30 a.m. coach. Once we were in Stoke, we had to get another bus from the bus station to the track. Looking back, it was quite the ordeal. But at the time, that was our normality. I'd been competing for about a year when the Stoke comp came around, mostly in high jump and long jump and, given that Mum didn't drive, we did all of our travelling on buses, trains and National Express coaches.

It always felt like an adventure; a really cool thing that me and Mum got to do together. Just the two of us, against all the odds. I loved Birmingham comps the most because usually I'd be competing in two events – high jump and long jump – so Mum would splash out on an overnight stay in a hotel. We didn't have much money then, so it was a special treat. I still love a hotel breakfast now, but back then it was the best thing ever.

There was nothing quite so glamorous about Stoke, though.

It was pouring with rain when we arrived; the type of rain you just know is set to last for the entire day. But I didn't really care; I just wanted to get to the track and get started.

Up to then, whenever I'd competed in Northern Premier or Liverpool Harriers competitions, they would have me starting the high jump, running over mid-event to do the hurdles, going back to the high jump, doing the long jump, doing the relay . . . it was the scattiest thing ever. I was a kid who loved the sport and who wanted to do each event, but the chaos of it all used to drain the life out of me. It was exhausting. And because of that, I wasn't doing as well as I could in each individual event.

The turning point came when I found out that a girl called Sophie in my training group had secretly entered a different competition to me one weekend. While I'd spent mine being pulled in multiple directions, she'd spent hers doing most of the same events, but for one single outcome. One aim.

Katarina Johnson-Thompson

A pentathlon. It made perfect sense.

For some reason, Sophie hadn't mentioned her pentathlon plans to anyone else in the group. We were all friends, and my mum and hers were always chatting, but there'd been no mention of her doing a pentathlon.

Now it was in my head, it was all I wanted to do. It was a chance to bring everything together and see what I could really achieve.

When the opportunity came to do one in Stoke, I grabbed it.

This time, I'd be competing on a level footing with everyone else. There'd be no advantage given to someone in the high jump because I was too busy doing hurdles or anything like that.

In Stoke, that was the focus for me. More than it being about 'I've found my event', it was, 'let's see what I can do'.

It was exciting, if a little nerve wracking. I'd never thrown a shot put before. Nor had I run 800m – I never even used to do two laps of the track as a warm-up. Now I was going to do both those things for the first time, in an actual competition.

As expected, the rain stuck around for the entire day. We couldn't afford that much athletic kit at the time, but Mum had brought one change of clothes for me, so after the high jump I went into the changing room to wring out my soaking wet kit and hang it up to dry while I changed into the dry set. Later on in the competition, I swapped more dripping wet kit for a set that was still damp from the morning.

My lasting memories of my first pentathlon are the shot put (I threw 7.80m; really embarrassing) and the 800m, where I had to beat a girl called Hannah Dickson to get on the podium. She was the girl to beat in that pentathlon, but she wasn't great at the 800m – none of us were.

Unbroken

I remember running as hard as I could, and every 10m or so I'd turn around to see where she was.

Somehow, I came away from that day with a first-place finish in the Northern category and sixth overall (they ran the regional and national championships together). I was absolutely buzzing. I'd finally been able to put all my events together in a sequence and I'd loved it so much.

With the medal around my neck and two lots of soggy kit in my bag, Mum and I watched everyone else get into their cars and drive off while we waited for a taxi back to the bus station to start the long journey home. It was a brutal day.

But I was so happy to be doing it. And most importantly, I felt like a proper Harriers athlete, with my bag full of athletics stuff!

From Year 6 until my late twenties, I was an athlete more than I was a person. It's a perilous imbalance. Why? Because any time I lost, or performed poorly, I became a *bad* athlete. It would become my new identity: an athlete who fails.

For me, not winning in athletics wasn't just a sporting failure, it was a personal one. It's something I struggled with for a long time. But it wasn't until much later in my career that I started to ask why.

In the beginning, I had no need to question things, because it all came pretty easily.

After the competition in Stoke, I knew that I'd found my event. Up until then, I'd been doing really well at the high jump, getting age group bests and the like, and everyone had assumed that was going to be my way forward. But after Stoke I was pretty sure that multi-events were my actual thing.

Katarina Johnson-Thompson

That feeling only strengthened the following year, 2007, when I went unbeaten in all five of the pentathlons I entered and was top of the under-15 national rankings in the event. I was also still winning individual high jump and long jump competitions (and was top of the national rankings in those events as well). That year, I jumped 1.80m for the first time, which was higher than anyone else in the country competing at the under-17 level. In total, I won eight national titles that year.

The last pentathlon I entered in 2007 came at the English Schools Combined Events Championships in Exeter, where I scored 3,626 points. It was the most points scored by a girl in my age group in nineteen years, breaking a record set by Katharine Merry (who had gone on to win bronze in the 400m at the 2000 Olympics) almost twenty years prior. I set three new PBs that day, including one in the shot put where I threw 10.19m – a bit less embarrassing than my first ever throw in Stoke.

Looking back, I think that was the moment I knew for sure: I was definitely better at pentathlon than I was at high jump. And all that success just reinstated my belief: this is what I do. This is My Thing. This is what I'm good at.

Daley Thompson (the two-time Olympic decathlon champion, who I later used to lie about and pretend was my dad) was at the competition in Exeter that day and told the local reporters: 'Katarina should be delighted with the gold medal, but this should be seen as only the start . . . most of the successful athletes in this country, myself included, made our name in these events. They really give you a taste of what it feels like to win gold.'

Unbroken

We had a picture taken together, which my mum still has in her collection, alongside the newspaper report. I was on such a high, winning medals, being in the papers and having stars of the sport talking about me.

I felt invincible.

It came as something of a surprise, then, when I was beaten.

It happened in the summer of 2008 – a year that started with me winning the Merseyside Young Sports Personality of the Year at a big ceremony in the ECHO Arena, earning my first ever GB vest for a combined-events match in Paris in March, and being awarded Lottery funding. That funding was a huge deal for me: £750 every three months! I felt like a millionaire.

Then came the summer, and a long journey from Liverpool down to Ashford in Kent. By that point, I'd started training under a woman called Val Rutter. I'll always think of Stan as the first coach I worked with, but he'd never really coach me at competitions; instead, he would watch and then, after I'd finished, he'd tell me what I should or shouldn't have done. If things were going wrong, I'd usually look over at my mum and she'd offer what she could: 'Have you had your sports drink?' she'd shout. Or: 'Have a Haribo, it'll give you energy!'

But by 2008 I was having proper, structured coaching with Val. She's a former high jumper who held the Harriers' high jump record of 1.83m for thirty-seven years until I broke it in 2011. She was only 5ft 5in when she was competing, so Val's PB is equivalent to jumping six inches above her own head, which is mad. I improved a lot under Val, especially in my high jump and running. She's the one who first started really organizing my training for competitions and took me under her wing at a time when I really needed it.

Katarina Johnson-Thompson

We got a lift for the long drive to Ashford from Val's husband Rodger Harkins, who was also a coach, specializing in the 400m (he worked with Commonwealth silver medallist Lee McConnell). We travelled down the night before and stayed with the team for what was going to be my second international after Paris. This one was a Combined Events International and, even though I was only fifteen, I was competing in the under-twenty category, which meant I was potentially going up against athletes who were five or even six years my senior.

On the day, I came third, and set a new PB of 5,343 points for the heptathlon.

Was I pleased?

No. I was livid. Absolutely livid. Not so much at coming third, but at getting beaten.

I didn't understand it. How were these people better than me? What had they done to be better than me? I didn't care that it was one of the first times I'd taken on the 100m hurdles (in younger age groups, the hurdles were over 60m or 80m), or that I was one of the youngest there.

I'd always felt that succeeding in athletics was simple; if I tried harder, I would win. But I was trying my hardest that day, and people were just better than me. It didn't make any sense.

More than anything else, I hated the feeling that the result wasn't within my control.

I still remember the girl who won it: Léa Sprunger. A few years later she moved on from the heptathlon to focus on the 400m and 400m hurdles, but even so, every time I saw her I felt the pain of that loss all over again. It was my first big defeat, and I took it really badly. In public I tried to put on a brave face, but in private the tears flowed. I don't think I spoke to my mum, Val or Rodger the entire way home.

Mum endured a lot of journeys like that. A few years earlier, when I was thirteen, we had travelled by coach to a competition in Birmingham. It was my first national championships in high jump and I was competing against girls much older than me. One was already competing at international level. I missed out on the bronze medal by one jump and was absolutely furious with myself. I didn't speak to Mum the whole journey home; not a single word. I just sat there in silence while she tried to tell me how well I'd done.

For so much of my life, I'd be so hard on myself when I didn't win, and I don't really know where that came from. Some parents go wild on the sidelines, shouting non-stop, and that can be really overbearing. I saw a lot of that at the track, but my mum was never one of them. She was quite timid by comparison and just wanted me to be happy, so that edge of always needing to win didn't come from anything that *she* said or did.

I had no pressure from anywhere else to be excellent; I put it all on myself.

If someone beat me, I'd be overcome by shame and hide myself away until that feeling had passed. In my teenage years, I would deactivate my Facebook after a loss or bad performance; cut myself off from the outside world in as many ways as possible. I would sink deep within myself and no one – not even Mum – could bring me back up until I decided I was ready.

Why did I react that way? Maybe it's just because I'm competitive.

Katarina Johnson-Thompson

I can be the most chill person ever about things I'm not into, like playing cards. But if I care about something, I can get so fierce I get dizzy and my skin actually feels like it's burning. Mario Kart can get that out of me. I am obsessed with it. My boyfriend and I can spend hours playing it (to be a little more specific, we've racked up between 700–900 hours), although we had to stop doing the time trials because the level of competitiveness that brought out in us genuinely started to turn a bit toxic. We've never been close to splitting up over it, but if we were ever particularly annoyed at each other and one of us left the house for a bit, the other person would purposefully break all the time trial records. It turned from a shared fun experience, taking turns and pushing the boundaries of the game, to going behind one another's backs to one-up each other. So we don't do that any more.

Looking back, though, I think it's more likely I would react negatively to losses because of the label I had put on myself from a very young age. Athletics was my whole life. In primary school, that was what everyone was impressed with; it was the only thing that ever got me attention. The teachers were made up because I was winning all their competitions. The kids all wanted to race me and were really impressed that I was beating other schools. That followed me into senior school as well, where I knew that if people were going to describe me as anything it would be as *the athlete of the school*. More than anything else, that was my identity.

I clung on to that label so fiercely from such a young age, and I think that's because of the constant feeling that I'm on the verge of – or in the middle of – two different things.

I'm British and Bahamian. I've got a white mum and a Black

dad. When I'm filling out forms, there's no dropdown box for me: it's 'White/Black/Mixed/Caribbean/Other'.

I've definitely ticked the 'Other' box a few times.

It all ties into how I've spent a lot of my life feeling. I've had conversations with other people who are mixed-race, but because most of them have siblings, they always had a person to live through that experience with. In my family, I was the only person like that, because I was an only child in my mum and dad's relationship and the rest were either one or the other: white or Black.

I never had a shared experience, and growing up I was never exposed to books or TV programmes that resonated with my experience; nothing I could point to and say: 'Yes, that's how I've been feeling, too.'

One of the first times I saw a Black community in Liverpool was when Mum found me a Black hairdresser in an area of the city called Toxteth, a really ethnically diverse part of inner-city Liverpool. After our first trip to that hairdresser, I remember telling Mum that I felt really comfortable there, and her being a little bit taken aback by that.

I think she understood why, but I definitely didn't at that point. I didn't really think about it at all until much more recently.

When I moved to France in 2016, I was based in Montpellier, where there's a huge Black population, especially in the city centre. Just being there, I noticed that I was finding that other side of me – allowing myself to find it. It was one of the first times I started going out with my hair just in Afro; being and feeling completely free.

I think every mixed-race or Black woman has had a hair journey, especially if you grew up in the nineties like I did, when everyone wanted the relaxer which made your hair pin-straight. I had lovely, thick, curly hair, but I remember begging my mum, crying, please, please can I get this thing done, which chemically burns and frazzles your hair to make it straight and white, basically.

My mum had grown up with seriously thick, curly hair too, so in many ways she understood, and when I was around nine years old, she finally let me have it done. It totally ruined my hair. After that it slowly started to break off. It got shorter and shorter the more I fought to maintain the straightness – using hair straighteners every day and relaxing the roots every couple of months, fighting against my actual roots. It created a natural Afro bouffant at the top, which was a very particular style a lot of people will remember from my teens. It took a long time, and more than one trip to the Black hairdressers in Toxteth, to put it right.

At my primary school, there were only two of us who weren't white, and my hair was always quite the attraction for the other kids. They'd never seen Black hair before and when they touched it (which they did, regularly) it was a new texture for them.

As I got older and started to get picked by brands for adverts and photo shoots, my hair was still an issue. Even though I can now recognize and appreciate the beauty of my natural hair, for so many years I would play along with designers and photographers, who always wanted straight hair.

At one of my first shoots, I was being photographed alongside another athlete who had long, straight, blonde hair. We both sat down for hair and make-up at the same time and the stylist went over to her first. As he ran his fingers through her hair he smiled and said, 'We don't really need to do anything to your hair, we'll just leave it to fall how it is.'

Meanwhile, I was sitting in a chair with someone on either

side of me, pulling and yanking on my hair as they desperately tried to convince the curls to straighten out. It took them two hours to get it slicked back the way they wanted it and I was dying with embarrassment the whole time. I vowed to do my own hair before every photo shoot from then on – I was determined never to be that much of an inconvenience ever again.

I totally beat myself up about it.

After that, I would pay my own money to sew straight hair into my scalp before shoots. I knew they wouldn't have anyone who was used to styling Black hair and I would compensate for their mistake myself. I also wanted to blend in with what I saw in the media. I didn't really see any Afros; I didn't see any Black women with my style of hair getting used.

It was only really recently that I decided: I'm going to turn up to photo shoots with my own hair and they're just going to have to deal with it.

That feeling of not fitting neatly into a certain box goes beyond race. It probably started when I was that young kid playing with the boys on the street outside my nan's house. For a long time I never felt any different from them; I didn't even think about the fact I was a girl and they weren't.

But then things started changing. The boys would have sleepovers and I wouldn't be allowed to go because I was a girl. It threw me for a while. Eventually I had to accept that I was different from them. Not special-different, but certainly the odd one out in my little friendship group.

When I started secondary school at St Julie's Catholic High School, I felt like the odd one out again. At primary school I hadn't been interacting with many girls at all, and then suddenly

Katarina Johnson-Thompson

I was at an all-girls' school, surrounded by people who were seriously into make-up and clothes. It was scary. That's when I started to change a little bit. I started to think more about hairstyles and my appearance. I tried to blend in with the norm.

I've even felt caught in the middle of things within my sport because I'm a multi-eventer. When you go into a team setting, like with Team GB, you see the sprinters gathered together in one spot, the throwers in another and the jumpers in another. And I could go to any of them. Some people might see that as *more* inclusive, not less, but for me belonging everywhere has often felt like I actually belong nowhere.

Throughout my life, I've always carried a feeling of being the only one like me in certain places. And it wasn't really until my late twenties that I started to come into my own and feel confident enough to not care as much. But during those years of going from being a young child to a young athlete and a young woman? I always felt alone, like I was trying to find my place.

I started therapy in 2022. It has really helped me to understand my feeling of otherness and how it has shaped my personality, the things I do and say, and how I react to certain situations. Part of that has been exploring my need to please, to avoid conflict like the plague, and to be terrified of upsetting anyone. Now, I can see that I was trying to control other people's perceptions of me – that I was scared in case they thought of me in a particular way. So, I learned to overcompensate, and to go above and beyond what was necessary or made sense, just to show other people how 'good' and 'nice' a person I was.

For example, someone once told me that the first time they met me, I pretended to be on my phone just to get out of talking to them at a competition. And when I think back to that weekend, I remember being really stressed. I thought I'd pulled my hamstring in the hurdles and I didn't really want to speak to anyone. At the time, I could have just explained that to this person and said, 'Oh yeah, that was probably the case. I was pretending not to talk because I didn't want to that day.' Instead, I kept them there for ten minutes explaining everything that had led up to that moment.

Now I know I didn't need to do all of that. I could have been fine with: 'Yeah, I was having a bad day, I'm sorry about that. Hopefully we'll get a chance to talk in the next couple of days.' But instead, I tried to control the situation. Now I recognize that it's OK if someone's opinion of me isn't the best; it doesn't really matter. Since I've started to apply that to everything I do, even athletics, I feel a lot calmer because I'm not trying to control the stuff that's outside of my control all the time.

'Control the controllables' is a phrase I'd heard many times in my life before therapy, but it didn't make sense to me then because I could only apply it to my training, and not to my personality. I have spoken to a lot of sports psychologists over the years and done a lot of good work with them. But the work I've done in therapy has been completely different.

Maybe that's because it hasn't been done with a sporting professional who's trying to give me the tools I need to compete, but with a psychotherapist who's helping me to understand why I react the way I do to any situation and whether that's something I need to change. Sometimes, I feel like sports psychologists give you a little bandage so that you can go out and compete. But then you're on autopilot mode and it all feels a bit performative. It's not sustainable, either.

You might finish competing and feel like it was really good, yet deep down you still have the same problem. Bandages only work a certain number of times before you need to be rescued and put on the right track, and the whole cycle starts again. It's a pattern.

Sometimes you have to go deeper. Sometimes you need to break the pattern.

But going that deep can be a risky game, because if you get to that deeper level within your consciousness and ask yourself why you put yourself through so much pain so often, sometimes there's no answer – you realize that you don't have to. You could easily convince yourself that your vocation, your passion, your *sport* isn't for you, and you could end up walking away from it entirely, simply to save yourself the pain. Luckily, I've found that when I ask myself that question, the answer for me has always been a different one.

Through therapy, I've figured out a lot of different things about myself, and as a result the way that I perceive myself as a person and as an athlete has completely changed. I've learned to value myself and my own opinions. I can still listen to those of others, but I now have the ability to separate them from my own thoughts instead of always accepting them as 'truth'.

I've learned to appreciate the woman I am outside of being 'KJT, the athlete' and to understand that I am worthy of people's love, affection and respect no matter what happens on the track. I've learned to value what makes me different instead of trying to erase or blur it. To not apologize for it, or take on any responsibility for how others might respond to it. Because that's on them, not me. I've learned to be more like my dad on that bus in Netherley. 100 per cent, authentically myself.

Unbroken

The work isn't over; I still speak to my therapist every week, and there are still some things I know I need to work on.

But every so often I think back to the young girl and athlete I used to be – the one who was scared to stand out, embarrassed by her difference, desperate to blend in – and I can see just how far I've come.

3
Body Image

EACH NIGHT BEFORE A COMPETITION FOLLOWED THE SAME PATTERN.

I would wait until everyone else was in bed, put on my competition kit, and run downstairs to the living room where the biggest mirror in the house was hanging on a wall above the fireplace. Then I'd climb onto the couch and stare at myself in the mirror opposite. A few years earlier, in 2004, we'd moved into my nan and grandad's house, and they didn't have any full-length mirrors, so standing on the couch was the only way I could see how I looked in my kit.

I never saw what I wanted.

I'd pinch the flesh on my inner thighs, pushing it back to create a 'thigh gap'. Then I'd move my legs and be disgusted by the jiggle that was created. All the while, my brain ran wild with negative thoughts: *Look how fat you are. All the others are thinner than you. You can't go out and compete looking like this.*

Unbroken

Then I'd sink down into the cushions on the couch and cry.

It became a ritual. I couldn't help myself; I had to do it. I knew I'd get upset over it but I'd do it anyway just to see whether this time might be different. Whether this time I might like what I saw reflected in the mirror. Then I'd stare at my legs and think, *They don't look like other people's legs.*

Sometimes Mum came downstairs and found me. 'Katarina, get off the couch, you look fine,' she'd say.

But I never believed her. I'd tell her that there was no way I was competing the next day. 'You can't make me. I don't want to go out there looking like this.'

The funny thing is, I never carried that attitude through to competitions; it stopped there. I think just saying it out loud to my mum was like a release. And once those thoughts were out of my head, I felt lighter. Calmer. I would be able to go to bed and not think about it any more. The next morning I'd get up and compete as though nothing had ever happened. It's almost as if, subconsciously, I knew I had to get those thoughts out of my system, because if I didn't, they might come out on the day and ruin my performance.

I was in my early teens at this point and, like many other girls growing up in the Size Zero era, was convinced that I was fat. I was never fat. But when you're around different age groups of girls – some who have been through puberty, some who haven't, some who are professional athletes, some who are naturally skinny, some who run all the time – you're surrounded by a lot of different body shapes and sizes.

At the same time, when you're a young athlete you're very aware that your body is getting looked at, whether that's by spectators, boys you fancy at the track, or coaches who think that maybe if you lost a bit of weight you might perform better. You're intensely aware that your body is the thing that is driving your performance, but at the same time you're becoming increasingly aware that your body is something that's attractive to people, even if you don't fully understand that yet.

It's a lot to process.

The relationship between female athletes and their bodies is often a complex one.

Society puts so much pressure on women to be smaller and smaller. To not take up too much space. To find our 'beach body' or 'bounce back' after having a baby. All of that is about fitting into an accepted narrative of what size and shape is valued as attractive or worthy.

And that's just for women in general. For sportswomen, there's a whole extra layer of stress. By virtue of our professions, our bodies have to be on display all the time, regardless of how we're feeling on any given day, whether we want to be put under an unrealistic microscope, commented on and scrutinized by coaches, fans and the media. There's a certain 'ideal' for what a female athlete should look like, regardless of whether it actually makes sense for the sport she competes in. How much muscle should she have? How much body fat should she carry? And if we don't meet that ideal, our bodies become the headline, above and beyond the incredible feats we achieve with them. The fear of that happening can have damaging consequences, both mentally and physically.

The teenage body issues I dealt with from 2008 onwards were hard for me, but they were equally tough for Mum. As a young dancer, she'd been through her own struggles over food and dieting, which led her to a lifelong sensitivity around body image; you'll never hear her passing comment on the way someone looks or their weight, not even casually. She's painfully aware of the danger of saying the wrong thing. So when I started going through similar struggles, she was desperate to help me through it, but she didn't know how.

I cringe so hard when I think about it now, but when I was fifteen years old we came across a local guy named Phil, who ran a business out of his garage selling milkshakes which were supposed to help you lose weight. He called it 'Philtastic'. Mum agreed to take me to see him and he stood me on the scales to see where I was at. I saw the number and burst into tears. I was the heaviest I'd ever been. 'It's OK,' said Phil, 'we're going to help you.'

I begged Mum to let me try the milkshakes and we left armed with a small supply. I don't blame her at all because, back then, we didn't really have any information – I didn't have a nutritionist or any guidance with regards to diet. We were just doing what we thought was best. For the next few months, I'd have a milkshake for breakfast, then a proper lunch ahead of my training session after school. Once I got home from the track, I'd have another milkshake or a 'nutrition bar' for dinner. I'd seen all the adverts on TV saying you could lose weight by eating two bowls of cereal a day, which sounded so easy that it was tempting, but using Phil's products seemed like a way to do it while still getting some fuel in.

I followed that diet for months. Then I started getting niggly injuries that I couldn't explain, like shin splints and little stress fractures. Eventually, I think it was Val who told me to come off it but, almost as a replacement, she said we would dial up the running instead. So before training we'd head off for a ten-minute run around Wavertree Park, just to make sure we burned through a few more calories. Thinking back, it might have just been a way to appease me or make me feel better, but in my head, it was simply confirmation that, yes, I was fat and I did need to lose weight.

I look back on that period as the first phase in my body image journey, and it was one that I actually returned to later on in my career. But before that happened, I became obsessed with a different aspect of my body: muscle. I was around sixteen or seventeen at the time and I had started lifting weights in the gym alongside my training sessions on the track. I knew I was strong. I knew I had muscles – probably more than most boys my age. And I started to think that maybe that was a bit intimidating. That maybe I was too 'masculine' to be fancied by boys.

The women I saw in magazines and on TV who were celebrated as being attractive didn't look like me. They didn't have visible biceps or calf muscles that popped out above their ankles. And their thighs looked tiny in comparison to mine. At the time, I had no idea that airbrushing was a standard thing in the media. I just accepted the idea that being smaller – taking up less space – was something to aspire to. But I was six feet tall and I had muscles, and I was living in an era in Liverpool when indie music was king and skinny boys in the skinniest of jeans were leading that movement, while I was starting to gain recognition as an athlete, with people talking about national championships, where I knew I'd be in the public eye – and, against that backdrop, I felt enormous.

My school, St Julie's, was girls-only until the sixth form, after which it became mixed. That's when appearance and fitting in suddenly felt more important than ever. I remember being in a class one day and one of the boys said, 'Your calves look hectic,' which means, 'Your calves look massive.' I was mortified. His words stuck in my head, and from then on I became super aware of everything I wore, making sure my calves were always hidden from view. Skirts were out of the question for a long time.

It wasn't only comments from boys or deliberately negative takes on how I looked that left their mark; even something meant as a compliment could have me fretting for weeks afterwards. During that same period, I was at a hairdresser with my mum when the woman doing my hair said something about the muscles in my legs and how powerful they looked. She was praising them. But as soon as the words came out of her mouth Mum saw my face drop.

You know when you get hot with a comment? That was me. I was burning. From that moment on I was either silent or monosyllabic when the hairdresser tried to chat. I wasn't deliberately being rude, I was just lost in my own head; drowning in a pool of self-loathing. The hairdresser wasn't even *trying* to make me feel the way I did. She was genuinely paying me a compliment. But no one could convince me. Not even Serena Williams could have sat me down and made me believe that looking strong was a good thing. I was a teenager, desperately trying to blend in and be like everyone else. Standing out from the crowd was terrifying.

The muscles that were helping me to succeed on the track were stopping me from fitting in away from it. But what could I do? I couldn't lose muscle, because then my performance would deteriorate. It was like what I'd gone through when I'd struggled with thinking I was fat, and knew that if I didn't eat, then I couldn't train properly, only this time it was more focused on the work I was doing in the gym: if I didn't lift weights and get stronger, I'd fall behind all the other girls who were. I was caught between the desire to do one thing and look a certain way and knowing that doing so would negatively affect the thing I most loved doing.

Looking back, it could easily have led to me stopping athletics entirely; not because I didn't love it, but because everything else in my life didn't love it – it just didn't fit into what I was experiencing. I can't say why I didn't, exactly – I guess I'm just grateful for the person I was raised to be, because I was strong-minded enough to resist a force that drags so many teenage girls away from sport.

It probably helped that I was doing so well on the track. At nineteen years old, I qualified for my first Olympic Games, and it was at London 2012 that I first saw the kind of career I could have from athletics. If I hadn't been experiencing that sort of success, I might have thought: *Why do I look like this if it's not benefitting me in any way?* Astoundingly, in the UK, 65 per cent of young girls drop out of sport entirely by the time they finish puberty – double the rate of young boys. It's scary sometimes to think that, if it wasn't for the level of my performances, I could have easily been one of them. If things hadn't been going well, or I'd gotten injured, it could have tipped me over the edge. Basically, I just didn't want to look like I did at the time.

Competing at the Olympics kept me in the sport, but it also left me comparing myself to the elite athletes I was lining up against, and that sent me back to a place I was so familiar with when it came to judging my own body: feeling fat. After 2012 I was no longer worried about the muscles popping out of my shoulders or legs, because I was more concerned with how I looked standing alongside athletes who I saw as being so much leaner than me.

Athletes at the Olympics are in the shape of their lives. In 2012 I was nineteen years old with chubby cheeks. I was still growing into my adult body and I could see I was different from the athletes around me, but I didn't know how to change it. That was terrifying for me because the stakes were suddenly so much higher. I wasn't competing in front of a small crowd on a club night at the Harriers any more. I was basically standing in a bra and knickers for the entire world to see. Exposure therapy? Completed it!

One thing that definitely didn't help was the kit. Those Olympic kits are basically sprayed on. I always have to take two sizes up, which automatically puts you in a bad headspace at a time when you're meant to feel at your very best. It's something I've voiced to the brand now, as an adult – that the fit of this kit needs to change – but when you're a young athlete it can really mess with your head.

The feeling that I was too fat to be an elite athlete spilled over into 2013. In my first competition after signing for Nike, which was a huge deal for me, I was competing at the British Grand Prix in Birmingham and racing in the women's hurdles, which meant I was going up against professional sprint hurdlers. The night before that race I was so stressed about how I would look lining up next to these elite athletes. It was almost back to the days of standing on my nan's couch and crying at the sight of myself in the mirror. It's mad really – I was more scared of my own body than of how I would actually perform against these experienced sprinters. It's funny to think that when

Katarina Johnson-Thompson

I was younger, I hated my body because it was too developed for those around me; that flipped almost entirely as soon as I turned professional, and suddenly my body wasn't developed enough. These women were incredible. After a competition, I used to have a ritual of going online to look at the pictures the photographers had taken of me. I know now that that's not healthy, and that it's basically impossible to get a flattering picture of anyone going over the hurdles, but at that time I was almost addicted to comparing myself with the athletes around me.

The following year, I was selected for my first photo shoot with Nike (the same one where I was alongside the blonde athlete who looked like an *actual model*). It was an advert for a sports bra and I was incredibly nervous about so much of my body being on display. In the months leading up to it I basically went on a crash diet and lost loads of weight. Pictures of me taken in 2014 show how skinny I became in comparison to the year before. Funnily enough though, I think that was probably the year that I finally became more comfortable in my own skin. It wasn't something I was completely conscious of. I didn't wake up one morning and suddenly feel completely at ease with my body. But looking back, I just know that 2014 was the year that I thought less about it.

That could be for a couple of reasons. First, I was getting loads of compliments and being put forward for more photo shoots, which obviously helps with confidence levels. Secondly, and probably the more likely, is that 2014 was the year I suffered my first serious injury: a stress fracture in my foot. It ruled me out of a home Commonwealth Games which I had been so excited about. Suddenly, how my body looked became less important than how it stood up to the rigours of a sport that demands excellence in all areas: speed, strength, power and endurance. Perhaps the natural toll of doing my job is what forced me to reconsider my relationship with myself.

Either way, I don't remember having those same thoughts about my body after that year. It's not like I suddenly accepted myself for who I was and it was all happily ever after. No – I think it's just that our relationships with our bodies change as we age, as do our priorities. As a young athlete I didn't give much thought to what was best for my body in terms of health and longevity, whereas those things have become so key for me as my career has progressed.

These days, I'm also much more clinical about things. I'll look in the mirror and think to myself: *What can I do to improve my performance? Is this good for my career?* Whereas before, I'd look at my body and think to myself: *What might someone else say about it that I can change right now?*

Now, the only reason I'll change something about my body is if I'm confident that it will improve my results. And I've come to terms with that. I can openly state that my left calf is skinnier than my right calf, and that's OK because I ruptured my Achilles tendon in 2020, and it takes a long time for that muscle to return to the same point it was at before. It sometimes seems crazy to me that I'm willing a muscle to be bigger, given how scared I was to put on muscle in my late teens, but that's what happens: today, I look in the mirror and see little things like that, and I know they're tiny details that only a coach or a physiotherapist really cares about.

When I think of my body now, I don't think: *fat, skinny, tall, small*. I think about injuries and health, and what I can use it for. My body has been through so much, not just in the twelve years I've been a professional athlete, but even before that, when I was still finding my way in the sport. And now, I'm really trying to start to look at it as a thing that I'm so grateful for. I'm grateful that this body has given me such a long, happy career. You can talk about all the injuries I've had, but, each time, I've been able to bounce back and still use this body. Not every athlete has had that opportunity.

So, I'm trying to really harness that feeling of being grateful for the body that I've got, the body that I'm still using, the body that allows me to undertake my crazy training, the body that launches itself over obstacles and pushes itself to its limits, all to try to win medals. I'm really trying to create a sense of love so that when I'm talking about my body it's not like: 'Ugh, injured again.' It's not easy, but I want to secure that sense of love I have for it, because it's helped me to do so much. My body is my life, my income, my most trusted and fragile and powerful companion. Humans only get one body, and mine has allowed me to turn something that I love into a career that has brought me so much joy. Something that has changed my entire life. My body is remarkable.

I think that's something worth thinking about.

Part of being grateful and appreciating your body is making sure you look after it in the right way – something that I learned early on would mean sometimes putting it above my desire to fit in with everyone else.

As a teenager, I not only went through the stage of wanting to blend in physically with those around me, but I also wanted to be able to live my life in the same way they did theirs. At one point, when I was around sixteen years old, I asked

Unbroken

Mum if I could get a Saturday job. I've got no idea how it would have worked when I was competing so often on weekends, but I wanted to be like my friends; so many of them were working in shops or cafes in town on a Saturday and then meeting up after work to go out.

Mum was dead against the idea. 'If you need money,' she said, 'I'll give it to you.' (Not that we had any to spare – although she never let me know that.) She knew that a job would be a distraction from athletics, and she could see the bigger picture of what might lie ahead *if* I could stay focused – something that's a serious challenge when you're a teenager and all your friends are busy enjoying the here and now.

But Mum was good at bringing that picture back into focus. I remember once needing a new pair of trainers and going into a sports shop with her, where she went straight to the bargain bin. My heart sank as she started rifling through the discount shoes, looking for a pair that were my size. I think she must have noticed, because suddenly she stopped her search, looked at me and said, 'One day, Katarina, you'll have the pick of shoes in this whole shop.'

I'm not sure I believed her.

Soon, it got to the point where people in my friendship group would be going out every weekend, like clockwork. I would join them *maybe* three times a year, if that. One of those rare occasions turned into a night that one generation of Harriers will never forget.

Someone from the club was having a house party which I decided to go to, despite the fact I was competing for the Harriers the next day. I hadn't been at the party for long when Mum got a phone call. Her stomach lurched when she heard the voice of one of my friends on the other end of the line. Something was wrong, they said; I'd collapsed and was out for the count. They didn't know what to do.

Mum was out the door almost before they'd finished speaking. She got a taxi to the party, picked me up (literally) and told the cab driver to take us straight to the local hospital. A couple of my friends from the party came with us, but nobody would tell Mum anything – to this day, she's still convinced either that someone spiked my drink or that I had an unknown allergy to something. I think it was more likely that I just didn't know how to drink in the same way my friends did. It was something I did so rarely that when I did go out and there was alcohol involved, I felt like it was my one chance. I had to make the most out of it. Stupid, really.

Mum sat by my bed that night and watched as I had my belly pumped and was put on a drip to try to rehydrate me. By the time the doctors were happy to discharge me, it was the early hours of the morning; not long before I was supposed to be taking part in a long jump competition for the Harriers. I felt terrible, but there was no way I was going to let the club down. I went home, showered and got my kit ready. One slice of toast was about all the fuel I could manage before we headed to the track.

My first two jumps were no jumps. Fouls. I just couldn't hit the take-off board right. But on my final attempt, I somehow managed to nail the take-off and jump a decent distance. In the end, that competition was one of my biggest victories, but I definitely didn't hang around to bask in it. Mum asked a friend of hers to give us a lift home and I sat in the back of the car in silence, counting down the minutes until I could crawl into bed. 'Is she OK?' asked Mum's friend. 'Oh, she's not feeling very well,' Mum replied, keeping the details of my night in A&E to herself. She did tell Val at the club about it, though (thinking it was probably wise to do so before I competed). 'Another year or so and she won't be able to do any of that,' Val had said, her eyebrows raised almost as high as her hairline. 'Not without her name being all over the papers, anyway.'

That weekend taught me that I couldn't get away with that stuff; I couldn't go out with my friends the night before I was competing. And I definitely couldn't drink like them. Was it a sacrifice? At the time, I probably felt so. But as you grow older, you realize that it's really your choice – you're the one who has to deal with the outcome of eating too much fast food, or drinking to excess and trying to train with a hangover. And it's just not nice. It's not worth it – not even in terms of it stopping you from being the best athlete, just in terms of you wanting to stay in bed when what you have to do is get up and work hard.

Even now, people still ask me things like: 'Do you have to watch your diet? Do you have to not drink? What's it like being an athlete when you're not allowed to do this or that?' But I choose not to drink during the season because, ultimately, I'm going to have to pay the price when I'm going to training in the morning with a headache. I've learned what my choices can lead to.

When I was nineteen, all my friends planned a big group holiday to Mallorca Rocks – a live music event that used to take place in Magaluf every summer. They were going in the summer of 2012, at the same time that the London Olympic Games were set to take place. I was devastated. It was going to be our first girls' holiday. I wanted to go with them so badly but, while they were booking their flights, I was desperately trying to qualify to compete at those Olympics.

Mallorca Rocks was a huge thing for me to miss and at the time I was really jealous of them all, flying off to have fun and go out partying every night. But when I look back on that summer now, all people talk about is London 2012. What I experienced at my first Olympics – a home Olympics – was a once-in-a-lifetime opportunity. The other stuff I can do right now, or when I retire – when I've got the time to do it with my friends.

That experience woke me up to the fact that it's OK to miss out on things, because what I'm doing on the track is ultimately more important in my life. It opened my eyes to see that there's sacrifice everywhere; if I had gone to Mallorca Rocks, I'd have missed out on the experience that changed my world for ever.

I suppose with regards to my struggles both with body image and with FOMO as a teenager, qualifying for the Olympic Games in 2012 was the key event that resolved them, or at least set me on the path to that being the case. And, in many ways, I feel so lucky that I was in the right place at the right time to do that.

The entry standard for me to get to the Games in 2012 was 6,150 points. Now, it's 6,480. That's a big jump. What nineteen-year-old is going to be able to get that today? I don't know if I would have ever qualified. And the difference that 2012 made to me is astonishing. Before the Games, I had no brand sponsorships and basically zero recognition. Adidas would send me kits to compete in, but I had zero financial backing from brands.

But the exposure that I received at those Olympics created brand interest in me. I signed a Nike deal on the back of that interest, which earned me more money than I'd ever seen in my life and allowed me the freedom to become a professional athlete.

I was lucky. These days, things are different. While there is more of a focus on body inclusivity, there are also new pressures for young athletes around social media, followers and presenting yourself in a certain way online, even if you're not like that in real life. New athletes are finding it tough to get sponsorships. I know of one instance where an athlete broke an under-23 record for her event but, because she doesn't have over 10,000 followers on social media, brands wanted nothing to do with her. How is that fair? That system isn't based on merit, it's based on clout – and since when has access to sport been a popularity contest? The struggle is definitely a different one for younger athletes now and, to be honest, I don't know which one I would rather face.

Athletics is not in a great place right now. It's fighting with itself to be a professional sport, but it doesn't have the financial clout or correctly packaged product needed to be truly professional. It's almost as if it's clinging on to the product it showcases at the Olympics – which is great, and makes athletics the blue-riband event of the Games – but it doesn't showcase itself properly the rest of the time in order to transcend the Olympics, so it's stuck in limbo between professional and amateur. The reality is that athletes who want to compete for top honours have to live and train as professionals to stand a chance. So I was pleased to see World Athletics – the global governing body of the sport – announce before the 2024 Olympics that they were going to award prize money to gold medal-winners at the

Games. But that's the tip of the iceberg. A lot of the athletes who I see day to day are struggling financially. It's really hard and I feel sorry for young athletes. I just don't know how they can do it with the pressures of social media, performance, money and education. I was – and I am – very fortunate to have come through when I did.

But it's more than timing that got me to a first Olympic Games and everything that followed. As every single athlete and sportsperson will tell you, we don't do any of it alone; there's always a team of people who play crucial roles in helping us along the way.

And my team contains some very unique, and very special, individuals.

4

Relationships I

'Hey, Barrie, I'm ahead, only the 800m to go. Guess what I'm thinking of?!'

I was in Italy competing for Great Britain at the 2009 World Youth Championships, and I was about to win my first global title. It was my third international competition, but the first one that was actually against people my own age (under-18s); I'd previously been competing against athletes who were mostly older than me. I was on a team with athletes I'd watched beating everyone in the country at various national championships; people like my now-partner Andrew Pozzi (or Pozz, as I like to call him), Jodie Williams and Jack Meredith. We were all in Italy together to take on the rest of the world and it was incredibly exciting.

Before I'd left for Italy, a man called Barrie Wells had made me a promise: 'If you come home with a medal,' he said, 'I'll introduce you to Steven Gerrard.' The Liverpool FC captain was my hero. I loved the passion he showed on the pitch and had covered my school books with pictures of him. A few years earlier, I'd been to my first ever Liverpool game (a riveting 1–1 draw against Middlesbrough) with one of my cousins and he had scored one of the most insane goals of his career, smashing the ball in from about 35 yards out. Meeting him in person would be a dream.

The competition went about as well as it possibly could have for me. I collected PB scores in almost every event and I built up a really good cushion of points before the final one, the 800m. While we were chilling in the rest room waiting for the race, I got my phone out and sent Barrie that frantic message.

Back in the UK, Barrie started panicking, realizing that he'd have to actually live up to his promise. He was a season ticket holder at Liverpool but he'd never met Gerrard and had no concrete route to him. But when I came back with the gold medal, he knew that he had to make it happen. It took a bit of time, and a lot of pleading with the chief executive of the club, but eventually we got an invitation to Melwood, Liverpool's training ground, and I got to meet my hero (as well as our star striker, Fernando Torres).

'Any chance you can leave us your medal?' Gerrard joked as we posed for a picture. 'I've not won any this year so we could use one around here.'

When I first started in athletics, it was just me and Mum, finding our way in a new world we knew nothing about. At the beginning it all felt like a great adventure. But to progress in any sport you need people around you who know the ropes and can help you find the right path. You also need people who will be there for you, win or lose. I've been incredibly lucky to find those people. And once I find them, I'm the kind of person who clings on to them as tightly as I can.

I will always be grateful to Val for what she did for me in those early years. She took me under her wing at a time when I knew nothing about athletics and she propelled me to the success that led to me getting Lottery funding and my first GB vest. And she was still around for me to talk to at the Harriers – even now, Mum bumps into her at some events and they always have a good chat. Val was a schoolteacher, and she definitely had that air about her when she coached, but I was never really scared of her. I was about to encounter something a bit different.

In the midst of my tumultuous teenage years, I started working with a coach called Mike Holmes, a former weightlifter-turned-throws athlete who had first joined the Harriers in 1969 before turning to coaching in the 1980s. A decade later, he led British high jumper Steve Smith to Olympic and World medals. He also spent six years as GB National Senior High Jump coach and was the first UK coach to have two athletes jump over 2.30m. His technical knowledge was impressive and I really believed he could help take my high jump to the next level.

A big guy who often hid beneath a baseball cap and reserved his bearded smiles for the rarest of occasions, Mike Holmes could be really intimidating, especially to those who didn't know him. Even Jessica Ennis-Hill, whose coach Toni Minichiello once brought Mike in to do a high jump session with her after the 2011 World Championships, was terrified of him. 'He had a way of dragging me down to earth,' she wrote in her post-2012 autobiography.

Katarina Johnson-Thompson

Once you get to know him, as I did, you do see a softer side; he can be like a big teddy bear. But you have to work incredibly hard to see that side. Initially, the idea had been for me to work with Jess's coach, Toni – someone who Mike was very close to. The four of us (Mike, Toni, me and Mum) had a few meetings together with British Athletics to discuss my future, and working with Toni was a very appealing option at the time.

Mum and I were still newcomers to the sport, really, but we knew how good Jess was – especially after she won the World Championships in 2009 – so working with her coach seemed like the right thing to do. Not only that, but Toni was telling us that he thought I could be even better than Jess, with the right guidance. He was based in Sheffield, so we discussed a few options, including my moving to a college there or my staying in Liverpool and the two of us travelling to in between locations. In the end, he came to Liverpool once and I went to Sheffield once.

Between all the commuting, Mike was keeping me ticking over as a favour to Toni. He was pretty much retired at the time, but he didn't mind filling in until we felt ready for me to move to Toni full time. Toni even came with me to the World Youth Championships in 2009 where I won gold in the heptathlon, while Mike stayed at home. But the move to Toni never happened. Things started going well with Mike and it didn't make sense to change everything – and leave Liverpool – when I'd already found something that worked.

Coaches all have different approaches to getting an athlete ready to compete. Mike's was: we get to the track, we absolutely kill ourselves until we're crawling out, we go home, we rest completely the next day, and then we come back the day after that and do the same again. And we do it and do it and do it and do it and do it, until we need to stop. Then we have the biggest taper out (where you decrease training volume and intensity in the lead-up to a competition) and the performances will come after that.

For the eight or so years I was with Mike, that was my way of life. The winter is when you do all your hardest work as an athlete: when you lay the foundations for the speed, strength and endurance that you hope will bring you medals once the season starts. With Mike, those winter sessions could look like this: we'd start with 50-50-50s, where I'd sprint 50m, then jog 50m, then walk 50m. We'd go around the track four times doing that as a warm-up. Then there'd be hill sprints; a brutal way to build up your strength and speed endurance while killing your lungs at the same time. After that, we'd get to go inside and warm our frozen hands and feet while doing core work and plyometrics, like box jumps. Finally, we'd always finish with what we would describe as 'something shitty'.

We never knew what it was going to be. And we'd never ask because we wouldn't want to have the dread that came with knowing. Sometimes I'd be going up and down hills carrying other athletes on my back as a weight instead of a weighted jacket. Other times it would be step runs, where you'd bound up the first block of the Wavertree steps, do fast feet up the rest, run across the top, run down and around and repeat that three times. Then rest and then do it three more times again. Or we'd do 60-metre turn abouts, which was sprint 60m, rest for 20 seconds, then go again, and do them in sets with a rest of between three and five minutes, depending on the session. We had a group record to try to beat, which was from when

Mike used to coach Steve Smith. We desperately wanted to beat that group record, which was twenty-four turn abouts. So we'd start out with two sets of four, go to eight, then two sets of five . . . and we'd build and build and build each week until we were doing a continuous twenty-four. Sometimes the 'something shitty' was jump tests, where Mike would get out training logs from all the athletes he'd coached who became British record holders in the high jump and we'd try to beat them in all sorts of things: standing long jump, standing triple jump, two steps and a jump, four hops and a jump, two hops and a jump . . . We'd be trying to beat the numbers in those logs and trying to beat each other at the same time. I had the group record in most of the tests, besting people like former international high jumpers Debbie Marti and Susan Moncrieff, whose PBs were 1.95 metres (the old British indoor record). So when I beat their training PBs, it gave me the confidence to believe I could best their actual PBs.

The attitude and mentality around the group was always: *Better, better, better. You can do better.* Mike pushed us and we pushed each other. All we wanted was to work the hardest, do the most, be the best, every single week. That was a good vibe to be a part of. It seems mad when I think back to those days, when it would get dark at 4 p.m. and we'd be out in the rain and wind for hours on end, but I used to love those winters. The Harriers only had a little four-lane indoor facility so we could never do much inside – we'd come in and do some core work to warm up and then be back out in the freezing cold. I don't know how I did it then and I don't think I could do it now.

Coaches today still talk about Mike's training for how brutal it could be; it's legendary within the sport. It was a lot heavier than the training I'd been used to before – not in terms of running, there was actually less of that – but in terms of plyometrics (or jump training) and just using up every single ounce of energy that you had to give. Mike would push and push, but we always felt he knew the exact moment to pull back and stop before you broke.

The one thing that all of his athletes understood was never to expect a compliment or a pat on the back from Mike. Usually, he would go in on the negatives: 'You need to do this,' or 'What the fuck was that?' If you were capable of doing something, he expected you to do it. If you didn't then it was: 'What the hell is happening? What's going on?' There was no give. He'd want the absolute best from you all the time. If you ever managed to do something that pleased him, there'd be silence and an expectation that you would repeat whatever you'd done. But still no compliment. The compliment was that there was no critique. You were made up with that. Ready to go!

It was one of those relationships where you were constantly fighting to impress. Constantly working for that positive reaction – even a word or a nod would do. As a young kid, that's exactly what I was doing. At first, it was just with him. Eventually, it was with the rest of the world too.

Barrie had a different personality. He was always smiling and telling stories, and that was apparent from the moment I first met him in 2008. He's fifty-three years my senior, but I now consider him to be a great friend, confidant and part of my extended family. One of the biggest athletics fans and statisticians

Katarina Johnson-Thompson

I know, Barrie believed in me at a time when even UK Athletics (the national governing body of the sport) weren't that sure about my prospects of making it to the top.

He'd spent a large part of his working life creating and building successful financial services companies, but in 2008 Barrie felt he'd reached a crossroads; he wanted to put his time, funds and energy into something he truly loved. He wanted to give his money away in his own lifetime, so he could enjoy seeing the difference it made.

That summer, while in Beijing to watch the Olympic Games (he's been to every Olympics since Munich 1972, bar the Covid-hit Tokyo Games in 2021), he decided to set up a charity aimed at helping young athletes on their journeys to the Olympic Games. Sport is his passion – Olympic sport, specifically – and, with London 2012 coming up in four years' time, he put aside £2 million to put towards grassroots sports projects and selected a group of British athletes who he would help in their quest for success in London.

Barrie set up a meeting with Baroness Sue Campbell, who was then Chairperson of UK Sport. She helped to arrange a series of meetings for Barrie, one of which was with Niels de Vos, the chief executive of UK Athletics. Barrie met Niels armed with a list of athletes he wanted to speak to in order to decide whether to back them.

Niels looked down Barrie's list of names, nodding: 'Dai Greene, Jessica Ennis, Jodie Williams . . . Katarina Thompson?' (I didn't add the Johnson part into my name until a few years later, when Mum changed her name back to Johnson, and I thought it was silly not having her name as part of my own.) The nodding stopped. 'That,' said Niels, 'is one you shouldn't sponsor.' Niels explained that I was just fifteen years old and they didn't really know what I was capable of at senior level yet. 'Go for Hannah England instead,' said Niels, 'she's a genuine medal prospect over 1500m.'

During the previous twelve months, Barrie had been following my results in *Athletics Weekly* magazine and he'd been getting more and more excited by what he saw: I was strong in high jump and long jump, I was decent at the hurdles . . . and then there was the 300m. At the beginning of 2008, Val had me running over that distance indoors and I was getting good times. When I beat a young athlete who was being looked at as a rising star, Barrie's excitement over my potential went up a notch. 'I want to go with Katarina,' he insisted.

In our first meeting with Barrie, I was quickly won over. He knew everything about athletics, including all my stats, and his enthusiasm for the sport – and me – was infectious (it still is). He's a big Liverpool fan, too. It was hard *not* to get on with him. He asked lots of questions. He wanted to know about my training, about what was important to me and where I wanted to get to in the sport. 'And one more thing,' he said. 'Who are your heroes?'

That year, because of the Beijing Olympics, I'd become obsessed with watching and reading about athletics. I'd come to it all so late – and that wasn't just in regards to athletics, but to Olympic sport as a whole. I'd only really discovered all of it once I started in the sport, so understanding its history felt like an important part of truly appreciating what it was all about. Part of my obsession involved looking up athletes who had played big roles in the sport's history, and one who I latched on to was Steve Prefontaine. A legendary

American long-distance runner who became famous for his aggressive, gritty running on the track, he helped spark a running boom in the US in the 1970s. I gorged on the films and documentaries made about him and loved the motivational quotes he became renowned for. Before my races I'd look up my favourite ones to help me get fired up.

I told Barrie all about my love for Steve Prefontaine and repeated the quote that resonated with me (and probably all heptathletes) the most: 'The only good race pace is suicide pace . . . and today looks like a good day to die.' Barrie looked pretty surprised to hear this fifteen-year-old quoting Prefontaine at him! We chatted some more about the sport and then he asked me what I really needed — what was it that would make a real difference and help me get closer to achieving my goals?

The first word that came to mind was transport. Mum didn't drive (yet), and the various bus and National Express coach journeys were becoming trickier. I wanted to learn to drive as soon as it was legally possible to, but the cost of lessons was a lot for me and Mum to cover — let alone then getting a car for me to drive once I'd actually passed my test. Barrie said that as soon as I turned seventeen, he'd pay for me to have driving lessons. In the meantime, he'd cover the cost of us travelling by taxi whenever we needed to.

At that point, Mike's shoulders dropped and his whole demeanour softened. In a matter of seconds Barrie had turned from potential disruptor into someone who was going to have a really positive impact on my ability to train and perform. Barrie also said he'd help out with the cost of my kit, as well as pay for both Mike and me to join a weight training club, where the facilities would be much better than those at the Harriers. I couldn't believe how lucky I was. It was one of the first times somebody had wanted to help me in that way.

The driving lessons in particular are something I'm forever grateful for. I passed my test at the first attempt, and the minute I could get on the road, life became so much easier. I saved up most of my British Athletics funding to buy a car – a black Chevrolet Matiz, by the way, which Mum still has – and Barrie helped to pay for the insurance, which would have cost more than the car. The very first day I got it, I drove to Leeds for a javelin session with Mick Hill, the former British number one and four-time Olympian, who was helping me at the time. I had no fear being on the road at all. It was something that I had wanted for so long. It meant that after training, instead of a fifteen-minute walk back through the park to get on the bus for another forty-five minutes, I could just jump in the car and be home within twenty minutes. The ease of getting from A to B bought me hours of time back, and that meant hours of recovery.

All Barrie asked for in return from the athletes he sponsored was that we gave up six half-days a year to go into schools and speak to kids about our sport. It was part of a project he set up called Athletes4Schools which was designed to get kids excited about Olympic sport. I was sceptical. Why would anyone want to listen to me? I was still a school kid myself, and I didn't see myself as being anywhere near the level of the other athletes Barrie sponsored, like Jess Ennis, Beth Tweddle and Liam Tancock. They were genuine medal contenders. Even Jodie Williams, who was younger than me, was more on the right track than I was. She was insanely talented and won everything as a junior. She was probably my first female inspiration in athletics. I could see why kids would want to sit and listen to someone like her, but me? I couldn't understand it.

Barrie would always give me a massive build-up when he introduced me to the kids: 'This is Katarina, she's from Liverpool. She's not going to be the champion of Liverpool, the champion of Merseyside, the champion of England, the champion of the UK, the champion of Europe. She's going to be champion of the whole wide world.'

'N-o-o-o-o!' I'd laugh. 'Stop building me up!' It seemed to work though. The kids would sit there quietly with their legs crossed and listen to me talk about what I did and how I got into it. At the end, they'd all wave their arms in the air to ask me questions. It all felt very weird at that stage of my life.

Over the years, Barrie's role in my career has changed. I might not need his financial support any more, but he brings other things that are just as important when you're dealing with the extreme highs and lows of elite sport. At every championship I compete in, there's one thing I can be certain of: at some point when I'm setting up my blocks on the start line for the hurdles (the first event in the heptathlon) I will hear the words: 'COME ON THE KAT!' being shouted down from the stands. Somehow, no matter where his seats are in the stadium, Barrie will always get close enough to that start line to shout his encouragement. I almost wait for it now. Then I'll look up to see where he is and raise a hand to let him know I hear – and feel – his support.

I've been hearing that shout for sixteen years now. The best thing about Barrie is that he doesn't really care if I win or lose; he's just there to support me. Obviously, it's really nice if I do win, but if I don't, he's never done what some other sponsors do and taken money away. He's here for the journey. You don't find many people like that.

I became a patron of Box4Kids when he set up the charity in 2010. It uses executive boxes at sport and entertainment venues to give seriously ill and disabled children a day out to remember. Barrie has helped to teach me the importance of helping others, and whenever I can, I'll be a host at one of the boxes. It's something I really enjoy doing; a way of supporting Barrie and giving the kids a great day (I hope). It's emotional to hear what the kids have been through or are about to go through, and I'm always totally in awe of their strength and positivity. Seeing the smiles on their faces and the joy they get from the day gives me as much of a lift as it does them.

If someone is 'my people' then that's it for me. We're in it for life. I'm a loyal person by nature; I've had the same group of friends since school, two long-term relationships and four coaches in my entire senior career, one of whom I was forced to leave. When I like you, I like you, and that's that.

The group of friends that I made at my secondary school, St Julie's, is one that I cherish. The dining hall was filled with big round tables and there used to be eleven of us that sat around ours. Over the years, that number has whittled down to five people who have stayed close to and been there for each other as we've gone from teenage girls to women – from people trying to get somewhere in their lives to people who *are* somewhere in their lives.

Between the five of us – me, Lauren, Liv, Charlotte and the incredible actress Jodie Comer – we have lived all over the place. I lived in France for a while, one of us lived in San

Sebastián and now lives in Berlin, and Jodie lives pretty much everywhere! But we keep in touch via a WhatsApp group, aptly and very maturely titled *Hoes in Different Area Codes*. I'll admit I'm not the most active in the chat during athletics seasons, but I know that if I ever feel a certain way about something I can send a voice note and ask the four of them whether I'm validated or not – and once the season is over, I'm on it as much as everyone else.

People know Jodie for her amazing work on stage and screen. I'm in awe of her talent, but to me she will also always be the funny, incredibly kind and genuine person who I first met in Year 8 and grew closer to as our school years went on. I knew what My Thing was, and she knew hers too. While I spent my free time at the track, Jodie was at drama school. I enjoyed school, but I wasn't the most focused student. I was a bit silly. Sometimes a bit naughty. I was never suspended or expelled or anything, but I just wanted to have a laugh, and I didn't care passionately about my results at any point, not in the same way that I cared about my results in athletics.

At the same time as I was finding more success on the track, Jodie was doing the same thing in the acting world. At one point she actually stopped going to drama school, perhaps because she had surpassed what they were teaching by that point and was already auditioning for roles. I thought it was pretty unfair that I could never do the equivalent; just stop training and say, 'I'm ready to compete.' But that wasn't the case at all; she had just developed so quickly that she'd already advanced to the next stage of her career.

I guess the difference between my career and hers is that there can be opportunities for child actors, whereas I felt I was committing myself to a life of having to train for ever before I got the chance to turn it into an actual career. Now I know the reality; that, actually, Jodie is constantly training. Every role she takes on is a new challenge and something she has to train for. She is such an inspiration to me, not just because of how amazing she is at her craft but because of the journey she's been on. I can very much relate to it; I know how many buses, trains and coaches she's taken to get to auditions for roles that she hoped would give her the opportunity for her talents to be seen by bigger and bigger audiences.

We get asked about each other in interviews a lot these days, and I don't mind. But there are times when people try to use me as a way to get to her and I can see it from a mile off. I'm very protective over our friendship and who I talk to about her. I feel incredibly lucky to have people I've known all my life as my closest friends. I'm really grateful for their friendship and the way they just take me as I am. That realization – that our friendship wasn't based on me being a good athlete or winning medals – was a really important one for me.

It came after the 2017 World Championships in London when I recovered from a near-disaster in the high jump to finish fifth, just 78 points away from getting a medal. It was the first time all my friends had come to watch me compete and I'd really wanted to get on the podium for them. We went on a night out afterwards and I was feeling really sad about it. 'I'm sorry it wasn't a better experience for you,' I told them.

But I was wrong. They'd had the best time. They were genuinely so amazed just being in the stadium and seeing what I do in real life. That was the first time I actually saw that in real life; that they didn't care at all where I finished, they were still my friends. And they were just so proud of the fact that I was there. I'd never really understood that until that point, and it was a really big moment for me. That said, when I have a really good comp, getting PBs and scoring big points, sometimes I wish I could be in the crowd with them, experiencing it the way they are.

That's what happened at the 2019 European Indoor Championships in Glasgow. It's probably one of my favourite competitions across my career; I won with a big score, my nan was there and my friends and family were just having an absolute ball. You could spot them from a mile off in the crowd, all wearing bright red hoodies with TEAM KJT splashed across the front. In the gap between the morning and evening sessions on the day of the pentathlon, my friends all went to a pub and got drunk. They were already buzzing to be there watching me, but they came back even more buzzed! That was one time I felt annoyed I wasn't with them, experiencing the same as them. I'm quite a loner by myself down on the track, and I had looked up at them and seen that they were having the best time. Afterwards, I went to see them and heard all their stories: 'You'll never guess what happened with the fridge and this and that . . . !'

We have completely separate memories of the same events.

The low times are obviously when you need your friends the most, and my friends have helped me through all of mine; the various injuries, the devastation of Beijing in 2015 and, maybe most importantly, the isolation of recovering from an Achilles rupture during Covid. On 1 January 2021, I was staying at my nan's house while I recovered from the surgery on the ankle tendon (I never imagined I'd be so grateful for her stairlift until that period), and because of her age and the fact that she was quite fragile with dementia by then, Mum and I had to isolate ourselves so that we didn't put her at any risk of catching Covid. It was a very lonely time. My friends were all going on a New Year's Day walk, which I obviously couldn't join in on because a) I couldn't walk and b) I had to be careful of getting too close to people. But later that day, there was a knock on the door and there they were, with a bottle of prosecco and five glasses. 'We thought you might need this.'

I hobbled outside and we sat on the low wall at the front of the house and had a drink together.

Seeing my friends grow, change and thrive, while we're all still there for each other, is something I'm very grateful for. There's something so comforting about being surrounded by people who've known you for such a long time and been by your side through so many experiences, whether that means physically being there or just being a voice on the end of the phone. I'm really lucky to have that – as I said, it's something that I really do cherish. I'm doubly lucky in that I've found it in athletics, too. There's a small group who are my core friends in the sport. They're people who have been there since we were in the young athletes league competitions and are still in the sport.

Alongside Pozz – who I'll come back to later – my closest friends in the sport are the sprinter Adam Gemili, the pole vaulter Holly Bradshaw, sprinter and long jumper Zak Skinner and the long jumper Jazmin Sawyers (Jaz). Jaz and I used to battle it out so much as youths, because she did pentathlon before deciding to specialize in long jump. We've met head-to-head at competitions as far back as 2007, including at the English Schools and Young Athlete League finals, one of my first experiences of high-stakes competition. Jaz was one of the first athletes I ever saw start a clap to involve the crowd: *What? How? Wow!* We've competed with and against each other through every age group, in senior comps and on the international stage. That's why I really love being in the same training group as her now; it feels like a full-circle moment.

Just like Barrie, Pozz and my schoolfriends, Jaz is 'my people'. And I'll always, always, always go above and beyond for them. When I was younger, I was so caught up in trying to appease and please everyone around me; I cared so much about their opinions and what they thought of me. As I've got older, my relationships have taught me that the only people whose opinions really matter to me are the people I'm closest to. The rest is just noise that I don't need to listen to.

Sport can be a lonely place at times, especially a sport like athletics where most of the time it's just you and your coach. When things are going well, it doesn't matter so much, but when you're in the trenches of dealing with an injury, defeat, or struggles with your form, you need those people around you who can help pull you out of the darkness.

I'm the type of person who tries to deal with things myself before I talk to anyone else about them. I close myself off. Lock myself away. Bury myself in books and music. But eventually, I come out of that place, and that's when I need my friends and family. That's when I need those people who I know don't care about points or medals; they care about me.

At the 2009 World Youth Championships, I didn't have Mike alongside me. He had prepared me for the competition but he was still talking about being semi-retired. Mum and Nan

Unbroken

came, though – they were so excited to watch me compete on such a big stage wearing a Great Britain vest.

I felt the same way. I was sixteen years old and had not long finished my GCSEs, and now I was boarding a plane to Italy to compete for my country. Not only that, but I was doing it alongside my friends and athletes I really looked up to, like the sprinter Jodie Williams. She was someone who was almost expected to come home with a gold medal (maybe even two, as she was competing in both the 100m and 200m). Jodie had dealt with a lot of the issues I was about to face regarding media and the pressure of expectation, and at an even younger age. For the first five years of her career she was unbeatable, and went on an insanely impressive streak, winning 151 races in a row. But me? I was a bit of an outside shot. I thought I might be able to finish in the top three if I had a good day, but first place? I could dream . . .

It turned out to be a really good day. I set five new PBs, and scored 5,750 points, which was the highest points tally at under-18 level in British history; it also put me second in the all-time World Youth rankings. I was disappointed with my shot put (I threw it 10m), but my long jump of 6.31m would have been good enough to win gold in the individual event!

All I had to do in the final event – the 800m – was stay ahead of the Latvian girl, and the gold was mine. I didn't run my fastest 800m, but I didn't need to; 2 minutes 20 seconds was good enough to secure me the gold medal (and my meeting with Steven Gerrard), and as I crossed the finish line I collapsed in a heap, trying to take in what had just happened. It was the biggest championships I'd been to and I was coming home with the top prize! (Naturally, it went straight to Nan so she could show it off to all her neighbours.)

Katarina Johnson-Thompson

It was so exciting to be part of a winning team. Jodie won gold in the 100m and 200m, as expected, and Ben Williams won the triple jump. The combination of heptathlon and triple jump gold medals was one that caught the attention of the media. The senior World Championships were coming up in Berlin the following month, and chief among the British athletes expected to win medals were Jess and the triple jumper, Phillips Idowu. Ben and I were being talked about as the ones who could follow in their footsteps.

Ben's response to that was one I never forgot: 'I don't want to be the next Jonathan Edwards or Phillips Idowu,' he told the journalists. 'I want to be the first Ben Williams.'

I took a mental note of that one.

Flying home from Italy, I felt on top of the world. A gold medallist on the world stage. It's a great place to be, but it's rarely somewhere you stay for very long. I learned that pretty quickly.

5

Manifesting

'Absolutely not!' I said, glaring first at my mum, and then at the offending computer monitor in front of her.

On screen was an email from British Athletics, congratulating me for being selected as part of the British Olympic Association's Ambition Programme for London 2012. That meant I'd get to visit Team GB's preparation camp where athletes from all different sports got themselves ready to compete at the Olympics. I'd also get to have a look around the Olympic Village in Stratford before any of the athletes arrived. On top of that, I was going to get tickets to two of the athletics sessions at the Olympics later that year.

I couldn't think of anything worse.

I'd already decided I was going to be at the Olympics. But not as a visitor or tourist. I was going to be there as a competitor. I was going to be an Olympian. It was something I'd been manifesting ever since 2011, when I'd visited the building site that was to become the Olympic Stadium as part of a group of athletes taken on a tour of the site by the then-head coach of British Athletics, Charles van Commenee.

As we walked up to it, I felt a bubble of excitement building in my belly. It was a humongous structure, and from the outside it looked almost ready to go. But once we got inside we saw how much work there still was to do. The floor was mostly mud and rubble and there was no running track in place or infield laid down.

To me, that didn't matter. I looked around and saw what it would become: a stadium packed with people, a brand-new track sweeping around it and, in the centre of it all, me, wearing the GB kit and standing on the start line for the hurdles on day one of the 2012 Olympic heptathlon.

I asked someone in a high-vis jacket and he walked me over to the exact spot where the start line was planned to be. I stood there and closed my eyes. I saw myself setting up my blocks. I heard the crowd roar as I got into position. And I savoured the silence as I waited for the sound of the gun.

BANG.

It was me versus seven other faceless athletes. I was fastest out of the blocks. I flew over every hurdle with ease, powered by the epic noise inside the stadium. I was an Olympian.

I'd never really used visualization techniques before then, but that visit to the Olympic Stadium in 2011 gave me everything I needed to build a mental pathway towards my first Games. From that day on, whenever I closed my eyes to go to sleep, I saw myself standing on that start line. During training sessions, I'd envision being in that stadium and hearing that crowd. It was all I would focus on.

Unbroken

It didn't matter that I was eighteen years old and dreaming of competing in an event where most athletes don't reach their peak until their mid- to late twenties. It didn't matter that I'd only been training four times a week, fitting it in around school, or even that I'd come sixth in the 2011 European Junior Championships, having hardly competed in 2010 because of injury. It didn't matter that I wasn't exactly in my flow.

In my head, I was going to the 2012 Olympics. And not as a tourist.

In 2012, I was incredibly focused. It was the first time in my life that I tried to manifest something just by visualizing it over and over and over again, and it paid off.

At that point, I believed that visualization was foolproof. All I had to do was envision it and it would happen. It gave me a kind of fake arrogance that I could somehow manifest my entire life. And when it worked, it felt amazing. I'm someone who likes to feel in control, and believing in visualization gave me that feeling in such a powerful way. I never once thought about what I would do if (or perhaps when) it stopped working. At the time, I was just happy riding the wave, letting it take me to the one and only place I wanted to be.

I'd been inspired to start using visualization by a Will Smith video I watched on YouTube. He used to post videos offering his words of wisdom on various things, and I would watch them a lot. I even noted down every line from one of them in my journal. It started with 'Skill is only developed through hours and hours of beatin' on your craft' and ended with 'Our thoughts, our feelings, our dreams, our ideas are physical in the universe. If we picture something and commit ourselves to it, that is a physical thrust towards realization that we can put into the universe. The universe is not going to push us around. We are gonna demand that the universe become what we want it to be.' I liked how he spoke – it was very motivational – and I took his words as absolute gospel. In one, he was talking about belief and how, before anyone else believes something, you have to believe it. He just kept on repeating it: 'You have to believe in order to be able to do it.' I used to listen to that video all the time, and I believed that it worked. After all, Will Smith said that it did!

Eventually, I was using visualization for most competitions that I did, and was setting PBs. They were only small comps, as I was coming up, but to me they felt like the Olympics, because that was all I'd ever experienced at that point in time. It could have been a national championships or an English Schools final, but it would feel like an Olympic final to me in terms of nerves, the level of competition I was going to face and the presence of an audience of my teammates and loved ones. I'd hype myself up for those events as if they were the Olympics. And over time, I did that on a bigger and bigger scale until it reached the point where I wanted to compete at the actual Olympics.

Mission 2012 is what Mike and I called it. That, or Mission 6150 – exactly the number of points I needed to qualify for the Games. In one running session, Mike was repeating it over and over: '6150, 6150, 6150,' and I got so confused, thinking he was telling me I had six lots of 150 metres to do to finish the session. I was like, 'Ugh, really?!'

It started in the winter of 2011, shortly after I finally dealt with a knee problem that had been causing me pain since 2010. It's called patella tendinopathy. It's when you suffer tiny tears to your patella tendon (the one that joins your kneecap to your shinbone), which then thickens as it heals, making your knee stiff and painful. For young athletes, it has to be managed really carefully to avoid it becoming chronic. That meant plenty of rest, and missing out on things I desperately wanted to be part of.

That included the 2010 World Junior Championships, held in Canada the previous summer. I had been devastated that I couldn't go. At that age (seventeen) I felt everything so deeply, and social media didn't help. All I saw on Facebook were photos of the GB team together, many of them the same athletes I'd competed with at the World Youths a year earlier. There were full-blown albums of them all having the best time while I was stuck at home. At one stage I had thought I might have been able to make it back in time to compete at the Commonwealth Games in Delhi later in 2010, but it had eventually become clear that that wasn't going to happen either.

So, at the start of the 2011 season, Mike and I planned a tentative comeback, hoping that the rest and rehab work I'd done would be enough to allow me to compete again. I'd already decided it was, though. I was done with missing out on major competitions. No matter how my knee felt, I just decided that it wasn't going to be a 'thing' for me any more. No one was going to take those opportunities away from me again.

That was the year I discovered painkillers. It started with over-the-counter anti-inflammatories before a comp. It was amazing. One little pill and suddenly I was pain-free. After that, I'd think: why not take them before a high jump session? Or before plyometrics? They started to become part of my pre-training ritual. I never became addicted to them, but I think all athletes rely on them to some extent – certainly more than we should. When you get past a certain age, it just becomes part and parcel of elite sport because of the toll that training takes on your body.

I had teammates at the time who took them and said, 'If you're in pain before a competition, then just take them for this short period of time.' Then you realize that it works, and you start doing it when you're not competing because you just want to get through a training session or whatever you need to do that day. Then it becomes a coping mechanism that you're using more often than you ought to.

It wasn't just painkillers, either. I remember seeing a British Athletics doctor when I pulled my quad. He gave me some sleeping tablets, saying that when you sleep better, your muscle recovers quicker. I loved them. I was going through a period where I was worried about competing, and that was affecting my sleep; but when I took one of those little pills, it knocked me out, and I didn't have to lie in bed worrying all night.

It's so easy to get into the thought process of: *This is just life. This is what you need to do to be an athlete. To compete at the highest level.* And while I wasn't an addict, there was shame. At the time, I didn't tell Mike that I was taking any pills. I didn't even admit that I was in pain. I knew that if he found out, he'd tell me to stop training, and I had already decided that I wasn't going to miss another year.

It was my choice to do that, and my performances definitely suffered as a consequence. I did three heptathlons in 2011 and the highest score I could manage was 5,787, to finish sixth at the European Junior Championships in Tallinn (when my nan made her infamous comment about it not being as much fun when you don't win). Two years earlier, I'd scored almost the same when winning the World Youths, and that was with the lower hurdles that you compete with as a younger athlete (which score fewer points).

By the end of 2011, I had come clean with Mike about my pain. It wasn't worth hiding if the guilt around doing so was affecting my results; I knew I couldn't afford to go through another year like that again.

A doctor advised me to try platelet-rich plasma injections (PRP), which is a procedure whereby blood is taken from a vein in your arm and then 'spun' in a machine to separate it into its various components: red and white blood cells, plasma, platelets, etc. The platelets are then collected, concentrated and mixed into a blood plasma liquid base, before being injected directly into the injured area. Because platelets are responsible for healing tissue, the extra concentration of them in the injection is supposed to speed up recovery time.

Mum and I took the National Express coach down to London where the specialist administering my treatment was based. I still have nightmares about lying in the doctor's office and seeing him walk over with the biggest needle I'd ever seen. I practically passed out when it went in. But it worked! It really worked. I could train pain-free, which made such a big difference to me mentally – no more worries about the potential damage of pushing myself hard or whether I was doing the right thing by taking painkillers. For the first time in almost two years, I felt ready and able to push on to the next level.

From then on, it was all about the Olympics. There were only three spots on Team GB's heptathlon squad and one of those belonged to Jess, no questions asked. Another British heptathlete named Louise Hazel was the 2010 Commonwealth Games gold medallist and had secured the qualification score at a comp the previous summer, so she had the second spot. That left just one spot with two athletes vying for it: myself and the 2006 Commonwealth Games champion, Kelly Sotherton.

She was thirty-five years old and had swapped heptathlon for the 400m in 2010 after struggling with a serious back injury, but wanted to return to the combined event for one last run at the Olympics. Some people might have looked at my PB – 5,787 points in 2011 – and thought that 6,150 would be too big a reach but, to me, it definitely wasn't. Because I believed I was better than 5,787.

I wanted to be at London 2012 so badly, and Mike felt the same. It was like we were in cahoots with each other; it was us against the world. That winter, we went super hard in training. Pushing harder and harder. Doing whatever we could to ensure I'd start 2012 capable of adding 400 points to my total. I used to keep diaries where I would note down my mindset right before a comp. That winter, it turned into a stream of numbers. Each evening, I'd open it up and write down different combinations of scores that could get me to 6,150. There were so many ways to do it, and that alone made me believe it was possible.

By the end of March that belief had almost doubled in strength, after I set a new British junior record in the pentathlon at a competition in Cardiff. That wasn't the best part though; the best part was that my score of 4,526 that day was over 300 points higher than my previous pentathlon PB. It felt like a breakthrough. After that, Mike and I earmarked 6 May 2012 as 'The One'. That was the date of the Multistars competition, hosted in the beautiful town of Desenzano del Garda in Italy. It was The One; where we felt I'd have the best opportunity to achieve Olympic qualification. There was enough time before it for me to recover from Cardiff and then put in a good block of training. Plus, it was early enough in the season that even if things didn't go to plan, there'd be time for another shot at it.

Every night, I would go to bed thinking about 6 May. Every morning, I would wake up having dreamed about it. As the day drew closer, my excitement levels rose. Mum was coming, and so was Barrie, who was missing Liverpool's FA Cup final against Chelsea that weekend. Not only that, but he was flying *Ryanair* to do it! The pressure was really on when I found that out.

The first day went well. I set new PBs in the hurdles, shot put and the 200m, and I went to bed that night feeling like Mission 6150 was well and truly within my grasp. But when I opened my curtains on the morning of day two, I was greeted by the worst sight: fat raindrops falling from the sky.

I hate jumping in the rain. And day two always starts with the long jump. In soggy conditions, the best I could manage was 6.14m, about 30cm down on my PB. In the space of time it took to complete three jumps, my hopes of securing the Olympic qualifier had disappeared. And my motivation followed. At that point, I wanted to stop. If it had been left up to me, I'd have called a taxi and headed to the airport there and then. What was the point of finishing, when nothing I could do was going to be enough to get me that Olympic qualifying score? Mike's calm-but-firm manner came to the rescue: 'You can't stop now, Katarina,' he said, 'finish what you've started.' It was the right decision. By the end of the comp, I'd scored 6,007 points, which was a good score: a new PB for me and a British junior record, breaking the one Jess had set by 97 points.

At that point, Kelly Sotherton had pulled up with an injury in the 200m, and looked like being out of the picture. I'd achieved the Olympic qualifying B standard. But that's only enough to qualify you for the Games if no one else from your country has the A standard, and two British athletes already had that, so I wasn't any closer to London 2012. I was devastated. I'd let everyone down: Mum, Barrie and Mike, especially. I held it together until the end of the competition; then I sank down at the side of the track. I'll always be grateful for what happened next.

With my head in my hands, I suddenly felt someone approach me. I looked up and saw a man I didn't recognize. He introduced himself as the organizer of an athletics meeting in Kladno, a city in Czechia which was hosting the Czech stop of the IAAF Combined Events Challenge. 'We would love you to come and be part of it,' he said, 'and I promise the weather will be better than here.' I'd never heard of Kladno before, but I thanked him as I wiped the tears away from my eyes and said I'd discuss it with my coach. It was an immediate second chance at qualification.

Three days after I got home from Italy, *that* email from British Athletics landed in Mum's inbox.

I was fuming. Didn't they believe I could do it? Mum sat and listened as I let off steam, including what I thought she should say in her reply to British Athletics (if I remember correctly: 'Katarina has declined this invitation because she is going to qualify outright and *be* at the Olympics' – you can't say I wasn't confident). Her actual response was a bit more subtle: 'Thanks for considering Katarina for the Olympic Ambition Programme,' she wrote. 'It is a fantastic opportunity but Katarina has her heart set on obtaining the qualifier and going to the Games on her own merit. She feels it would be too heartbreaking, and kind of bittersweet, if she was to go as an observer and not a participant.'

Then, just as Mike and I started thinking about Kladno, I received another invitation, this one to the prestigious Hypo-Meeting in Götzis, Austria, an annual combined-events competition that is essentially a rite of passage for any multi-eventer. I was thrilled. Jess had won at Götzis the previous two years and Denise Lewis had won in 1997, so British heptathletes had traditionally done well there. I was so excited to be invited to compete at a place I'd heard so much about; I'd basically decided that I was going to accept before I even got to the end of the email inviting me.

But Mike had other ideas. Götzis was at the end of May and that was too soon, he said. If we went straight into that competition so quickly after competing in Italy, I'd be tired. I also wouldn't have time to do much more in terms of training, which would likely mean just getting the same score again. If I wanted the best shot at getting the qualifier, I needed more training *and* more time to rest. That meant missing Götzis and aiming for Kladno on 10 June instead.

That plan also meant missing the World Junior Championships in Barcelona that July, which I'd have been able to compete at if I went to Götzis and didn't achieve the Olympic A standard.

But the time gap between Kladno and Barcelona was much shorter; if anything went wrong, it would be impossible to recover in time to compete in the heptathlon at both. Choosing to go to Czechia instead of Austria not only meant that I was pinning all of my hopes on one last competition, but also that I was effectively saying no to the potential for a World Junior Championship gold medal, which is just about the best thing you can win as a junior athlete (because, realistically, even if you make it to the Olympics, you're not there to win at that stage of your career).

Choosing the right path at that point was a real lesson for me: both in patience and in learning how to make the right decisions. I had to ask myself, what did I really want that year? And what was my best chance of getting there? The answer was the Olympics, and my best shot was at Kladno. As upset as I was about missing Götzis, as well as the chance to win a World Championship in Barcelona, they were both sacrifices I had to make. London 2012 had to be my sole focus.

Kladno was my last chance. I went there knowing it was make or break. Do or die. The only good pace was suicide pace.

The organizer I'd met in Italy had promised me better weather, but he couldn't have known that comp weekend was going to be one of the windiest the city would see that summer. We arrived at the track and were greeted by grey skies and gusts of wind so strong they bent the trees sideways. But that weekend, it had no impact on me. Nothing did. It was as if there was a forcefield around me, protecting me from anything that could affect my performance. We lined up for the 100m hurdles with the wind blowing straight at us. So what? I won it in 13.62 seconds, a new PB. And the rest of the day followed the same path. I jumped 5cm higher than I did in Italy. I threw the shot put further than I ever had before. And I ended the day with a fast 200m, despite another strong headwind pushing me back. It was just me, in my flow. Not one person or thing outside of that mattered.

I woke up on the morning of day two knowing that I was in a really good position, but the weather was not on my side. The wind had dropped off, only to be replaced by the rain. But this time, it made no difference. I refused to let it. I jumped 6.41 metres, putting myself a big step closer to qualification, and then I threw a PB in the javelin. As jazzed as I was, it still felt surreal. Was this really happening? Nothing could stop me that day. It was like there was a special pathway opening up just for me, and I was running through it like I was battery powered.

It's the best feeling as a heptathlete to be able to build and build throughout a heptathlon. It's like being on the game show *The Weakest Link*, where you can 'bank' your money as you go along, only I was banking points; building and banking, building and banking, building and banking.

Going into the 800m, I knew I could run it in 2:30 and still get the score I needed. I can't tell you how much more enjoyable the 800m is when you know you don't *have* to empty the tank completely to win it. Of course, I ran it hard anyway. I knocked 4 seconds off my PB and cleared the Olympic standard by 100 points, ending up with a whopping 6,248 – 241 better than my previous PB and the best score by a junior athlete, bar the legendary Carolina Klüft, since 1989.

Mission 6150: accomplished.

Twenty-eight athletes started the competition in Kladno and

only twelve finished; that's how grim the conditions were. But nothing was going to stop me from getting that score. That's just the mood I was in that weekend.

How do you mentally prepare yourself for a home Olympics in the space of eight weeks? I honestly wasn't sure it was possible – and I'm still not. But we did what we could to make sure I was at least physically ready to compete on that huge stage.

Part of that meant a change of plan. Happily, I would compete at the World Junior Championships in Barcelona after all. But instead of doing a full heptathlon, which would have been too much just three weeks before an Olympics, Mike said we were going to compete in the long jump and hurdles. My long jump had been improving rapidly, but I was still only ranked at tenth in the world (at junior level) going into the competition. I thought I might be in with a shot at the top five though, or maybe top three, if I really hit the board right. On my third jump in the final, that's what happened. I landed a jump of 6.81 metres! It felt like everything had come together just at the right time.

Incredibly, it put me in first place. Jaz had a big jump that was close to 7 metres but was a foul, so then I just had to wait for a German athlete to make her final jump; she came extremely close, but she didn't beat me. She jumped 6.80 metres and I won the competition by 1cm. I couldn't really believe it. I thought I'd sacrificed my chances of being a world junior champion by competing in Kladno, and now I had a gold medal around my neck – and in the long jump of all things! It was mad. A completely unexpected bonus.

One of the best parts of that day was standing on the medal podium alongside one of my closest friends in the sport, Jaz,

Unbroken

who had made it onto the podium too, winning long jump bronze.

Winning gold brought a bit more attention to me going into the Olympics than I'd expected. Suddenly, journalists were asking me about the long jump instead of the heptathlon – questions I didn't mind at the time, though later on in my career they would come to be a source of frustration. Thankfully, I wasn't alone under the spotlight. Adam Gemili had won gold in Barcelona too, running the 100m in 10.05 seconds, a new championship record, and he was going on to compete at London 2012 – together, we were the youngest members of the GB athletics team. I'd had no media training at all (I still haven't) so I was completely myself when I was talking to the press. Completely open. Completely honest. Completely vulnerable. At that stage, it was fine; it was only a few years later, when the media started trying to build a rivalry between me and Jess that I felt some started taking advantage.

Come to think of it, maybe *that* was my media training. But more on that later.

When I think back now to how I approached 2012 and how firmly I believed that I would be competing at those Olympic Games, it seems mad. Yes, it was based upon a belief in myself as an athlete and the confidence I had built from seeing my PBs and scores improve year on year. But it was also based upon a belief in something far less tangible: that I could manifest my success. That seeing it, feeling it and thinking about it was enough to make it happen.

And for a good portion of my early career, it worked. Obviously I was putting in the hard work in training too, but mentally that was my foundation. The problem with it was that it was purely outcome-based. It wasn't about how I got there – what I had to do to get over the hurdles quicker or clear the bar in the high jump. It was about crossing the finish line first or standing on top of the medal podium.

That's a precarious base on which to build a performance. Because winning is not always within your control. How *you* perform is, but how others perform is not. So now I just try to manifest me doing everything correctly. I don't try to manifest me standing on the podium with a medal because that's just a dream. It's a nice dream, but I don't think it gets you any closer to actually achieving it. You need to do the things, too; you need to manifest what needs to be done in order to get that end result.

But as a teenager heading into my first Olympics, I firmly believed that I could manifest my entire life.

Going into London 2012, I felt sort of untouchable. There was a lot of attention on me, but it wasn't a burden. It was fun, and I didn't feel any pressure. I felt like I'd already won just by being there.

After so many years of focusing purely on being the best, it felt a little strange going into a competition without a specific goal in mind. The night before going into the Village, I wrote in my diary: 'What do I want to achieve from this?' I spent a good half an hour trying to think of the right answer, but the truth is I didn't really know. Because I didn't know what was waiting for me inside that stadium. I didn't know what experience I was about to have, and I didn't know the impact it would have on me. At that point, all I knew was that since

Unbroken

that day in 2011 when I'd stood on an imaginary start line and had seen myself running hurdles at the start of an Olympic heptathlon, this was all I'd wanted. I'd manifested it. I'd visualized it. I had made it happen.

And now it was about to become reality.

6

Fame

I FELT THE VOMIT RISE IN MY THROAT.

Oh fuck, not here. Not now.

Mouth closed. Deep breath in through the nose. Breathe out. Deep breath in. Breathe out.

It was 3 August 2012: day one of the Olympic heptathlon. I was so nervous I felt physically sick. I was going to vomit. My whole life had built up to this, and I was actually going to puke.

I'd felt OK at the warm-up track earlier that morning. A little nervous, sure, but my excitement levels at that point were enough to override any wobbles. But then it was time to make our way to the main stadium for the 100m hurdles, the first event of the heptathlon and the start of two long days of competition. It was a ten-minute walk from the warm-up track to the Olympic Stadium, although one athlete was spared the extra load on her legs; Jess had been provided with a golf buggy for the journey. I was lucky to be invited to join her.

Unbroken

As we approached the stadium, we started to hear the noise emerging from inside. The closer we got, the louder it became. I remember playing music to settle my nerves. 'Not Nineteen Forever' by The Courteeners was the first song to come up when I hit shuffle; a song that became the anthem of my youth. It still reminds me of the best times with my friends and of that day: Day One of my Olympic journey. But in that moment, the noise was like no other crowd noise I'd ever heard before – not in real life, anyway. It sounded like the roar from a Colosseum as two Roman gladiators prepared for battle. I tried to concentrate on the music, remain calm and stop my mind from spiralling.

The lead-up to that first race was the worst bit of the whole Olympic experience for me. I always get most nervous before the hurdles anyway, because that's the event with the biggest jeopardy; you can sprint out of the blocks, hit a hurdle and fall on your face and then that's it, your whole heptathlon is done. So that was part of it. But mostly, I was nervous about being in front of that many people: 80,000! I'd never had that many sets of eyes on me before. I had no idea what it was going to feel like or how my body was going to react. What if I just fainted? I'd be mortified.

There were five heats for the 100m hurdles and I was in the fourth one, before Jess got her Olympics under way in heat five. The other Brit, Louise Hazel, was in the heat before mine and just as she and the others in her race were preparing to get into their blocks, I made my way into the final call room underneath the stadium alongside the others in my heat. It's a weird feeling being underneath a stadium. Usually, you can't hear much from there at all; maybe a faint hum of noise from above which gets slightly louder if something exciting happens, but nothing more.

A little while after the heat-three girls had gone into the stadium, we suddenly heard an explosion of noise. They had little TV screens in the call-up room so I went over to see what was going on, and that's when I realized: that noise was for Louise. The crowd had seen an athlete arriving in a Team GB kit and completely lost their minds. My stomach lurched.

Mouth closed. Deep breath in through the nose. Breathe out.

And then it was our time. I was just leaving the final call room when I heard a voice say, 'Kat!' I turned around and saw a familiar face. 'Hey, Kat, you all right?' It was Arwel Williams – Taffy – from Liverpool Harriers, the same Taffy who'd told my Mum she could still bring me training in the wind and rain way back when I first joined. He was working as an official at the Games. Seeing him put me in a different, calmer headspace instantly. It was just a normal event, after all. Yeah. That only lasted until the moment I walked out of the tunnel and laid eyes on the crowd for the first time.

Oh shit.

Why are there so many people?

Normally when we do hurdles, there's nobody there. It's the first event of the morning session and people are still making their way to the stadium. Getting their snacks. But the stadium was full. There were people everywhere. Constant noise. It was a lot to take in.

Mouth closed. Deep breath in through the nose. Breathe out.

I made my way towards the lane I'd been given: lane 9, the last one in the row and the one closest to the crowd. The sun was out and I could feel it warming my skin, but I was covered in goose bumps. I did a few warm-up jumps, trying to shake out the nerves as much as warm up my muscles. That's when I saw the camera making its way along the start line. It stopped in front of each athlete, allowing the stadium announcer to present them to the crowd and giving the athlete a chance to soak up some applause. Some smiled and waved. Some did very little.

What would I do? Why hadn't I thought about this bit?! I watched as the camera got closer and closer to me, stopping at Dafne Schippers in the lane next to me. I knew her well – she'd won the World Juniors in Canada when I was out injured and the European Juniors the following year, where I finished sixth. She was The One To Beat at youth level. Dafne played it cool for the camera – a little grin and wave and that was it. Then it was my turn.

As the camera arrived in front of me I gave an awkward double-handed wave down the lens.

'And in lane 9, from Great Britain, Katarina Johnson-Thompson!'

Not to be arrogant, but . . . then the crowd exploded. The noise was incredible and there were Union Jack flags waving everywhere I looked. I raised an arm and just started laughing. The cheers just kept on coming. The words in my head spilled out of my mouth: 'Oh wow!' I'd never heard that kind of reaction to my name before. It was crazy.

Eventually, a hush fell over the crowd. The starter called, 'On your marks,' and I took a brief moment to try to settle myself before walking over to my blocks.

'Set.'

Oh, fuck.

And then the gun, followed immediately by an alarm sound,

like someone had just tried to walk out of the supermarket without paying.

A false start from the Estonian athlete in lane 6.

It was the best thing that could have happened. If the race had gone on that first gun, I'd have been a nervous wreck, and raced like one. The false start gave my mind and body the chance to realize this was just another race. We've done it before, many times.

And then it was back into our blocks.

Mouth closed. Deep breath in through the nose. Breathe out.
BANG.

And it had started and now there was no stopping it. Not the 100m hurdles. Not the Olympic heptathlon. And not me.

Life would never be the same again.

Regardless of what had happened before it, London 2012 was the launchpad for my athletics career. It was the first time I fully understood what a career as a professional athlete could look like: 80,000 people cheering your name in unison, a tangible electricity passing directly from them to you, lighting up your entire body. It was addictive. Once I experienced it, I wanted that same feeling again and again.

Being on that stage brought me recognition and opened doors to a new life. A life where athletics would become more than the hobby it had been up to that point. It was already my identity – it had been My Thing since I was five years old – but it was about to become my career, too. Was I ready for it? On the track, maybe. Off it? Not a chance.

A few weeks before those Games, while we were being kitted out together at Loughborough University, Team GB javelin thrower Goldie Sayers had told me to take the Olympic experience in as deeply as I could, because nothing would ever be like it again in my life. And she was right. I first thought about her advice the day I arrived at the Athletes' Village in Stratford. People ask me about it all the time, and I don't know how else to describe it: the Olympic Village is insane. It's like a kids' playground except for athletes. At the London Village, there was an arcade room, mega Jenga, pool tables, the huge Olympic rings, and the biggest dining hall I'd ever seen, serving every and any kind of food you could ever want. There was even a 'pub', although the only drinks it served were soft ones from some of the biggest Olympic sponsors. The place was lit up by the brightly coloured kits of hundreds of different nations and it buzzed with the unique soundtrack of thousands of excited athletes from all over the world.

That first day I was running about exploring like an excited kid on Christmas Day. I saw Princess Anne being shown around and spotted Chris Hoy (or Sir Chris, as he's now known). Everywhere you looked, there were faces and names that I'd only ever seen on television before. I had to calm myself down. It was only a couple of days before the heptathlon started and I didn't want to get to the start line of the hurdles already fatigued, so I told myself to be sensible: focus on competing and save the exploring for afterwards. I was sharing an apartment with fellow heptathlete Louise Hazel and the distance runner Jo Pavey, who was competing in the 5,000m and the 10,000m. We had lucked out and had a prime location – we could see the stadium from our rooms, which was really cool, especially after dark when it was illuminated (luckily, they supplied blackout blinds in the room so it didn't ruin our sleep). For the two days of the heptathlon competition, I had my own room. After that, Jo moved into my single room and Louise and I shared the twin.

Heptathletes get some preference when we're competing because the hours are so long. Often on competition days, I wake up at 5 a.m. to eat, digest and get to the track an hour before warm-up, and I don't get back at the end of that first day until 11 p.m., or even later sometimes. Then I just grab my spikes and whatever I need for day two, leave everything else a mess and try to get some sleep.

Some comps are worse than others. At the Rio Olympics in 2016, I remember starting my ice bath at 1 a.m., which was horrendous considering I had to get up at 4 a.m. the next day because our accommodation was fifty minutes (!) away from the track. Anyone watching might not notice it, but at the start of day two, all heptathletes may as well be the zombies from *The Walking Dead*. The only silver lining is that everyone feels the same. But it's not great when the long jump, the first event on day two, is one of your best events – yay for me.

When my alarm went off bright and early on the morning of 3 August 2012, I was wide awake and alert immediately. No caffeine required! It felt like Christmas morning as I put on my GB kit and made my way to the vast dining area (which was pretty quiet given it was pre-7 a.m.) for breakfast. It was a buffet-style layout with more options than I'd ever seen in my life, catering to the diets of athletes from all over the world. But I played it safe with my usual scrambled eggs, granola and yoghurt. Plus coffee, more out of habit than anything else. My brain was already wide awake and buzzing about what lay ahead that day. Though I had no idea just how

Unbroken

momentous it would feel once we actually arrived at the stadium and heard that noise, nor just how much my nerves would jangle once I was on the start line of that 100m hurdles.

The moment I crossed the finish line of the hurdles and saw my time on the scoreboard, I breathed a sigh of relief. I'd made it through the most perilous event unscathed *and* I'd got a good time to boot (I equalled my PB of 13.48 seconds, finishing level with Dafne). My adrenaline was still pumping, but now I was just riding the wave. I wanted more; more of the crowd, more of the excitement, more of this incredible feeling. It wasn't like anything I'd experienced before. We went straight into the high jump after that, and every time Jess, Louise or I sailed over one of our warm-up jumps, there was an immediate roar from the crowd. Warm-up jumps getting a cheer was completely new to me – what was this insanity? I loved it! I almost found myself cheering along with them. They were just screaming for everything, it was amazing.

And unlike the hurdles, this was my event! My comfort zone. Usually in a high jump competition you have to get the crowd going, but not that day. That day, they were starting their own claps. Queen's 'We Will Rock You' was blasting out of the loudspeakers and the crowd were stomping their feet and singing along. Hearing that while waiting to jump was like drinking a double espresso. The sun that had beamed down on us all morning had been replaced by clouds and rain for the start of the high jump, but that didn't bother me at all. I cleared 1.80, 1.83 and 1.86 metres before Mike suggested going to 1.89 metres – a PB for me by 1cm. By this time, everything else in the morning session had finished and so the entire crowd was focused on our high jump competition. I stood on my mark and stared at the bar, seeing myself soar over it and hearing everyone go wild.

And then it happened. I cleared 1.89 metres for the first time, in front of 80,000 people. As I landed on the crash mat, a wall of sound came down around me. I clenched my fists and put my hands over my eyes in disbelief. After two events, I was in third place. Bronze medal position. It was beyond all my wildest dreams. I remember being interviewed after the high jump; the reporter congratulated me on being in third place. 'Yeah,' I said, 'but the shot put's next, *hahaha*.' When I spoke to the media, I just said whatever came into my head with no thought for the fact that it then got broadcast to the world.

The high jump was the last event of the morning session, meaning there was a long gap to the shot put at the start of the evening session. Part of me was devastated about that, because I just wanted to be out there again, feeling that buzz from the crowd.

But I have to admit, another part of me was thrilled; it meant I stayed in third place for hours.

In the gap between the morning and evening sessions, some heptathletes go back to the Village to sleep, but a lot of the time it's too much of a rigmarole to go back and forth; you don't really want to do any extra unnecessary walking, so other athletes decide to stay in the rest room. The rest room is a special room that's only for combined eventers, where we can get a meal between sessions (everyone eats *a lot* after the high jump) and chill out or just sleep.

Some rest rooms are good and some are terrible. At the 2023 World Championships in Budapest, the rest room was amazing:

Unbroken

we had coffee machines, our own cubicles with a blow-up air bed, towels and pillows, and they actually turned the lights off when it was time to sleep. In stark contrast, the rest room at the Rio Olympics in 2016 was just one big space, with pathetic little blue mats on the floor for beds, and daylight flooding in the whole time.

In 2012, Jess was given her own private rest room, and I was really lucky that she allowed me to be there too. It was a huge space so it wasn't like we were in each other's faces or anything, but I still made sure to keep as much distance as possible between us. Jess was on her own journey in 2012 – and an intensely pressured one at that. So while she was helpful to me in terms of letting me be around her and observe, she'd never give advice. I'd never ask, either. You didn't really see her talking to anybody during those two days of the heptathlon in London. She was completely in her own zone, either by herself or with her coach Toni. I think she had to do that to block out all the noise. It was a big gesture for her to allow me into that space, and just being there was more than enough for me. I didn't dare try to talk to her in that scenario. I was young and I was there to learn. I was wise enough not to disrupt her flow and wary of doing anything that could even remotely overstep; even if, looking back, it would have been helpful to ask her questions.

The long jumper Greg Rutherford was one of the more experienced athletes who was really going out of his way to give everyone advice in that crazy environment. He's always been that way. I'll never forget a kind message he sent me a few years later, after I did three no-jumps at the World Championships in Beijing, and an interview he gave to the press basically telling them to give me a break.

Katarina Johnson-Thompson

By the time the final event of the day arrived – the 200m – my third place was a distant memory. I had thrown 11.32 metres in the shot put, 50cm down on my record in Kladno, putting me back to twentieth place overall. I knew it was something I had to work on, so I wasn't surprised. Also, this was my first ever senior international. I was up against seasoned athletes; people who I'd been watching compete against each other on TV for the past two years. Their PBs in every single event were better than mine, so I had no expectations whatsoever. I wasn't annoyed to be getting beaten. I was just loving being there. Case in point: the 200m. Generally, I always won the 200m, but in London I was in the fifth and final heat of the night alongside Jess and Dafne, who was the Dutch record holder over 200m. She had beaten Jess in the same event at Götzis earlier that year.

It was 9 p.m. by the time we walked out for that last event, but the crowd were just as exuberant as the morning attendees had been at 10 a.m. One of the reasons I feel so lucky to have had the 2012 experience that I did is that unlike some athletes who only got to perform once and their Olympic experience was over, I had a full two days of being with all these different crowds – four of them, because there were morning and evening sessions each day. Everybody was so excited to be there so every single session was electric.

For the 200m, I was in the outside lane again, but this time the camera came to me first, and a huge roar went up in reaction to my name. I looked down the lens and grinned before giving a wave and repeating my words from that morning: 'Oh wow.'

Honestly, the feeling on those start lines is something I will never, ever forget.

When the start gun went off, there was an explosion of noise that felt like it carried me straight into the bend. Just as I came off it, into the home straight, I suddenly saw something swing past me on the outside. *What the . . . ? What is that?* I initially thought it was another athlete, until I realized I was in the outside lane!

It was the camera for the side shot – something I'd never experienced before, because they tend to only have them at the biggest competitions. It didn't have any interest in me; it was simply zooming past to catch up with Jess and Dafne, who were streaking ahead of everyone towards the finish line. I ended up dipping for the line to nab fifth place, and I set a new PB of 23.73 seconds. It was a great way to finish day one, but there was a small part of me that wished I'd been in one of the earlier heats. Louise Hazel had gone in heat two and won it by a distance, despite running a second slower than I had. She'd had that magical moment, crossing the finish line in first place as the crowd went wild. Whereas I'd been dipping for fifth. I really wanted a moment like hers.

My mind and body were on such a high that night that it took some time for sleep to come. I was in fourteenth place and loving every single second of performing in front of that crowd. I could see Jess doing her best to block it out, allowing herself just a brief wave to acknowledge the wall of noise that greeted her every appearance, and I wondered if I would be able to do the same if I was ever in her position. I couldn't see it. I didn't see myself as ever being that kind of athlete. I felt like I was always going to be the type to absorb the atmosphere and use it to my advantage rather than trying to shut it out.

Inside the Village we were somewhat cut off from the madness that was happening outside. I knew that Jess being in first place at the end of day one would be big news, but I hadn't realized the knock-on effect it would have on me – that is, until the morning of day two, when I decided to reopen Twitter on my phone. I hadn't looked at it for three days before the competition, when I had about 1,500 followers. By Saturday morning that had gone up to 30,000.

Oh my god. What's happening?

I quickly closed it again. I had to focus on what was coming next – the long jump – not my follower count. I was jumping in Group B, placed right after Jess in the order. It was wild. Every time I prepared to start my run-up, Jess was walking back to her seat, having completed her jump, and the crowd were going mad, doing a little Mexican wave as she passed them. It wasn't Jess's fault – she wasn't even looking at them – but I found it hard to concentrate. My best jump was 6.19 metres, which was enough to put me ninth in the long jump and twelfth overall, with two events to go: javelin and 800m. I threw 38.37 in the javelin, which was a little bit down on the PB I'd set in Kladno (you know, when my soul was on fire). That left me in sixteenth place overall, with one event to go.

All that was left was the 800m. This time, I was in the penultimate heat. I felt the usual dread as I prepared myself for the race – you know it's going to hurt – but now it was coupled with a tinge of sadness. My two days as an Olympian – the best two days of my life – were almost over. I gave the camera one last smile as it focused on my lane. One last wave to the crowd. Then, it was go-time. I worked my way to the back of a leading group, sitting in fifth place as we went around the first lap. I was in my rhythm, about to make my kick for the finish line, when there was a huge roar from the crowd. I had no idea who they were shouting for; I only realized later on that it must have been Greg Rutherford winning gold in the long jump. When we entered the home straight, I kicked. Hard. I overtook two competitors, then another one. Suddenly I was chasing down the leader, Brianne Theisen, but the finish line beat me to it and I finished in second place. When I saw the time, I was so happy; I'd knocked 4 seconds off my 800m PB, and finished in fifteenth place (it's since become thirteenth; two athletes were later disqualified for failing drug tests) with 6,267 points overall – a small increase on my score in Kladno and so another new PB.

Once I had my breath back, I made my way over to the front of the mixed zone (the area where broadcasters and written press wait for interviews with athletes) and waited for the final race. Jess had built such a good gap to second place that it amounted to a 15-second lead, so I was pretty confident she would get gold, but you still know that anything can happen once the gun goes. She went out fast. Too fast. When she got caught by a few chasers it got a bit scary. But once they hit the final 200m she broke away and there was nobody else who was going to win. Seeing that moment from close up was amazing. And as I saw all of Jess's emotions finally pour out of her, I felt mine rising up too.

I cried the whole way round the victory lap, which all the heptathlon athletes do together. I'd seen up close the pressure that Jess was under. I'd watched how she'd handled it so well and kept her emotions in check for two whole days. Now she was letting it all out, and it made me want to do the same.

As we walked around that stadium, absorbing the noise and

love from the crowd, the enormity of what Jess had done hit me. Seeing her and everyone in the stadium so ecstatically happy was one of the most surreal, inspirational moments of my life.

It was the moment that I knew: I want this moment again. I want this moment for me.

The madness didn't end when I finished competing.

In the days after the heptathlon, I was invited to all sorts of events and I'd only taken my Olympic kit into the Village with me – nothing dressy at all. I arranged to meet my mum and nan in the big Westfield shopping centre, right next to the Olympic Park, so we could catch up and I could go to Topshop to buy a new dress for the night. I had no idea that just being in the Team GB tracksuit would be like ringing some sort of alarm bell.

We were mobbed. People were shouting my name and asking for pictures. It actually got pretty scary; there were so many people surrounding me. Eventually, security came and got me out. To this day, I've never experienced anything like that. It was insane. It got even weirder later that night when I went to an event at Adidas House. Steven Gerrard was there and he knew who I was! I was blown away. The Liverpool captain. The man whose name I'd had on the back of my shirt when I was a kid now knew who I was. What was going on?!

A few days later, I went to the O2 Arena with Barrie, where the gymnastics competition was being held, and the same thing happened again; we were swamped by people requesting pictures and autographs. At one point we dived into a restaurant to try to get a bit of space and air. When the police came over I thought it was to help me, but they asked for a picture too.

Unbroken

I've never really felt 'famous' but, in 2012, I think every athlete wearing that Team GB kit felt a bit like a celebrity. Anywhere we went it was the same: people recognizing you and wanting pictures taken. I remember going to BBC Radio 1 for an interview not long after the Olympics and bumping into the actor Blake Harrison, who plays Neil in *The Inbetweeners*. I was starstruck, but really wanted a photo with him. Before I could pluck up the courage to ask, he actually asked me for one. I was in shock! I wasn't used to it at all and it sometimes made me quite anxious. Even now, if too many people want pictures in a public place, I get the same feeling; my body goes into high alert and I just want to escape.

Anyone who knows me knows I don't like being the centre of attention. Being tall has never helped with that. My coaches have always told me to stand tall and be proud, but I'll literally hunch to try to blend in with the crowd. Despite how much I enjoyed competing in front of 80,000 people that summer, I don't like personal attention. To this day, it's something that I really hate, because I'm a natural introvert. I'm comfortable with people I know, or in small groups; I find it challenging going to big events where I don't know many people. In the spring of 2024 I was invited to a Net-a-Porter event, and the invite was just for me, no plus-one. I was apprehensive, but thought I'd try to challenge myself and go – I thought, *I'm grown, I should be able to do things like this.* But at the start of the evening, there was a moment where I was just standing by myself thinking: *Oh my god, why am I here?* It was the worst; I felt isolated for what felt like for ever (though in reality probably wasn't long at all) before someone came over and spoke to me. And after that moment, I really enjoyed the evening, and was glad I pushed past that fear and momentary feeling of isolation.

I'm never the one to just bowl in and start a conversation, though. I get anxious thinking about what questions I should ask. Is that inappropriate? Is that overstepping? I don't want to seem like I'm not bothered but, also, I don't want to ask personal questions. I go through all these different things in my head. Overthinking it. So I just say nothing to avoid having the regret over saying the wrong thing. And then I come across as rude.

My boyfriend Pozz is the opposite. It's so nice to be around him in social situations because he'll be chatting away, asking loads of questions, and then if I see someone's responding, I know, OK, this is safe, and I can jump in. You can see the difference between us at the end of something like a British Championships weekend, where we'll be trying to get to the car to leave and Pozz will stop and speak to every single athlete along the way. We'll move five inches closer to the car and then he'll stop and chat to someone else. In the end, I'm OK with not continuing the conversation and saying, 'All right, I'm going now . . .' But he can't do that. It usually ends with me waiting by the car door for him to finally stop talking.

Some people might struggle to understand how an introvert can go out and thrive on competing in front of thousands of people. But I don't see competing as a related thing. I'm an introvert, and I can be a professional athlete, because what I'm doing is nothing more than movements that I've practised a thousand times. That's basically all that athletics is: movements under pressure. It's not like social skills. It's not being the life and soul of the party.

When you go into the mixed zone and it's just one on one, it doesn't feel like anything big. Whereas I don't love public speaking, or any scenario where there's lots of eyes looking at you, just waiting for something that will come out your mouth. For me, that's much scarier than running and jumping over a bar.

At big international competitions, British Athletics name a team captain who gives a speech to the whole team on the eve of the event. Generally, it's someone with a fair bit of experience who can speak about what they've learned along the way, give newer athletes on the team some useful advice and get everyone pumped for the competition. I've lost count of the number of times I've been asked: 'Are you going to be team captain this year?' I was invited to do it once, but I said no.

It was an honour to be asked, but it's just not something that feels natural to me. It used to be decided by a voting system and even then, when I gave my vote, I'd openly ask anyone planning to vote for me to vote for someone else.

Laura Muir was team captain for the World Championships in Budapest last year but she wasn't in the holding camp before it started (the longer distance athletes often train in altitude right up until they compete). So British Athletics decided that, as Laura wasn't going to be there in person to deliver her captain's speech (she did it via video link instead), they would also pick six prefects to deliver a speech in the final team meeting. I was picked as one of those six, alongside a lot of extroverts. Before the big meeting, we all got together to discuss what we were going to say and I was really stressing over it. We were addressing personal development questions: Has anyone ever felt like they weren't enough? Then someone would stand up and give an example of a time they felt that way. It was supposed to be something that brought us together.

Katarina Johnson-Thompson

When it was my turn to speak, I opened my mouth and – I don't know how else to say this – what came out wasn't my normal voice. It was like my throat had closed up and I had to really strain to get the sound out. It was embarrassing on another level. I'll happily speak to young athletes one on one and answer any questions they have, or pass on advice if I feel it could be helpful. But too many sets of eyes and ears in one go just makes me anxious. And that's the last thing I need before I compete.

When I was younger, there was definitely a period after 2012 when I was excited by the idea of fame and all the media opportunities that came my way. But as I got older and understood the realities of what it means to be 'famous', I knew it wasn't really for me. I see fame and recognition as two different things. Recognition for what you do is always lovely, and makes you feel like you're doing something worth talking about. But on the other side of it, fame still stresses me out a little bit. It gives me anxiety when someone comes up to me and I don't know where the conversation is going. Nine times out of ten it's really nice, and they're just saying, 'Well done, we loved watching you,' and I love those kinds of conversations. But that tenth time can be really awkward and disjointed.

Around the Olympics, it always goes up to another level because that's when track and field gets the most attention, and it's just not what athletes are used to dealing with. I feel like if people go into the sport for that type of fame, then they're in the wrong industry. Some people thrive on it and lean into it, like Noah Lyles, who won the 100m gold in Paris 2024. He wants all the recognition in the world to be able to invigorate the sport, and rightly so; those individuals are the people who are carrying it. But I'm introverted, and nervous around new people. I'm not even good at first conversations with people I do know. So when it's just interactions in the street, or people shouting 'Are you that famous one?' at me on a plane, I'm just like, *Oh my god, I want to die, because now everyone's looking* – and how am I meant to answer that? I mean, clearly not, because you don't know my name!

It's fine when I'm in a stadium and I've got control. Like when it's my last long jump, and everyone's watching, I don't mind starting a clap, because it's something that I'm comfortable with and something I've practised doing. But in a social situation, when I don't know where the conversation is going or what's going to happen, I just get really nervous.

After an Olympics or World Championships, I do end up turning a lot of media work down, because I feel like that's not really what I do it for. For me, the moments I have with my family and friends afterwards are everything to me – as much as the moment of actually competing.

Six weeks after London 2012, I was sitting in a lecture hall at Liverpool John Moore University, having just started my degree in sports science. It was the strangest feeling.

Student life hadn't got off to the best start for me. I'd missed Freshers' Week because I was at Bisham Abbey, rehabbing an ankle injury that I picked up just before the Olympics (I'd rolled it pretty badly, but it wasn't my take-off leg, so I was able to compete). And then I saw on Twitter that a couple of the girls who I was sharing halls with had been talking about me. It wasn't anything nasty; just chatter about me being in their halls, in the room next door to one of them, and about how they'd never seen me in real life before. I wasn't used to that sort of thing. It felt like everyone was talking about me, and I hated that feeling.

By the time lectures started, I was already back in training, to the point that I was missing more than I was making. It wasn't long before I started to wonder what the point of me being there was.

Three weeks in, I said, 'I can't do this. I can't concentrate here. I can't do both.'

Doing that victory lap at the Olympics and experiencing all the emotions that come with 80,000 people cheering their hearts out made me realize that athletics was it for me. It was all I wanted to do. I had always loved the sport, but until then I had still viewed it as a hobby. Seeing what Jess achieved in London changed that. I wanted the same things for myself one day and I knew that meant it couldn't just be a hobby any more; it had to be my life.

I'd juggled training with school and then with college but I didn't want to do that any more. I wanted to be able to give all of myself, all of my focus to becoming as good as I could be. So it frustrated me when I was sitting in a lecture hall, knowing that I could be at the track working on becoming a better heptathlete instead.

The way I saw it, I could be an average student and an average athlete at the same time or I could commit to one of those things and try to be the best in the world at it.

There was no competition. My heart wasn't in university, it was in athletics.

I spoke to Mum about it and she was really supportive. She had gone back to studying later on in life and said that I could always do the same if I wanted to, once I was finished competing.

That was all the encouragement I needed to make my final decision. One lecture in, I quit.

For the first time in my life, I was a full-time athlete. I didn't have to fit in training sessions around lectures or worry about getting assignments written. I had one job to do, and it was the best one in the world. One that didn't feel like a job in the slightest.

I had already been to an Olympics, but it felt like my athletics career was really just about to begin, and I couldn't wait to see where it took me.

What I didn't yet realize was how much it would teach me, too. I was about to learn more about the sport – and so much else besides – than I knew was possible.

And struggle with it more than I ever expected.

7
Belief

I LOOKED DOWN AT MY SHOES, TRIED TO KEEP MY STOMACH CALM and attempted again to focus.

I took a breath, and the fresh Moscow air rushing through my lungs brought me back to earth. It was August 2013 and there was only one person standing between me and a medal at my very first senior World Championships. And I knew her well.

As a junior, Dafne Schippers had mostly gotten the better of me, and at London 2012 she'd put on an impressive performance in the heptathlon, beating Jess Ennis-Hill to win the 200m and finish tenth overall. Thanks to the hype generated by a home Olympics, I was pretty well known in the UK, but in heptathlon circles everyone was talking about the twenty-one-year-old Dafne and her incredible performances. She was getting PBs all over the place, and at the end of day one in Moscow had run the fastest ever 200m in a World Championships heptathlon.

Unbroken

It was Dafne who was the next best thing in the heptathlon, not me.

Now, a year after London 2012, we were both vying for the medal at the World Championships in Moscow and it had all come down to the final – most brutal – event of the heptathlon, the 800m. Of the seven events in the heptathlon, it's always the one that hurts the most. It's the one that pushes your heart and lungs to their maximum, and serves as the knockout punch for legs that feel heavy and sore from two long days of competing.

Although I was only twenty, I was used to aiming for a specific time over the two laps and trying to get a certain number of points. This time, I had to run it at least 3 seconds faster than Dafne if the bronze medal was to be mine. That meant I had to go out as fast as I possibly could and hang on for dear life. Even then, there were so many different scenarios that could potentially play out, because the top five athletes going into that race were all so close.

Just the thought of it made me feel sick.

I went out hard, pushing more and more as the race went on. I knew I was ahead of Dafne, but it was impossible to know by how much, so I just tried to keep on pushing, demanding more and more from a body that was screaming at me to stop. I crossed the finish line in second place and fell to my knees, gulping in as much oxygen as I could. In interviews afterwards, my voice was so hoarse it sounded like I'd been smoking seventy a day. I could barely breathe without coughing.

Dafne followed me across the finish line a second later and immediately collapsed to the ground. She'd gone so hard over the final 300 metres that she needed medical attention. I'd taken 3 seconds off my PB to finish in 2:07, which even Mike was happy with, but Dafne had smashed her PB by 7 seconds to finish in 2:08. That meant the bronze medal was hers, and it was a big one; the first heptathlon medal won by a Dutch woman in World Championship Athletics history.

Meanwhile, I'd gone from fifteenth at the Olympics to fifth in the world and fighting for medals, in the space of a year. I'd also added another 200 points on to my total. I was pleased with my performance, but my overriding feeling was one of frustration. I was annoyed that I hadn't gone into the event looking for more.

I should have believed more in myself.

I'd approached Moscow 2013 with the same mentality as I had London 2012: that I was still a young athlete who was primarily there to learn and have fun. There was still plenty of time to progress and work my way up to the medal podium. What I didn't appreciate was that the year after an Olympics is often one where there's a lot of transition. Many athletes reassess their whole lives after an Olympic Games. Some retire. Some change coaches. Some lose motivation.

Ultimately, that meant that a lot of people who had competed at the Olympics in 2012 weren't in Moscow, and so the standard was lower than it had previously been. I should have realized that; I should have changed my approach and been more focused – Dafne clearly was. After Moscow, I changed my laptop wallpaper to a picture from the World Championships of Dafne proudly holding the Dutch flag and me, in the background, trying to get out of the shot. I wanted that moment for myself. It was the first time I used a negative thought or moment as a motivational tool – something that I would do again after the next World Championships –

because I thought it would help me on the days I needed a push.

Six years later, at the European Indoor Championships in 2019, I remember wanting to pass on a similar message to Niamh Emerson, a British heptathlete who was only nineteen at the time. I wanted to tell her that just because she was young, it didn't mean that she couldn't be in contention for the medals. A lot of people tell young athletes that they're just at championships for experience, maybe to take the pressure off. But I genuinely believed in her capabilities. I told her that she could do really well at those champs given her previous performances, and that she might just catch one and go on a break.

I took the gold that day, but Niamh won silver with 4,731 points; the best pentathlon score ever recorded by a teenage athlete.

I wish someone had said something similar to me in 2013. I don't think it would have added any pressure. There's a big difference between 'you should win' and 'you can win'.

But ultimately, the experience I gained in 2013 is one that I'll carry for a lifetime. I left Moscow secure in the knowledge that nothing would ever be as terrifying as starting an 800m race when I had no idea what was going to happen or what I was capable of.

The time had come to switch up my mental approach: from now on, I was going for those medals.

The comparisons to Jessica Ennis-Hill started the moment I broke her British junior record in Italy, when I was trying to qualify for London, and they only increased after the Games.

At that early stage of my career, I was excited to be compared to Jess; she was the biggest thing in sport at the time and the poster girl for British athletics. That kind of success was what I wanted for myself, so I completely bought into it. But it was also daunting. People say that if you can see it, you can be it, but I'd witnessed the level that Jess was at first hand, and it still felt a long way away from mine. How would I ever get that good? How would I close the huge gap from fifteenth place to first? The jump from 6,200 points to 6,900 felt too massive.

Yet despite my worries, in the two years following the 2012 Olympics, the gap steadily started to close. I changed from the smiley young kid who was just excited to be there into an athlete capable of winning medals. People were looking at my performances and filling in the blanks, saying, 'If she just does this, this and this, then she can be a champion.'

It was a fractured look at a potential champion. And that's not how the heptathlon works.

But at the time I was believing it; Mike was believing it; everyone was believing it. After all, coming out of London 2012, everything was different. I'd never had a 'normal' job; I never earned a salary, and before my first Olympic Games I didn't have a sponsorship contract with anyone. Adidas would send me bits of kit to wear, but there was no financial backing to go alongside that. The only funding I had going into London 2012 was from British Athletics and Barrie, whose support was for specific things, like getting to training and competitions. I had no money for anything else though.

After the Games, Adidas said they wanted to sponsor me because I'd done so well that year, but Nike were also keen. The brands then got into a bit of a battle with one another, which actually worked out pretty well for me as the package offered kept getting better and better. In the end, I signed a contract with Nike that made me feel like I was set for life, even though I was a long way from that. I was a bit like one of those lottery winners who will probably lose all of their winnings within a year, but I'd never seen that much money in my entire life. And that was part of the reason I felt able to quit university. I felt like I was getting paid more than I would if I was to finish my course and get a job. I felt as though they were paying me to be an athlete, which gave me the confidence and freedom to commit to it, which I was so excited to do.

Money aside, London 2012 had given me a taste of what to expect from future championships and it was all I could think about. That Olympic heptathlon was (and remains) my favourite competition ever. Full stop. The feeling you get after winning the World Championships is obviously better, but the elation I experienced during that Olympics is the best feeling I've had while actually doing the event. It was the most fun. It was the best crowd.

And it was with a lot of the friends who I've still got now: Pozz, Adam Gemili, Holly Bradshaw. That heptathlon was when I decided that it was what I wanted to do all the time. When I realized the true extent of how amazing professional sport could be.

I had about two months off after London, which I filled by rehabbing the ankle niggle I'd picked up before the Games, travelling to the Bahamas to see my dad, and embarking on my brief experiment with university life. But then it was straight into the hard winter graft.

The option was still there for me to move to Sheffield and be coached by Toni Minichiello, but it didn't make sense for me to make such a big change. Mike had got me to the Olympic Games and helped me add hundreds of points to my score. And

I was happy at home in Liverpool. In turn, Mike postponed his retirement and said he would help me for as long as I needed. We were a team and it felt like we were starting the next stage of an exciting journey together. We decided to focus on strength training and improving my throws. I'd been in third place at London 2012 before the shot put, and twenty-second afterwards; it was a big wake-up call.

I qualified for the 2013 World Championships in Moscow by winning the European U23 Championships in Finland that July. That win took me from being the young athlete who'd get excited to finish her season and sit at home, watching the World Championships on TV, to someone who was now routinely competing in them.

By the time Moscow concluded, my perspective had shifted even further. After disappointing performances in the high jump, where I knocked off the bar with my hair extensions (my hair causing me pain again! I'd made the mistake of putting it in a ponytail for the high jump, something I've never done since), and the shot put, I had one of the best second days I'd ever had. I set PBs in the long jump and javelin before that bruising 800m battle with Dafne. It gave me a strange kind of confidence to know I could come so close to a medal, finishing fifth in the world despite coming thirty-first out of thirty-three athletes in one discipline (you guessed it: shot put). And I knew where I needed to improve. Mike and I had already worked so hard on my throws that season, so my performance was frustrating, but I was one step away.

We went into that winter with a renewed sense of purpose, and new goals. At the start of 2013 we'd been quite conservative about things, just aiming to press on a little further and

Unbroken

keep on building. But after adding almost 200 points on to my score at the World Championships and finishing 28 points away from a medal, we approached 2014 rather differently.

We basically started attacking PBs. We wanted PBs in everything. We were trying all these different events, attacking the triple jump, the 400m, the 400m hurdles, just doing everything. We were going in. We wanted it all. Why? Because we could. I'd had a really good winter and I was in great shape. So, why not? And it paid off. That indoor season, I nabbed the British record for the high jump (1.96 metres) and set a new PB in the long jump too (6.75 metres). It was my fifth PB of 2014 and it was only February. But the biggest surprise came the following month at the World Indoor Championships in Sopot, a seaside town in northern Poland.

My intention was to go to Sopot and compete in the pentathlon – I was desperate to, actually – but after setting all those PBs early in the year, I picked up a bug and was too ill to participate in the qualifying event. I had, though, achieved the qualifying distance in the long jump, so we decided to go and see how I would match up against the event specialists. I had no real expectations but thought that if everyone else had an off day then perhaps I might be able to sneak a medal.

A few days before the long jump competition I'd had to sit and watch the pentathletes compete, which was a pretty miserable experience. It's one thing being stuck at home injured and missing out, but being there, being fit, and still not being able to compete was probably even more frustrating. Some forty-eight hours later, my mood had done a complete flip. I set another new PB in the long jump (6.81 metres), and somehow won a silver medal! It was my first senior medal and it didn't come in

Katarina Johnson-Thompson

either of my events (the pentathlon/heptathlon), or even in my strongest discipline (the high jump). I was thrilled – surprised, but absolutely thrilled.

Mike and I were on a roll. And with the Commonwealth Games taking place in Glasgow that summer, excitement started to build about what I might be able to do in front of a home crowd. London 2012 had captivated the entire nation. They loved the heptathlon and were excited to see more British success. So when Jess announced in January 2014 that she was pregnant and would be missing the Commonwealth Games, everyone's gaze shifted from her to me.

At that point, I believed I could do it. Mike believed I could do it. 'Yes, we can do this. Yes, we are ready' became our mantra. Every session, Mike would instil in me that I was good. That I was the best. That I could beat the best. And I took that as the truth because, remember, he's naturally a very negative man, so if even *he* was saying that then it must be true. I still had to do it when it counted the most though – in an actual heptathlon.

My next opportunity came in Götzis at the beginning of June 2014, two months before the start of the Commonwealth Games and almost a year since my last full heptathlon at the World Championships in Moscow. The prestigious combined-events competition in Austria was one that I'd been wanting to compete at for years; I felt like I'd almost missed my moment. But I tried to temper my excitement with the knowledge that it would be a tough competition, with a lot of the same athletes who I'd been up against in Moscow set to take part.

It went better than I ever expected.

Unbroken

On day one, I set four heptathlon PBs (including in the shot put!) and an outright PB in the 200m, going under 23 seconds for the first time ever. It left me in second place, 15 points behind the Canadian athlete Brianne Theisen-Eaton, the defending champion and silver medallist in Moscow. Day two was even better. After a 6.70-metre long jump (the furthest I'd ever jumped outdoors) and an outright PB in the javelin, I was in third place behind the Belgian athlete Nafissatou (Nafi) Thiam (the European junior champion) and Brianne. With only 30 points separating the three of us, what happened in the 800m would ultimately decide the final placings.

In Moscow, I'd been terrified of going into the 800m with something at stake. This time was different, because I'd been there before. It was still daunting, and I still knew it was going to hurt, but the fear of the unknown was gone. I knew I could handle it. Brianne pushed hard on the first lap but I stayed close to her. And when I felt the time was right, I made the kick for home and overtook Brianne to win the race, and the overall title.

When I crossed the finish line I was in disbelief. Had I really just won Götzis? The list of previous winners read like a who's who of the greatest heptathletes in the sport's history and now my name was going to be added to it. I hadn't just gone through my rite of passage, I'd hurtled through it. My overall score of 6,682 was the highest mark in the world since Jess's Olympic win in 2012. Only two British athletes – Jess and Dame Denise Lewis – had ever scored higher than 6,682, and both of them had gone on to win Olympic gold medals.

Looking back now, it's mad to think about what happened over just two years: I went from scoring 6,200 in London, to

6,400 in Moscow, then up to 6,600 in Götzis. It was just going up and up and up. It was exciting. I was the number one heptathlete in the world.

Those years after London were full of change. So many of the heptathletes who'd competed in 2012 had retired by the time Moscow came around a year later. That, combined with my rapid rate of progress, was how I suddenly found myself finishing fifth at the 2013 World Championships and then top of the pile in Götzis in 2014. The popularity of the heptathlon in the UK after 2012 had increased so much that everyone was desperate to find out who 'The Next' was going to be, and my performances in 2014 (and at the start of 2015, when I won the European Indoors) were enough to make them believe it was me. My transition from young athlete to expected medallist was suddenly complete, and at just twenty-one or twenty-two years old, that was a lot to deal with.

I used to try to make sense of it all by writing my thoughts and feelings down in my journal before and after every competition, but what I really could have done with was an experienced voice around me to help guide me through those years, when everything around me was changing and I had no idea how to keep pace with it.

I was determined not to get carried away after Götzis. Winning there meant everything to me, and at the same time it meant nothing. I wanted a major title to my name.

But the media saw it differently. After my performance in Götzis, as the number one ranked heptathlete in the world, they made me the favourite to win heptathlon gold at the Commonwealth Games in Glasgow the following month, and more sponsors started emerging too. New brands wanted to get involved. One even plastered the slogan 'You'll never run, jump, throw alone' on the side of the Liverpool Ferry, next to a picture of me. I became more recognized, too. I'd be sitting having a coffee with Mike and Mum, and people would start approaching me, wishing me good luck. It felt like I was the main character in a movie and everyone was waiting to see what happened next.

It all added to the weight of expectation I was starting to feel. There was a lot of talk about the Commonwealth Games being a repeat of London 2012, in terms of both the atmosphere and the amazing crowds, and I was excited for that. But I tried to play down the 'favourite' tag as much as I could, just to take some of the pressure off myself. 'My goal this season is to win a medal at the Commonwealths,' I told the BBC. 'Next year, at the 2015 World Championships, that's when I need to be winning stuff.'

With two weeks to go before the Commonwealth Games started, I competed in the long jump at a Diamond League event in Glasgow – in the same stadium where the Games were going to be held two weeks later (the Diamond League is an annual series of elite track-and-field competitions where you run for yourself rather than your country). It was close to the Games, but we thought that it would be a good opportunity to familiarize myself with the environment and get used to competing there. It turned out well; I jumped 6.92 metres, 11cm further than I'd ever jumped before. It was also, at that stage, the second furthest jump in the world that year. Everything just added to the feeling that I was in the best shape of my life, and that this was my time.

Everyone always says that there's a fine line between reaching the top of the mountain, being the strongest, fittest, and fastest you've ever been, and falling off the edge of it. I was about to find out why.

Less than a week after competing in the Diamond League, I was in the middle of a training session, when I felt a sharp pain in my foot. I sat down and took my spike off straight away to see if I'd maybe trodden on something, but there was nothing there. When I woke up the next morning, I couldn't walk on it at all.

An X-ray showed a stress reaction in my left foot, which is often a warning sign before a full stress fracture occurs (when there are tiny cracks in a bone that develop over time, as opposed to a bone break that happens immediately on impact). At first, I was told I had a choice as to whether to put up with the pain and compete in Glasgow anyway. And for a time, I actually considered it. After all, my family were all coming up to watch me. They'd already booked accommodation and travel and they'd be gutted if I wasn't there. 'If it cracks, it cracks,' I thought, stupidly. 'At least I will have tried.'

But when I talked it through with Mike and doctors from British Athletics, they made it clear that there were risks to my long-term health if I did that, and that I could be damaging my future athletics career. I was devastated.

All those PBs. Becoming the number one heptathlete in the world. I should have been happy about those things, but even as they were happening, I'd been keeping everything contained – because all I wanted was to win gold in Glasgow (regardless of what I'd said to the press) and now that chance was gone. At the time, it felt like the end of the world. Like this was the biggest moment I'd ever have and it was being taken away from

Unbroken

me. But instead of dealing with my feelings then, I chose to block them out. While the Commonwealth Games were on, I went to a spa hotel in London for two days and tried to pretend nothing was happening.

Now I look back and think it was quite a childish way to deal with things, but it felt like the biggest upset at the time. I had been in the best shape of my life. I couldn't go from that to sitting placidly watching other athletes doing what I knew I could do better. I remember getting a message on my phone from my uncle George, who had recommended the hotel I was in. He was with the rest of my family in a cramped static caravan on the outskirts of Glasgow, dealing with crappy weather and cold showers: 'I can't believe you're not competing and we're in this rotten place!' It was meant to be funny, and now I can look back and laugh, but at the time it was horrible. I felt so bad.

The only glimmer of light was that there was a European Championships in Zurich starting around a month after the Commonwealth Games, and everyone was telling me that there was a chance I would be ready to compete in the long jump there. I went through weeks of intensive rehabilitation work in an oxygen chamber, used ultrasound therapy, had injections – all in the hope that my foot would be ready for Zurich. But a few days before we were due to leave for the competition, I had another scan, which showed that the bones hadn't healed as quickly as the doctors had expected. If I competed at the Europeans, they said, I still risked long-term damage to my foot.

It was really shitty. I'd spent a month dealing with the upset of missing Glasgow by focusing on another goal. Living in hope. In the end, it seemed as though I'd been taken for a ride. Like they'd thought: 'Just give her a little target so she's not too upset.' Instead, I just felt like I'd been lied to.

That was the end of my 2014 season, one that had held so much promise but ended in huge disappointment. I can look back now at what I achieved and recognize it as an amazing year, if only for the number of PBs I shattered (that 6.92-metre long jump is still the furthest I've ever jumped outdoors) and the world-leading score that I set in heptathlon.

But at the time, I couldn't appreciate any of those things. I was totally consumed by feelings of injustice and sadness at missing two major championships when I'd been in such good form.

As a young athlete, I so often based my self-belief on external things, like what other people said or wrote about me or the position I finished in a competition. At the time, I didn't realize how fragile that made it. Up until the injury to my foot, I had felt more confident in my own ability than perhaps ever before. I was on top of the world, doing exactly what everyone had expected of me. Maybe even more.

Then it was all thrown into doubt. Not by a bad performance, a missed jump or a clipped hurdle, but by something completely outside of my control. There had been no warning signs that I'd ignored. One moment my foot was fine and the next it really wasn't. It came down to chance. To bad luck.

That didn't suddenly make me a worse athlete. I was still the same Katarina who had set that score in Götzis and jumped 6.92 metres in Glasgow. It was difficult for me at the time to remember that and to understand that self-belief has to come from within, not from external rewards. You have to foster it within yourself.

Unbroken

I think understanding that is something that comes with experience or, in the absence of that, with the right guidance.

I was about to take a big step towards that understanding.

There's not much rehab work you can do for a bone injury aside from resting it, so at the end of the season I went on a holiday to Thailand that I'd been planning, and I returned on 1 October feeling mentally rested and itching to get back into training. Jess was back in training too, after having her son, Reggie, and part of me was relieved, thinking that her return might take some of the expectation off me going into 2015 – a World Championships year. It also felt surreal, though, because so much had changed since we'd last competed alongside one another. In 2012, I'd almost been watching Jess as a fan, while also trying to learn from her along the way. Now, that balance had shifted. Despite still being only twenty-one, I wasn't the young, up-and-coming athlete any more; I was expected to win, and I believed that I could.

Now, I was the one wearing the gold-plated spikes of the world number one heptathlete. I was the one who had won in Götzis at the first time of trying. I was the one who had set PBs almost every time I competed the previous year. But the heptathlon doesn't care about any of that. It only cares about consistency, discipline and being able to stay in the moment, no matter what happens over the course of two days of competition.

I was about to learn all of that, in one of the most public, and painful, ways possible.

8

Expectation

World Athletics Championships, 23 August 2015, Beijing 'Bird's Nest' National Stadium, China

Shit, we're in trouble.

I knew we were in trouble because I'd just seen my coach, Mike, take off his cap.

During a comp Mike generally has one facial expression. It's hard to tell whether he's happy, sad or fuming because his face never changes. But he's got one tell: if he's concerned, he takes off his hat. Whether it's a fisherman's hat, a cap, whatever. If he's worried, he takes it off.

I'd just landed in the sandpit after my second jump and when I looked over to where he was standing, I saw the one thing I didn't want to see: Mike removing his cap. My stomach lurched.

A split second later, there it was: another red flag being waved high in the air by one of the officials.

Two no jumps. Two chances gone. One left.

Unbroken

I walked over towards Mike (whose cap was bearing the brunt of his stress, squeezed tightly between his hands), my chest tightening with every step. We made a decision to move the start of my run-up back. We took it back, back and back some more. By the time we put my marker down, it was probably three metres behind the point where my previous run-ups had started.

I took a few big breaths and stared at the take-off board, visualizing my left foot planted perfectly behind the plasticine placed on the foul line. As I waited for my turn to jump, I tried to quieten my thoughts, but they were forceful, and loud. They told me to play it safe. To do whatever it took to get on the board safely and register a distance in the competition.

Then they reminded me that I was just 80 points behind the heptathlon leader, Jess, and that there was a gold medal at stake. A good jump now would put me within touching distance of it. I knew I had to run fast into the board to generate the speed I needed. If I held back, if I hesitated, I wasn't going to break six metres. I stood on my mark, looked down the runway and went through my usual cues: 'Jump out of the pit, don't even *think* about landing.'

I saw myself sprinting, hitting the board perfectly and flying way over the long jump pit, with the white flag of approval from the officials waving far below me.

One more big breath in.

And run.

Normally, when it's a no jump you know straight away because before you've even landed in the pit there's a red flag being waved high in the air. This time, I looked and there was no flag. I turned back to look at where I'd landed. The jump was massive – at least 6.80 metres – which would surely be enough to take

Katarina Johnson-Thompson

first place. As I stepped out of the sand, I allowed myself a small clap of celebration.

Then, out of the corner of my eye I saw a flurry of movement around the take-off board. Three officials were out of their seats and hunched over it, poking, prodding and pointing ominously.

As I got closer, I saw one looking at the board so closely his nose was almost touching the plasticine.

If this happened to me now, as a more experienced athlete, I'd tell them not to touch it. I'd take control of the situation. But as a twenty-two-year-old who was still finding my voice and place among the senior ranks, all I could do was stand and watch as they poked and pointed. It felt like a situation far beyond my and Mike's control.

And then, there it was: another red flag.

Three foul jumps meant I hadn't registered a single distance in the competition. And that meant no chance of a medal. No chance of proving that I had what it took to win on the biggest stage.

It was humiliating. A public failure like no other I'd experienced. But the worst was still to come.

From the moment Jess Ennis-Hill announced she was back in training, three months after having her son Reggie in July 2014, I was getting asked about it: How did I feel about her return? What would it mean for the sport to have the Olympic champion competing again?

My answer was always the same: 'Welcome back, here's all the pressure,' I'd smile as I mimed passing a huge pile of it from my plate to hers.

But it was naive to think that her return would automatically reduce the focus on me in 2015, or that we could just slip back into the roles of master and apprentice that had fitted perfectly in 2012. Things had changed. I wasn't the young kid being tipped for a bright future any more; I was an almost twenty-two-year-old who was competing with the best in the world, and beating them. Now, people were talking about Jess and me as rivals, getting excited about us going head-to-head at the 2015 World Championships and finding out who was the better heptathlete. I'd spent my days as a young athlete being compared to 'Jess at this age' and now people wanted to see how we stacked up as two elites (albeit ones at very different points in our careers). The pressure hadn't just shifted from me back to Jess, then. It had simply doubled in size and was now sitting on top of both of us. I'd watched her deal with it effortlessly in 2012. Three years later I was going to have to do the same. It was almost as daunting as the prospect of beating Britain's golden girl.

I don't think I've ever been as eager to get back into winter training as I was in 2014. It was partly due to all the PBs I'd set that year, but also because it felt like I'd had the longest time away from athletics while waiting for my foot to heal. By October, I had the green light to get going again. The winter of 2014, going into 2015, was the hardest that Mike and I ever worked as a pairing, and that's a pretty high bar. The European Indoor Championships were taking place in Prague in March 2015 and we had earmarked that as an opportunity to try to break the pentathlon world record of 5,013 points, set by Ukrainian athlete Nataliya Dobrynska in 2012.

We spoke about it constantly in training. Whenever reps were hard we'd talk about that goal. I'd think about it outside of training, too. I had an app on my phone where you could input all your PBs and it calculated your heptathlon or pentathlon score and I looked at it constantly, playing around with scores to see what would happen if I added five centimetres here or took two seconds off my time there. We were after it. By the time we got to Prague for the start of the competition, though, I was dealing with pain in my knee. It was bad enough to alert me but not bad enough to get me to pull out of competing; at that age I would just block out that sort of pain and get through it. I really wanted that world record and, knee pain aside, I knew I was in shape to get it.

Just like the heptathlon, the pentathlon starts with the sprint hurdles, although the race is over 60m indoors compared to 100m outdoors. Then it's on to the high jump, shot put, long jump and the dreaded 800m to finish. It's an incredibly long, intense day. I got off to a strong start in Prague, setting a new PB of 8.18 seconds in the hurdles and followed that with a 1.95-metre high jump – a championship best. I was really happy; it felt like everything was going to plan. After two events I had a lead of almost 200 points – something I knew I needed before the shot put – and a strong total of 2,259 points.

As usual though, the shot put brought me back down to earth. I threw 12.32 metres, which equalled the furthest I'd thrown that season but it was the shortest distance of the thirteen athletes in the competition and meant I dropped into second place overall, behind Nafi Thiam, who had won a bronze medal at the European Championships I'd been so desperate to go to in 2014. I felt confident going into the penultimate event though. Long jump had been going so well for me that I always felt I was on the verge of pulling out a big distance. As I stood on my mark and looked down the runway towards the take-off board, I felt my body relax: *This is what I do; this is what I know.*

From the moment I planted my left foot and took flight, I knew it was good. I tried to gauge the distance as I stepped out of the pit. It looked close to my best ever, but how close? I looked at the scoreboard, waiting for the official distance to flash up . . . 6.89! A few centimetres off my best ever, and the furthest ever seen as part of a pentathlon competition. I allowed myself a big smile and looked over to Mike, who gave me his nod of approval.

That jump put me back into the gold medal position on 4,076 points, within touching distance of Jess Ennis-Hill's British pentathlon record of 4,965. It also meant I knew exactly what I had to do in the 800m to break the world record: run it in under 2:11.86. That was it. It was totally doable. In fact, it was around 4 seconds slower than the time I'd run at the World Championships in Moscow two years earlier (2:07.64).

As I stood on the start line preparing to race, I held up my crossed fingers to the camera. Everyone knew exactly what I was aiming for. At the sound of the gun, I burst to the front of the pack. With two laps to go I was well clear of the rest; there was no one pushing me to go faster. No one on my shoulder threatening my victory. I was out on my own, cruising along.

Somewhere along the way I let my concentration slip, and, without realizing it, my pace. I crossed the finish line and looked at the digital clock on the side of the track.

2:12.78.

What?

I put my head in my hands. What had just happened? I lay down on the track in shock, only half aware of the official trying to hand me flowers for winning the gold medal and the giant furry (mole?) mascot standing behind me clapping.

When I got to my feet, someone threw me a Union Jack flag to hold up behind me for the pictures. I looked at the bank of photographers and tried to smile, but I was still trying to process what had happened. I'd won my first gold medal in a senior championship, and I'd set a new British record of 5,000 points. At the time, only one other woman – the world record holder, Nataliya Dobrynska – had ever got more than that.

But I'd finished 13 points shy of her record. And that was so hard to take.

In the moments after I crossed the finish line, the television cameras had focused in on the crowd and found Barrie and my mum looking just as disappointed as me (because they knew how much I wanted that record). 'Come on, Team Kat,' said the BBC's commentator, Steve Cram. 'Surely it deserves a smile.'

I don't think some people fully understand how hard it is to get scores like that over the line in events like pentathlon and heptathlon. A lot of athletes are capable of doing it, but *actually* doing it event after event after event, and getting it over the line, is so incredibly hard. That's why I was so sad. I'd accumulated all of those points to get to the moment where I could actually break the world record, and then I'd missed it. Of course I was happy with hitting 5,000 points and nabbing the gold medal, but I was gutted to be leaving without the record after coming so close. I tried to hold it together for the mixed zone interviews, but everyone could see the tears welling up in my eyes as I spoke.

Five consecutive events make for an incredibly long, intense day. You're basically going from one event to another, from the moment you arrive until you pick up your bags to go home. My

Unbroken

day in Prague was made even longer when, like all medallists, I had to go for drug testing. The problem was, I was so dehydrated from a long day of competing that getting 90ml of urine from me was like trying to squeeze juice from a week-old lemon. Everything I drank would just stay inside! In the end it took four separate wees for the testers to get enough from me.

Mike and I had been among the first ones in the stadium that morning, and we were the last ones to leave that night. By the time I was finished with the testers it was so late that all event transportation had stopped, and we had to make our own way back to the team hotel.

It was the longest day. And while it was so disappointing to fall short of the record, it was also promising for the rest of the season. We could see that everything was there. There was nothing major that needed fixing. No need for a serious discussion or dissection of what had happened; it was just little mistakes here and there. And that's sport, right? Sometimes it's hit and miss.

That night, some sponsors had organized an evening out and I headed straight out to join them as soon as I could, quickly making up for my dehydrated state at the end of the comp. It was a really fun night, and one of the first times I stayed out until the morning light. Luckily, with a few extra years on me, I didn't end up in hospital having my stomach pumped again, but the hangover was very real. So real that, even though I was due to fly back home with the rest of the team the following day, I booked myself a flight back to Liverpool and headed straight home to be in my own bed. A couple of days later, an email arrived from the head coach of the British team telling us off for being a disgrace to our nation . . . I'd missed the last night, but the rest of the team had obviously gone out again, and by all accounts it was an even bigger night than the one that had finished me off!

Straight after my win in Prague, Jess had tweeted her support: 'Well done, Kat!! Amazing performance! Sad to see my record go but couldn't have gone to a more deserving athlete!' For me it was a good tick in the box. A sign I was on the right path. For the media, it was much more than that; it was the perfect way to set up what they were hoping was going to be the first head-to-head between us since Jess's return, at Götzis in May.

I'd had experience with journalists by this point in my career, but I didn't yet fully understand the game. I didn't appreciate that they'd sometimes be looking for a particular headline, or even have the story half written before they even spoke to you. I'd always been completely open and honest in interviews but, over the months that followed, especially as the build to the 2015 World Championships in Beijing began to ramp up, I realized that what came out of my mouth didn't always appear on paper as I had meant it.

I'd give an interview where I would back myself to win in Beijing, without mentioning anything about Jess, and then the subsequent headline would suddenly read: 'Katarina Johnson-Thompson says she'll beat Jessica Ennis-Hill.' These were fresh experiences to me, and they were horrible. Even Mike – with his inbuilt, natural cynicism – was getting caught out by journalists. He told one that taking on Jess was 'like kicking the Queen in the shins', a line that was like manna from heaven for a press looking to create a rivalry between us.

I'd never experienced anything like it before. I'd had no idea that amount of pressure could even exist.

Unbroken

At the same time, I was still struggling with my knee. I'd been diagnosed with a tendon problem. The advice for tendon issues is usually to load them, so after Prague we spent plenty of time in the gym putting weight through my knee to try to facilitate healing in the tendon. But a month or so later, it still wasn't improving.

Further investigation showed that it wasn't a tendon issue after all; instead, what we found was a sharp bit of bone in my knee that was sticking into a bursa (a fluid-filled sac that provides cushioning and reduces friction around large joints) and causing me discomfort. Loading the knee wasn't the answer, then; rest was. That meant defending my title in Götzis was out of the question, and my full focus turned towards preparing for the World Championships in Beijing that August. The world would just have to wait a bit longer for the first showdown between Jess and me.

By the time Götzis took place at the end of May, I was back to doing light track work but I wasn't ready for a full heptathlon. Jess was in a different place. She scored 6,520 points at Götzis, finishing fourth in her first heptathlon since winning gold in London 2012, and qualifying for that summer's World Championships as well as the 2016 Rio Olympics.

I had no pressure on me when it came to qualifying for Beijing, as I had secured it with my heptathlon scores in 2014, so we decided to go straight to the Worlds without squeezing another heptathlon in between. Instead, we lined up a few events where I could get some competition practice and continued to train hard. In theory it was a good idea. In practice, nothing went to plan.

At the beginning of July, I competed at the British

Katarina Johnson-Thompson

Championships in Birmingham. I went into them feeling like I was back in good shape, but then I pulled my quadriceps muscle during the 100m hurdles, which meant another three weeks off training. It had already felt like we were chasing time going into Beijing, but now it felt like we were running up a steep hill to get there. I was approaching the biggest moment of my career so far, a moment when all eyes were on me and the head-to-head with Jess, having done minimal training (everything was just rehab), barely competed since March and not done a heptathlon for over a year.

I stepped off the plane in Fukuoka, Japan (where the British Athletics holding camp was located), knowing that I had ten days to prepare. Ten days to get ready for a heptathlon. I went to the team hotel, dumped my bags and went straight to training. Looking back now, it was madness – you need to let your body rest and relax after a long flight. But at the time, we felt we couldn't waste a single day. Normally, a holding camp is about making small refinements – tiny tweaks that might add a centimetre here or save a second there. But this one was all about catching up on the training that I'd missed. We were in panic mode.

Mike Holmes is one of the most inventive coaches in the world, especially when it comes to cross-training; coming up with creative ways to get you fit that don't involve pounding your body on the track. At the holding camp, we were doing a lot of high intensity training which got me into good shape physically. The flip side was how much that intensity was taking out of me so close to a major competition. I felt I didn't have a choice, though; I had to do what I could to catch up.

When I spoke to the media, I was honest about my situation.

Unbroken

I told them that, given my preparation in the previous three months, I had tried to lower my expectations a little bit. But I was also clear that I was still going to try to win gold; it was what I'd wanted from the start of the year, so it was what I was going to aim to get. If I was in that situation now, with the experience that I have, I would be able to rationalize things more, and say, 'I've had a bad year. This is the preparation that I've had. I don't know what shape I'm going to be in because I haven't competed much at all. I've had injury after injury and I'm happy to be here competing in a heptathlon again after such a horrible year, so let's see what we can get out of it.'

At the time though, I didn't want to show any weakness. I wanted people to believe I was still the person they saw setting a world lead in 2014, and almost breaking the world record in Prague. *I* wanted to believe it too, because at that point, in my head, I was someone who could go through competitions with sore knees and still win. So that was my approach: *I'm ready. Let's take it on.*

I had belief in myself. I'd envisioned it. I truly thought I was going to win the gold in Beijing.

It was seriously hot when we emerged at the Bird's Nest Stadium on the morning of 22 August 2015, the first day of the World Championship heptathlon. It wasn't even 10 a.m., but the sun felt like it was burning your skin the moment you stepped out of the air-conditioned call room.

I was in the third hurdles heat of the morning, with Jess going in the fourth and final one. As we lined up for the start of the race, I tried to focus on the lane ahead and the hurdles directly in front of me. But in the back of my mind, I knew that the next thirteen seconds or so would tell me a lot about my fitness and my chances of winning gold. It was 13.37 seconds in the end – a PB, despite a pretty slow start out of the blocks.

Given my preparation, I was happy with that. And, as always, I was hugely relieved to get the first event of the day out of the way. It always feels like you're being chucked in at the deep end having to do hurdles first; there's no qualification, no second chances if you slip up. It has to be right because you only get one shot at it. It's scary but, at the same time, that's sport. It's what we're all doing it for; to see who can handle that moment. Who can step up to it? It doesn't matter what you've been doing the rest of the season, the moment that counts the most is the moment that you're in. I don't love it when I'm doing it, but I love watching it. I love seeing what athletes have got at any given moment, because that's what I believe sport is about.

Jess is an incredible sprint hurdler and though she'd looked tense ahead of her heat, she crossed the line in 12.91 seconds – not as rapid as her London 2012 time, but fast nonetheless, and enough to put her straight into second place after one event, seven places ahead of me. I knew that the next event – the high jump – was a good opportunity for me to claw back some points. But it was almost a disaster. I set my opening height at 1.80 metres, which is usually a pretty safe one for me to come in at, but my first two attempts were fouls. I just couldn't get over the bar.

I had one more shot at it. One more attempt to avoid bombing out of the competition when it had barely got started. I'd been fighting all season to get to Beijing – I didn't want it to end with such a whimper. I could feel the adrenaline coursing through my veins as I started my run-up. As I got closer to the bar, I completely lost my rhythm and stuttered into my take-off. It was a horrible jump but, somehow, I found the strength to basically muscle my way up and over the bar. I shook my head in disbelief. What was going on?!

As I got back to my stuff I passed Jess, who said she'd been absolutely crapping herself for me. It was really nice of her to support me in that moment. She was such an inspiration to me in 2012, and I've only ever had the utmost respect for her and what she managed to achieve under such pressure.

I wanted to win because I wanted to win, but I also wanted to beat Jess. The media's portrayal of a rivalry between the two of us definitely influenced me and my young brain into believing that beating Jess right then and there was the answer to everything. Of course, I now know that not beating Jess in Beijing, when she was an established heptathlete and I was still young in the game, didn't mean I could never be better than her in the future – that beating her PB or the number of times she was World Champion could also come into the conversation. But at the time, the media had put that scenario into my brain: it was now or never. I needed to beat Jess in order to prove that I could be the great athlete everyone was saying I could be. And I'd bet good money that she wanted to beat me, too.

I cleared my next height (1.86 metres) with much less drama on the first attempt, then went up to 1.89 metres. Again, I failed it twice, putting all the pressure on a third and final attempt. With Jess leaving the competition at 1.86 metres, I knew that getting over this height would be a big win. Once again, my run-up was all over the place, and as I approached the bar I had to do a little shuffle to get my feet in the right position. It was a total mess of an approach.

Katarina Johnson-Thompson

But I cleared it! I couldn't believe it. How had I managed to do that?

Winning the high jump put me into second place, 30 points behind Jess with the shot put and 200m still to come on the first day. It had been a shaky and emotional couple of hours. Was it rustiness, because of a lack of competition and steady, consistent training going into Beijing? Maybe. But it was also my reaction to a high-pressure situation. It felt like everybody was watching the first official head-to-head between me and Jess, and I was desperate to show that I had what it took to win; that I was the same athlete who had secured the world number one ranking in 2014.

By the time my head hit the pillow that night, I still fully believed it was my World Championships to win. After four events I was still in second place overall, 80 points behind Jess. The shot put had temporarily left me in ninth, but in the 200m – the final event of the first day – I'd gone head-to-head with Jess and come out on top. With one of my best events up first the next morning, I felt like I was in a good position to maybe even take the lead. The other athlete who had been expected to challenge for gold was the Canadian Brianne Theisen-Eaton. She had come into Beijing having scored an incredible 6,808 points in the Götzis comp that I'd missed through injury, but her first day hadn't gone to plan and she was in fourth place overnight.

Waking up on day two, I felt excited for what was to come: three events left and I could potentially have a gold medal hanging around my neck. It was a dream that turned into a nightmare before my morning coffee had even kicked in. My first long jump of the day was a big one – close to 7 metres.

But it was a foul, meaning my foot had crossed over the plasticine-coated foul line on the take-off board. That in itself wasn't a huge deal. I'd been in similar situations before. Just a day earlier I'd left it to my third and final chance to clear two heights in the high jump.

I wasn't panicking. But then it happened again. Almost a carbon copy.

Shit, we're in trouble.

And then the story ended. The public know about the part that played out on screen. A third massive jump, a jump that would likely have put me into the gold medal spot – and then the lengthy, excruciating deliberations of the officials as they carefully examined the take-off board for any minuscule sign that I had committed a third foul.

And then the eventual dagger to the heart: a third red flag.

I couldn't believe what was happening. I hadn't seen any sign of a mark in the plasticine, but the officials were saying that the very top bit of my shoe had crossed. Mike called me over and said we would appeal the decision. Outwardly, he looked calm but I could tell that, inwardly, he was panicked too. Things had flipped so quickly. But there was no time to try to absorb it or process what had happened. I had to go and get ready for the next event, the javelin.

As I started my warm-up, I tried to block out what had happened. To carry on and compete as though the jump was going to be allowed. Because it still could have been. But in the moments before the javelin was due to start, I saw Neil Black, then the performance director of UK Athletics, go over to speak to Mike. My mind wouldn't let it be. I knew then that the decision had been made and had to know what the outcome was.

Katarina Johnson-Thompson

'I can't do this without knowing what's happening,' I told Mike. 'Yeah, it's done.'

My head was all over the place. I sat on a bench surrounded by the other heptathlon girls preparing to throw, but I wasn't really there. I didn't want to be there. I wanted to be as far away from there as physically possible. The moment the javelin competition was over (I managed 39.52 metres, a few metres down on my best), I picked up my bag, dumped it in the rest room and left the stadium. There was a big gap between the javelin and the final event of the heptathlon, the 800m, and in my head I was done, anyway. There was no way I was coming back for that race.

I left all my stuff in the rest room and went back to my hotel room. I don't even remember how I got there, my head was so messed up. The moment the door closed behind me, I threw myself onto the bed and broke down. All the emotions of that morning just came flooding out. I couldn't stop them. I was devastated. At some point, Mum joined me. I told her I didn't want to go back out for the 800m. I was adamant: I wasn't doing it. She'd been sent in to tell me I had to.

Mum had spoken to Mike and the media officer for British Athletics, who had made it clear that I had no option but to go back and finish the heptathlon. She was told that every British athlete had to speak to the BBC (the national broadcaster), and so I would have to do the 800m and then go through the mixed zone to give an interview. I still don't know if that's true or not. But what *was* true was that if I pulled out of the heptathlon without a valid reason, like injury or illness, there was a very real possibility that I would be disqualified from competing in the individual long jump event a few days later. It was the last thing I wanted to hear. For the next hour or so

I wavered between trying to block out what was happening, crying, or taking the stroppy approach, refusing to partake and refusing to care about the potential consequences.

It was a horrible time.

No one wanted to give me a medical note. Would an athlete's mental health come into consideration now? It certainly didn't then. I had no other option: I had to go back to the stadium and run the 800m. I eventually agreed to do so, but with one caveat – I wasn't going to race it. I wanted to be as fresh as possible for the long jump qualification round coming up in four days. The only reason I was going back was to make sure I could compete in the long jump competition, so what was the point in draining every last ounce of energy from my legs just to finish a few places higher than my current position of twenty-ninth? It seemed obvious: the sensible thing to do was just jog around.

I splashed my face with cold water, trying to erase the evidence of any tears; I gathered my things and I made my way down to the bus that ferried athletes to the track. The only problem was, I'd left all my stuff – including my accreditation – in the rest room at the stadium. The officials didn't want to let me on the bus without any ID (I have no idea how I got back to the hotel without it in the first place) and then, when I did eventually convince them to take me along, I couldn't get into the stadium. I told the security guy that I had to get in to run the 800m, but then I caught myself – why was I even fighting to get on this start line? 'Good. Fine. I won't go in. You let them know.'

In the end, I made a call to my agent, Greg, who spoke to British Athletics. Team management came outside and got me in. It was all systems go for the 800m I wanted to do less than any 800m I'd ever run before. As I walked out to take my place on the start line, alongside four other athletes who were also wallowing at the bottom end of the standings (there were three who didn't bother to start the race because of their lowly position), I spotted Barrie Wells near the front of the stands. He and his team always made big banners for all their athletes at the major competitions, and in my dark mental state I thought I'd make a joke of the situation we all found ourselves in.

'Come on, where's my banner?' I shouted up to him, smiling at the bleakness of it all.

It was the strangest feeling, jogging away from the start line when the gun went off. Not trying my hardest, not pushing myself, not allowing my competitive instincts to override the part of my brain that knew I was doing the right thing – all of it just reinforced the feeling that I had failed. That I was a failure. As I ambled my way around the track, all I could think of was the scene in *Game of Thrones* where Cersei is forced to undertake a public walk of shame to atone for her sins. She's stripped naked, her long hair is hacked off and she's left completely vulnerable as she walks through throngs of people shouting abuse and chanting the word 'shame' at her.

For the 2 minutes and 50 seconds it took for me to cross the finish line in last place, I felt like I was doing my own walk of shame. In my mind, the commentators could only have been saying as much: that I should be ashamed. That I'd messed up. That in my biggest moment I had shown everybody that I wasn't good enough. As soon as I crossed the finish line, I was beckoned over to the mixed zone by the British Athletics media officer to speak to the cameras. The interviewer was a guy named

Unbroken

Phil Jones; he was the BBC's trackside reporter for all the big events. I'd been interviewed by him many times before, which was usually a positive thing but, in this case, our familiarity almost made the situation worse.

As I walked towards him, I took a deep breath, exhaling for as long as possible as if I could somehow breathe out the intense emotions bubbling away inside me. 'This is the last place I wanted to be right now,' I told him. 'But I had to complete the 800 if I wanted to go to the long jump. So, that's not my fitness.' I laughed as I said it, but it wasn't long before the mask slipped.

'We know what a great talent you are,' said Phil. 'This is the biggest lesson you can learn, I suppose, cruel as it is . . .'

The kindness in his voice was all it took to press the release button on all the feelings I'd been suppressing since I got back to the track. My throat closed up so I could no longer speak and my eyes filled with tears. Phil saw what was happening and wrapped up the interview, leaving me free to go, but as I turned away he beckoned me back, putting an arm of comfort around my shoulder. At that moment I could hold back the tears no longer, but the cameras were still on me and caught everything, broadcasting my emotional breakdown live to the nation.

I've never watched the footage back. I've never watched anything from Beijing back. I can't. Neither can Mum – if she ever hears or sees anything about that competition, she feels physically sick. It affected us both.

I've always felt guilty that I didn't stay in the stadium that day after the interview, to do a victory lap with the rest of the girls. That's something I'd do differently, if I could. It was very uncool of me to leave before the final race started. I didn't want to see it, but sometimes heptathlon is about sucking it up in moments like that. In every career, you win some, and you lose some – but either way, you do the victory lap with the girls. I should have done that, but instead I left the stadium and went straight to Mum's hotel. I couldn't stop crying.

For the next few days, I didn't leave Mum's room. I turned off my phone so no one could contact me. We got room service for all our meals. I didn't want to see or speak to anyone. It all felt so public – my failure to get on the board, my tears live on television – hiding felt like the only way I could try to escape it all. I knew that if I saw anyone from the team, or any other heptathletes, they'd be sympathetic and kind, but I was in a state where that was all it took to leave me in pieces. Sometimes, when you feel like I felt during that time, you almost wish people would be cruel and unkind about your circumstances – just so you can feel a different emotion.

After three days in Mum's room, I had to emerge. It was time for the long jump qualification, which meant going back to the track and back to the same runway. I wasn't ready for it, but I was resigned to doing it, to getting it over with, to giving my body the permission to do what it had done a thousand times, without letting my brain get in on the act.

I was so nervous before my first attempt. What if it happened again? I played it incredibly safe – I don't think my foot even touched the board, never mind the plasticine – and managed 6.54 metres. That settled my nerves a little and on the second I managed 6.79 metres, which was enough to qualify me automatically for the long jump final the next day. It was a weird feeling. In some ways it could have added to my pain;

after all, if I'd put in that performance four days prior, I'd have probably won a World Championship medal. But mostly? I was just numb. The worst had already happened; nothing could hurt me more. I'd put out a social media post that morning with the hashtag #MondayMotivation, but that was a lie. It wasn't the way I felt at all. I wasn't re-motivated, and I wasn't excited about the long jump. I just wanted it all to be over.

I was jealous of all the heptathletes who had finished competing and were celebrating the end of their season, because I felt like mine had been such a long slog, only to be met at the end with nothing but a quick drink of water. Physically, I was exhausted from everything I'd done to get ready for Beijing and, mentally, I was done too. I was not in the right headspace to be out there competing.

In the final the following day I managed two jumps of 6.63 metres (my second was a foul), which meant an eleventh-place finish. I couldn't have cared less. The worst week of my life was finally over and, as I boarded the plane to fly home, I waved goodbye to Beijing, vowing never to return.

I blamed myself entirely for what happened.

It wasn't Mike's fault; he moved me back three metres and I still couldn't get onto the board. I was the one who didn't deliver. I was the one who had failed to live up to the world number one billing. I was the one who had lost ground in the head-to-head with Jess. And I felt like a bit of a dick, wearing gold-plated spikes while doing it.

I threw them into the back of a wardrobe when I got home, but I never forgot they were there. During Covid, I was doing a big clear-out at home, and I found them. In a bid to make fun of myself, I took a picture of them, posted it on my Instagram and asked people to tell me their worst sporting memories. I vowed to send them to whoever had the best story. I sent them to a girl whose story resonated with me; I hope that I've taken the bad luck from those spikes so that all that's left is good fortune, which she can reap the benefits of.

But that was years later. In the aftermath, I couldn't see a single shard of light in what had happened. I punished myself. For months.

Part of me thought I deserved it. Another part of me thought it would motivate me; that if I saw the image of my foot planted for that final fouled jump on my laptop screen every time I opened it, I'd feel inspired. But mostly, I just felt sad.

What happened at that competition changed me. It was something I didn't even notice until the following year when my then-boyfriend told me that I wasn't the happy-go-lucky kind of person I had been before. Beijing took a lot of the joy out of me. I was a lot heavier, mentally, emotionally.

It felt like I was carrying my failure around with me every hour of every day. And it was weighing me down, turning me into a different version of the person I had been before. It had been the worst experience of my life. I was twenty-two years old and had never experienced anything like it before. And it showed.

The impact lasted years. Memories of the long jump would haunt me every time I'd stand on the runway and stare down towards the take-off board: Would it happen again? Could it?

I think one of the reasons it left such a deep scar was that it was the first time my entire belief system had been destroyed. Up until Beijing, I'd always prepared for competitions in the same way: using imagery and visualization. I'd believed if you could see it, imagine it, believe and think about it enough, then it would happen. I had no reason not to. Manifestation had always worked for me. It got me to my first Olympic Games in 2012, fifth at my first senior World Championships in Moscow and a world-leading score in the heptathlon in Götzis in 2014.

But Beijing had broken the trend. Manifestation hadn't worked, and suddenly I couldn't bring myself to believe in any of it any more. The impact of that was huge for me as an athlete. It was like removing an essential piece of kit from my bag, or telling me I had to throw left-handed. All I could think was: *How do I compete now?*

I needed to find a new process and I had no idea how to go about it. It's something that ended up taking me years to figure out.

I was also left with a feeling of personal defeat that I'd never really had before. It wasn't like I'd lost to someone from another country; I'd lost to one of the nation's favourite sportspeople, who had just achieved something truly incredible, coming back from the birth of her first child to win a world title. It felt like it was everywhere. It was on the TV, it was in the newspapers, it was brought up during every single competition that we'd both do. Jess is Jess; she's big news. And I'm not saying it shouldn't be that way – it absolutely should – just that it felt like I couldn't escape it.

That really affected me. I'd had all those years of people saying that I could be better than Jess, and I wanted to live up to that. I wanted to prove that I could fulfil the high expectations that people had for me. But I'd lost the head-to-head with her in Beijing.

So how could I claim any of that to still be true?

As low as I was coming out of Beijing, I never even thought about walking away from the sport entirely. Maybe that was down to Mike's approach; he looked at what happened in Beijing through a very black and white, very factual – if conditional – sphere. It was: 'If this hadn't happened, we'd be here.' 'We were half a centimetre away from being world champions.' 'The gold medal was won in a lower score than you got in your last heptathlon.' 'These are the performances you can do. I don't see anybody else doing them.'

That way of looking at things helped me in one sense, because what happened in Beijing didn't feel fatal. It just felt like an awful mistake. But it didn't help me understand *why* it happened. Or what I could do to change things, or even to cope with the situation better.

Nowadays, I understand that athletes just have to learn how to deal with external factors, like the expectations that others might have of you, and you have to learn not to let them matter too much. To not allow them into your brain. I had allowed external factors to impact me in a big way.

In Beijing, my failure wasn't down to injury, or a lack of fitness or ability. It was down to me not rising to the pressure. The pressure of expectation. The pressure of going head-to-head with one of Britain's most loved athletes. I didn't yet have the experience to realize that that was the problem, nor the tools necessary to cope with it. I was so busy trying to escape the pressure that I didn't take any time to analyse it, and to try to take something useful away.

With 2016 – an Olympic year – on the horizon, that left me in a precarious position. I had a year to try to dig myself out of the hole I was in.

The only problem was: it was about to get even deeper.

9

Imposter Syndrome

Olympic Stadium, Rio de Janeiro, 12 August 2016

Am I even a heptathlete?

Can I really call myself a heptathlete if I can't do this?

My mind was full of questions. Questions about my ability. Questions about my right to compete with the best athletes in the world. Hours earlier, Nafi Thiam and I had set a new world record in the high jump and I'd broken the British record, clearing a height that would have won me an Olympic gold medal in the individual event a week later. Now I was questioning whether I should even be at the Games.

Life comes at you fast when you're a heptathlete.

It's an event that constantly humbles you. It's literally designed to remind you that however good you might be at one thing (or even two), there is always something that you're not so good at, or not quite the best at.

At the Olympic Games in Rio in 2016, I experienced that in

its most extreme form. I'd gone into the competition telling the world I was targeting top spot on the podium: it was gold or nothing. And the first two events had gone to plan; I was in first place after running 13.48 seconds in the hurdles – not my fastest but an OK time for me – and an incredible high jump competition that had brought out the best in me and Nafi.

Both of us had cleared every height at the first attempt and, when none of the other athletes registered a height in the 1.90s, it left just the two of us in the competition. In subsequent years we would become used to going head-to-head, familiar with each other's strengths and weaknesses, but in Rio it was a fresh battle, and we both came alive for it.

The bar was raised to 1.95 metres. I cleared it first time.

Nafi failed it once. Then twice. On her third attempt, she cleared it.

The bar went up: 1.98 metres. One centimetre higher than my PB, and the British record I shared with high jumper Isobel Pooley.

I was first up. One big breath and then I was into my strides. Building momentum, gathering pace as the bar neared, then calling on all that momentum to carry me up, up and . . . as I fell backwards onto the mat I saw the bar following me down. Damn.

Nafi's turn. I sat and watched as she powered herself high over the bar, the arch in her back making it look as if she had a few more centimetres in her still.

Game on.

I stood on my mark and looked at the bar, visualizing myself approaching it smoothly and soaring over with room to spare.

This time, the moment I planted my left foot for take-off,

Katarina Johnson-Thompson

I knew. I knew I was over. I knew I had the speed, the momentum, the height. As I fell backwards onto the mat, I punched the air with both hands. I'd done it! I was in disbelief. To pull out such a big performance on the biggest stage in the sport was a career moment, and the fact that it slightly foreshadowed what was to come during future battles between me and Nafi makes it even more special.

As I walked away from the bar, I allowed myself to smile and soak it in: a new British record, and we'd both hit a world record high jump in the heptathlon. I was delighted. After neither Nafi nor I could clear the next height of 2.01 metres, it meant I was in first place after the morning session, with Nafi in second and Jess in third.

I didn't stay on that high for long.

By the time the next event started, the face that had shown such delight that morning showed serious worry. I wore the expression of someone whose entire world was falling apart. That was how I felt; I'd gone from feeling like I belonged, competing alongside the best athletes in the world, to feeling like an imposter who could be thrown out of the Olympic Stadium at any moment. And it was all down to the voices around me.

My shot put competition started with a foul throw; I got my footwork all wrong and stumbled outside of the turning circle. The shot had travelled all of 10 metres, so part of me was relieved that it wasn't actually going to count. The next two were legal throws but only went as far as 11.68 metres. I'd thrown over 13 metres at a meet earlier that season.

Only two other athletes finished below me in the shot put. It's hard to describe what it does to you, going from being one of the world's best to being bottom of the pile. The only way I can describe it is that it humbles you to such an extent that if you don't have the tools to cope, it can break you.

I went from first to sixth place overall and I instantly knew what everyone else was thinking and saying about me on social media: Does she have the mental strength for this? Why doesn't she just do the high jump? Is she even a heptathlete if she can't do this?

At that moment in my life, it wasn't just the people on TV, on the internet and in the newspapers asking those questions. It was me, too.

When I got home from Beijing, I'd wake up every morning feeling like I had the world's worst hangover; full of self-loathing and regret. My mum, then-boyfriend and friends did their best to lift the gloom, but there was nothing anyone else could say or do. I had to process it in my own time and figure out a way through.

In some ways it helped that I had to start training again a few weeks after getting home. Usually, a World Championships would mark the end of my competitive season because mentally, after that, you're done. You're in the bin. You throw everything into peaking for that big event, so afterwards you need a rest and a reset before you start building up again for the following season.

In 2015, though, I had to wait a bit longer for my holiday, because my disaster of a year meant that I still hadn't scored highly enough in a heptathlon to qualify for the 2016 Rio Olympics. There was the option of waiting until 2016 to try to qualify, but neither Mike nor I wanted to do that just in case the shit hit the fan. We decided to enter the final heptathlon of the year in Talence, France, in the hope that we could box off qualification for Rio and put the season to bed with at least that positive to show for it.

So, while everyone else was out of their spikes and firmly into their off-season, I was back on the track in Wavertree Park, trying to get myself mentally and physically ready to do it all over again. I knew exactly what my aim was – 6,200 points, which was the qualification mark for the Rio Olympics – but some days it made no difference; the track was the last place I wanted to be.

One particularly wet and windy day, I finished a rep and dropped down onto the track. As I waited for my breath to return to its normal rate, I watched the rain continue to fall relentlessly from the sky, dampening the track almost as much as my mood. 'Another one,' I heard Mike shout, as he motioned me back to the start line for another set of 3x200m sprints. A series of fat raindrops dripped off the peak of his cap.

My mind went one way: I shouldn't be here. This time last year I was on holiday in Thailand. Now here I was, slogging away in the rain, while every other athlete I knew was relaxing at the end of a long, hard season. My body went another: back to the start line. Get set. Go!

Those few weeks of training were a real struggle. My head was still spinning from what had happened at the World Championships. Plus, it felt like everyone else had achieved their goals for the season and were reaping the rewards, resting their weary bodies and getting ready for an Olympic year. Meanwhile I was out in the pissing rain, asking my body for more.

Unbroken

The saving grace was that I knew it wasn't about winning in Talence. It was just about going through the motions and getting the qualifier. It was kind of chill in that respect. It wasn't like four years earlier when I'd been really fighting to get the qualifier for London 2012, because now I was a 400-point better heptathlete. I could afford to score lower than my PB on every single event and still get 6,200 points. No problem.

That was the theory, anyway.

Reality hit the day before the heptathlon started, when Mum, Mike and I were due to travel from Manchester airport to Talence via Amsterdam – a journey that should have taken half a day, at most. Instead, it ended up taking thirteen hours. Our flight from Manchester was delayed, meaning we didn't have much time to make the next one, and Mike refused to run to the gate (he's one of those people who's always last to board the plane) so we missed it! I'm definitely not still bitter about it. The next flight was not for hours, so we spent most of the day in Amsterdam airport before eventually arriving in Talence late in the evening.

It wasn't ideal in terms of preparation, but the first day of competition still went smoothly enough. I finished day one at the top of the standings on 3,850 points, a 22-point lead and well on target to hit 6,200. Day two, however, was a disaster. It started with a poor long jump, where I only jumped 6.17m after fouling my first attempt. And then BAM! While throwing the javelin, something in my leg popped, and I felt the most aggressive pain I'd ever experienced – a sharp, stabbing feeling deep in my thigh. I fell to the ground – I think I actually fainted – before a medical official came and helped me up.

Katarina Johnson-Thompson

I could hardly walk, let alone attempt to run the 800m.

That was it: competition over. Season done.

Of the two heptathlons I'd started that season, one had ended in infamy and the other in agonizing pain – I'd torn my adductor. Whether it was due to injuries or errors, I felt like I couldn't get through a full heptathlon unscathed. My outlook that year had gone from chasing world records and gold medals to getting beaten further and further down.

I didn't blame anyone except myself, because sometimes I would push through training when I knew I should probably stop, or at least say that my body was hurting. But I wouldn't voice it because I wouldn't want to let Mike down or seem like I didn't want to train. I pushed through a lot of stuff at different times and for different reasons but, ultimately, I hated the feeling of not completing something.

When I was a kid, one of my training partners used to stop a lot mid-rep, and I'd get quite annoyed about it. I just couldn't understand it. I remember saying to myself, 'I never want to do that. I'd rather walk across the line than just stop or give up.' Stopping mid-session is just something that I've always hated the thought of.

Even now, sometimes I'll push through a training session and think, *I've got away with something there.* And I'll know I shouldn't have done it. I'm not alone in that. I think it's something a lot of athletes do; they try to push until they can't.

It's just that some of us get punished for it more than others.

By the end of 2015, I'd reached the point where I could push no more. The knee problem that had kept me from competing in Götzis earlier in the year hadn't gone away; I'd been working around it and managing it all year, but it was still an issue. After Talence, Mike and I met with a specialist and it was decided that the best course of action – the one that gave me the best chance of an injury-free run-in to Rio – was to have it operated on.

Having surgery sounds like the perfectly terrible end to a perfectly terrible year, but to me it felt more like a positive step than a setback; I was fixing something that needed to be fixed. There was an opening with a really good surgeon in London at 6 a.m. the morning after I got back from an end-of-season holiday, and I grabbed it. I'd never had any operations before, so as I lay there being given the general anaesthetic that I knew would knock me out, I was petrified. But the next thing I knew, I was awake and the operation was over. The surgeon explained that he had shaved the sharp bit of bone that was causing me pain and taken something called the bursa out (apparently it grows back if you need it). The operation went smoothly, but I've never regained the feeling on one side of my knee. I can bang it on a table and not even realize until the bruise comes up; it's completely numb.

The rest of that winter was all about slowly building myself back up to fitness. I was on crutches for two weeks after the operation, and then it was straight back to work. I did all my rehab in Loughborough, so every Sunday night I'd drive from Liverpool to the university's campus where I'd stay until Friday. I really missed being with my usual training group in Wavertree, suffering through winter training with everyone, but equally, it felt good to be solving a problem.

Not many people outside of my immediate circle knew that I ended 2015 on the operating table, and I didn't want them to. After the year I'd had, the last thing I wanted was to bring more negative attention to myself, so I kept it quiet; no social media updates, no interviews.

Some six months later, at the end of May 2016, I was back competing in Götzis, back targeting the Olympic qualifying score of 6,200 points and, unfortunately, back keeping quiet about an injury. I'd missed the entire indoor season that year, because I wasn't able to start running again until January. But by the beginning of May I was ready to go, and relishing jumping pain-free for the first time in years. Physically, I felt like a whole new athlete, but mentally, there was something holding me back.

In the lead-up to Götzis, I was being followed by a camera crew filming for a BBC documentary called *Faster, Higher, Stronger: Katarina's Olympic Dream,* where I'd be interviewed by former GB sprinter Darren Campbell. The crew were present at some training sessions and competitions. Just before Götzis, Darren asked if I was feeling the pressure of getting the qualifying score for Rio. 'No,' I told him. 'But I'm not gonna lie, I'm terrified of getting injured . . . That's the biggest pressure on me this year.'

I *knew* my capability. I knew I was more than capable of scoring 6,200 points. What I was less certain of was whether my body could make it through a full heptathlon unscathed. I didn't recognize it at the time, but that uncertainty was like a virus coursing through my body and mind, sending my nervous system into overdrive and eating away at my self-belief.

Arriving in Götzis for the first time since 2014, when I'd walked away with the victory and a world-leading score, I couldn't have felt more different. Two years earlier, I'd spent the indoor season attacking PBs, pushing myself to new heights – figuratively *and*

Unbroken

literally – and I'd viewed Götzis as an exciting opportunity to test myself against some of the best heptathletes in the world, minus Jess. This time, PBs and finishing positions were the last things on my mind. All I wanted was 6,200 points, Olympic qualification, and to board the plane home injury-free.

The first morning of the competition, I was terrified. Almost sick with nerves. I hadn't run over ten hurdles in training all winter, so as I walked out to the start line my stress levels were at their peak. I didn't even dare look for Mum's face in the crowd – I knew she was feeling exactly the same as me anyway. We're both terrible at hiding the way we're feeling, so seeing her face would have only amplified my nerves tenfold.

It went better than I could have hoped. It felt smooth and fast as I crossed the line in 13.37 seconds, equal to my 100m hurdles PB. That meant over 1,000 points in the bank. The relief I felt at getting that first event out of the way was immense. The high jump was positive too, with a first-time clearance at 1.92 metres (a PB outdoors) putting me top of the leader board going into the shot put. At the beginning of May I'd thrown 13.14 metres – a huge PB – at my first competition back after surgery, so I was hopeful of a good showing in Götzis. But my first throw only went 11.55 metres and, from then on, I felt like I was chasing something that was simply out of my reach.

My second throw was a foul, and the third was so terrible it barely went over 10 metres. Every other athlete in the competition had thrown further than me, meaning I added just 631 points to my score, giving me 2,832 after three events. I went into the final event of the day – the 200m – knowing I had to score some decent points to get me back on track. To everyone watching, it seemed I did just that. I ran 22.79 seconds, a new PB and a time I was really happy with. But in doing so, I'd tweaked my quad. Again.

As I climbed into the big tub of ice to start my recovery for day two, Darren Campbell and the BBC cameras were right there watching. I smiled and joked with them as if nothing was wrong, even as my mind was racing towards the worst-case scenario of: What happens if I have to pull out?

I told myself not to panic. It was a tweak, nothing more. All I needed from day two was 2,268 points, that was it. A half-decent long jump and I'd practically be there. But my nerves the next morning almost stopped me from devouring my usual pre-comp scrambled eggs. As I stood on my mark preparing for my first jump, I couldn't stop thoughts of Beijing from clouding my mind. All I had to do was hit the board cleanly; that was it.

One of the most tentative jumps I've ever done resulted in a distance of 6.13 metres, almost 80cm below my best. The crowd cheered – in what felt like relief more than anything – and I couldn't help but laugh, embarrassed by it all. It was the last time I smiled that day. My second jump was a foul and as I landed the third at 6.17 metres, I grimaced in pain. The tweak was now a properly pulled muscle and Mike and I needed to have a serious conversation about the right next step: do we pull out, take six weeks off and try to find another comp? If we did that, I was probably going to miss the cut-off date for Olympic qualification. Or, do we finish this comp kind of injured, then at least we have the qualification and we can build into the Olympics as best we can?

As we spoke, the heavens opened, the weather reflecting my

darkening mood. With our decision made, I got my left thigh firmly strapped and warmed up for the javelin, jogging backwards to take any pressure off my quad. I needed to throw at least 35 metres to keep me on course for 6,200 points and managed 36.66, the second worst in the field.

By this point, it was fairly obvious something was bothering me, and Darren asked Mum on camera if there was a problem with my left quad. He'd seen me massaging it, trying to get as much blood flowing into the muscle as possible. 'I think it feels tight,' said Mum. 'She's not taking any chances . . . she's got to be very careful. She doesn't want to get any more injuries.'

Just like the surgery situation at the end of 2015, I didn't want anyone to know my reality, and Mum knew that.

All I had left to do was run 2:24.50 or better in the 800m; even with one working quad, that was doable. I eased around the track in 2:16.81 – the eleventh quickest time overall – which was enough to take my points tally to 6,304 and secure my place in Rio, at last.

In the mixed zone after the 800m I told the press I'd run it so easy because I didn't want to push and injure myself; that I'd just taken it as an easy day. It's the same in the BBC documentary; there's a lot of: 'Oh, we're just taking it easy in Götzis because it's all about 6,200, blah, blah.' I'm lying through my teeth! A few weeks after the competition, they filmed a catch-up with Darren back in Liverpool, and I'm on camera telling him everything's going great – I can't even watch it back because I know how much I'm lying.

Everything was kept a secret because it felt embarrassing to be talking about more misery when I just wanted positivity. I was also scared of showing weakness, and of the impact that it might have on my competitors. In athletics, it's kind of accepted that, if you admit your weaknesses, other people will latch on to them and use them as a way to beat you. I knew all about it because I'd done it to other people. You take what you can to create a story in your head that gives you an advantage. I knew how effective that had been for me on occasion and didn't want to give the same opportunity to any of my competitors.

That's one of the reasons I wanted to write this book: to tell the true story and fill in the gaps. At many times in my career, I've been really honest in interviews – laid my soul bare, even. But there have also been times when I have kept things to myself, maybe as a form of self-protection. And I feel that now is the right time to shed light on some of those things.

I left Austria with a certain sense of relief. I'd qualified for Rio, and that's what I'd gone to Götzis for. But the other thing that I'd really needed to take away from Götzis was confidence – belief in my own body. And I didn't have that; I was leaving a heptathlon injured again.

By mid-July, I was easing back into competition, trying to gradually rebuild my form and confidence before the Games. As part of that, Mike, Mum and I travelled to Manchester, where there was a low-key athletics meet taking place at a local club. We did some long jump training there during the day, and then decided we'd take part in the javelin competition at the club's open night. The aim wasn't really to compete as such, just to practise and get some throws in under pressure – but not too much.

That was the plan, anyway. Then, later in the afternoon, Jess turned up with her coach Toni and a full team of people, including a physiotherapist and a specialist javelin coach. Mike and I were both blindsided; it was the last thing we'd expected to happen.

It felt to me like an attempt to knock my confidence. I wondered whether Mike had mentioned to Toni that we were going to compete there, and Toni had made the decision to show up. I was still building my strength and form back at that point, and all of a sudden they turned up and seemingly took over the competition. Even Mike didn't know how to handle it. I went to ask him for feedback on my throws – since this low-key meet had turned into a veritable head-to-head between me and Jess and I was losing it – and he didn't have any answers.

Looking back now, I remember it as a really terrible experience; one that explains a little bit more about where my head was at during those years and why. I know people look at it as me just falling apart, and in some ways I did, but there was also a lot more to it; to me, at the time, it felt like an attempt to get in my head. In a way, it's something I now almost respect, because I know that using your experience to your advantage however you can is a part of elite sport; but at the time, I was completely naive to it. It was a very steep learning curve.

I left that night feeling really frustrated at everything. It might be that the whole situation gave me the motivation to not let that happen again and gain some control, because after that I felt like I was on a real mission. At the London Diamond League, I jumped 1.95 metres in the high jump and then 6.84 metres to win the long jump – an event in which Jess was also competing. It was the first time I'd not paid her any attention – she was just another athlete – and it changed our relationship.

This time, it was Jess's turn not to rise to the occasion, as she failed to make the top eight in the standings while I went on to win the Diamond League. With around three weeks to go until the Olympic heptathlon took place in Rio, I was heading into the holding camp at Belo Horizonte in a positive mood – at least, that's how it looked on the surface.

Deep down, I was living in fear. I went into every training session, every competition, worried about getting injured. In public, I was talking about wanting gold – and that was the truth – but at the same time, my confidence was the lowest it had ever been. I had zero belief that my body could make it through a heptathlon. My head was a mess. My blood pressure was through the roof and I had already lost so much weight that year (I was so skinny that Jaz refers to 2016-me as 'vacuum-packed Kat'). It was all because of stress. The stress of potential injuries, of not knowing whether I was going to get through a heptathlon, of the Katarina-and-Jess head-to-head that never was in Beijing. It was all of it.

On the first morning of the Rio heptathlon, I made my way to the dining area for breakfast. Mike was nowhere to be seen. It was early in the morning and there weren't many other athletes around, so I sat alone at a table with only my porridge, scrambled eggs and coffee to keep me company. A few minutes later, I was surrounded by Jess and her team. I hadn't seen them the entire time we'd been in the Village and now here they were, on the morning of the biggest day of my life, laughing and joking among themselves and barely acknowledging my presence.

I wasn't in the best place mentally, but by the end of that morning I was in first place after two events, having broken the British record in the high jump and matched the new world record by jumping 1.98m. Unfortunately, it's a jump that gets forgotten more than it gets celebrated because of what happened immediately afterwards: my aforementioned performance in the shot put, and the inevitable questions that followed. And, in my mind, I mainly remember the jump for a moment that happened in the heptathletes' rest room right afterwards.

Mike told me that he'd heard that Toni had been telling everyone that my performance in the high jump didn't matter; I was just going to go and throw 10 metres in the shot put, my head would go down and that would be it. He was apparently telling anyone who'd listen that I was going to crumble. When I heard those words, I took them on. They got into my head. It completely derailed me and brought all my fears to the fore. I believed Toni was right and that I had no chance. That was my headspace going into the shot put. At that moment, I should have been riding the high of matching a new world record high jump and using that momentum to take control of the shot put, but hearing those words instantly played into my biggest fear.

I did manage to rally to win the 200m, the last event of the day, leaving me in fourth place overall with three events still to come. But by the time I fell into bed that night, in my head it was over. I almost can't believe myself as I write this, but at that point I had already decided that the medals were out of my reach. I had given up on myself. It makes me so sad to admit that, but it's the truth.

I threw that competition away, based on how I handled the heptathlon. I jumped 1.98 metres in the high jump – which was a fantastic achievement – but then I allowed those comments to completely warp my interpretation of it. I took them to heart in a very real way.

Katarina Johnson-Thompson

If the same thing happened to me now, I wouldn't let people's perception of me and my shot put performance overwhelm my ability to compete. I look back at my younger self and wish I'd had more support and protection. But because of the person I was at the time, that perception had the power to destroy me mentally.

Something I know now, but that I didn't fully appreciate at the time, is that the heptathlon is the most humbling event of them all. It doesn't really matter if you jump a British or world record in the high jump, because the heptathlon is not just one moment, it's a collection of events. The chances are that in at least one of those other events, you're not going to be the best. And you have to learn how to accept that and deal with it. If you do something good, you've got to move past it. If you do something bad, you've got to move past it. You've got to stay in the moment.

I love that about the event, and I've learned how to deal with it now, but I still sometimes wonder what it must feel like to be the best in the world at something. When I watch other athletes train in Loughborough – my training partners or my boyfriend – I almost have an identity crisis. They're *the best in the world* at their One Thing, and wouldn't I love to have that feeling?

Funny, eh?

As a heptathlete, you can always be better. In everything. You get humbled all the time. I often put myself in situations where I'm competing against athletes who are specialists, especially in the throwing events, because I need to practise my shot put and javelin in a competition environment. I can't always do a full heptathlon (generally I'll only do two or three a year, mostly because it's so taxing on the body), so I'll enter them as individual events instead. It's a very humbling experience, every single time.

The longer I'm in this sport, the more at peace I am with being humbled. I just want to try to learn from every situation that I'm in. Progress, not perfection.

It's just like competing when I'm not in good shape or coming back from injury. When I was younger, I would really struggle to accept not doing well at a comp, regardless of how my preparation had gone, and I'd worry about how my performances might affect other people's opinions of me. That's exactly what happened at the javelin competition in Manchester where, the minute Jess and her team showed up, I lost sight of the fact I was there to practise and continue improving my form coming back from rehab. Now, as long as I'm on a path, I can grin and bear it when I'm not in good shape. I can go to Götzis knowing that I'm probably not going to score well but that I need to do it for various reasons, and not worry about how that might make other people view me.

Ego definitely comes into that. It's a weird concept as an athlete, because in some situations you need ego – you need to think you're unbeatable. But in other contexts, ego can get in the way of improvement, or of hearing advice from the right people. I don't think you can have ego when you train, for example, because every day you go to training your coach's job is basically to tear you apart: 'You haven't done this, you need to fix this knee, this angle is wrong . . .' It's a constant reminder that you're not where you need to be, and that you have to try to find ways to get there. For anyone who has too big an ego, that would wear them down.

Staying humble is vital. When you're in bad shape, or it's the start of the year, and training is kicking your arse every single day, you start to think: *Am I even good? Am I not cut out for this any more?* It's happened every year of my career; I come back after a winter break and I immediately question myself: *Am I going to be able to do this again?* It's one of the reasons I have so much respect for athletes who come back from having a baby; I can barely come back from September!

That said, most of the time you *do* need ego to compete, so you have to master the ability to switch it on and off as needed. You can't go into a competition thinking you're not where you need to be. You *have* to believe in yourself. There's a really delicate balance to be struck between ego and humility, and it's one that can be hard to find, especially as a young athlete.

In Rio, I was in such a conflicted place; desperate to win gold, but missing the belief in myself or my body that was necessary to allow that to happen. Ultimately, that's what led to my downfall.

By the time of the final event, the 800m, I was in eighth place and out of medal contention. I'd only jumped 6.51 metres in the long jump, well below my best, and I'd recorded the third-worst javelin throw in the competition – a result that brought that imposter syndrome flooding back into my brain. Am I even a heptathlete if I can't do this?

I knew what people were saying about me: 'She needs to fix her throws.' 'She should concentrate on the high jump.' It was hard to avoid it. People would message me, telling me about commentators saying negative things, thinking they were sticking up for me by letting me know. It's common knowledge what people are saying, anyway. You try to shelter yourself but you can only do so much – the minute you get back into the Olympic Village, your friends are telling you what's been said. In Beijing, I remember someone from the BBC telling me not to watch their coverage of the heptathlon back: 'We were just talking to fill up space . . .' they said. I knew what that meant . . . I'd been getting roasted.

In Rio, by the time the 800m came around, I had mentally checked out. I finished fourth, with a season's best time of 2:10.47, which meant a sixth-place finish overall, but my head was not right. Nafi Thiam was the new Olympic champion, marking the start of what's become an incredible senior career, and I was left feeling lost, wondering whether I had what it took to put together a well-rounded heptathlon.

On the victory lap, Jess and I had a brief chat and she told me she was probably going to retire. 'Me too,' I said. I was joking – or was I? I wasn't sure. It was a transparent attempt to cover up the rising sense of frustration and disappointment that had been building in me throughout the months leading up to Rio. Months of feeling like I was taking one step forward and two back.

As we went around the track acknowledging the crowd, my mind was racing. It was nothing like London. For a start, the crowd attendance was poor, but mostly there was this uncertainty about what was next and a sensation of failure. I was done with feeling the same way year after year after year. It felt like the third time I was coming away from a major season having failed to achieve what I should have. Even though I've learned from them since, I'd just been through three years of hell. Three years of injuries and public failures. Something needed to change. Something big. And it had to happen right there and then. There was no way I would return to Liverpool and start the same cycle all over again. If I was going to do this again, I had to do it a different way. I had to try something new.

I had no idea that around the same time, Mike was having similar thoughts. He and Barrie met just after the heptathlon had finished and Mike told him there and then, 'That's the last heptathlon she'll ever do. She's now retiring as a heptathlete and we're going to concentrate on high jump and long jump. No more heptathlons.'

In fairness to Mike, I had been saying the same thing, and had also lost confidence in my ability as a heptathlete. It's funny, though – hearing him say it out loud made me more defiant and strengthened my belief that I would come back and be the athlete that I wanted to be. And that meant moving away from Mike and finding a new coach. It was a scary decision and a really hard one to make, given how long we'd worked together – not to mention that he'd gotten me to two Olympics – but I felt it was the right one.

The day after the heptathlon, I was in the Olympic Village and sent Mike a message saying I needed to start afresh somewhere new. The way I went about it is something I kick myself for now, but at the time I just couldn't say it to his face. I wasn't mature enough to do the right thing; to sit down and have an honest chat. It was something I regretted for years afterwards, given everything we had been through together. But I'm hugely grateful that we have since managed to have that talk and make up, and that I got the chance to apologize for how it ended.

It was a strange feeling, not knowing what lay ahead of me;

Unbroken

where I was going to go, who was going to train me. I just knew that I had to leave everything else behind and start again. And when I say everything, I mean everything.

It was the only way.

10
Change

WE'D BEEN SITTING IN THE RESTAURANT FOR LESS THAN FIVE minutes when Jean-Yves Cochand, a French multi-event coaching legend, reached under the table and started rummaging through his bag.

'Aha,' he said, pulling out a bottle of red wine followed by four wine glasses. Seeing the look of confusion on my face, he explained: 'I have three passions in life: athletics, wine, and wine glasses. Because a bad glass can ruin a good wine.'

That was the vibe in Montpellier; totally chill and very, very French. It was October 2016 when I first went there with Denise Lewis, the former British heptathlete who won gold at the Sydney Olympics in 2000, to meet up with Jean-Yves and see whether he might be the right coach for me (and I the right athlete for him). Together with his fellow coaches, Bertrand Valcin and Bruno Gajer, Jean-Yves looked after a group of athletes that included Kevin Mayer, the French decathlete who had won silver in Rio, and Antoinette Nana Djimou, known to most as Nana, a double European champion in the heptathlon.

Before our relaxed lunch in the late autumn Montpellier sun, Jean-Yves had taken me through a shot put session. It was a bit of a tester to see if I liked it there and whether we could communicate with each other. Jean-Yves is probably best known for coaching Eunice Barber, the Sierra Leonean-French athlete who was once Denise's major rival in the heptathlon, but he's also a renowned throws coach, which I knew could really benefit me.

We spent an hour or so out in the throwing circle that day, throwing medicine balls to drill the correct pattern of movement, and I left it feeling positive. Jean-Yves and I seemed to understand each other well and I liked what he was saying about the changes we could make to my technique. The vibe at the track was relaxed but with serious undertones. Working hard was the minimum expectation, but once training was done for the day, a lot of the athletes in their training group would head to the beach or the lake, and go out for dinner together – it was the complete opposite of what I'd always done at home, which was to train and then spend the rest of the day indoors watching box sets and napping.

In many respects 'The Montpellier Way' felt a million miles from the pressure pot I'd been living in for the prior three years, and that was exactly what I wanted.

When Jean-Yves pulled out his bottle of wine at lunch, I was pretty much sold. It was exactly what I wanted: to change my life completely, even if it meant moving away from some of the places and people I loved. I was leaving behind my mum and nan, who I'd been living ten minutes away from since moving into my own place in 2014, and saw pretty much every day. I was leaving behind my boyfriend, who I'd been with since 2012. And I was moving away from my sausage dogs, Bronx and Chorizo, who had brought untold amounts of joy into my life since I'd got them a few years earlier (though Mum had already said she would look after them if I moved abroad). When my then-boyfriend and I broke up a little while after I made the move to France, he even said to me: 'It's only your mum you haven't got rid of.'

Aside from the time I spent in the Bahamas as a baby, I'd never lived anywhere except for Liverpool – I'd never even been to warm-weather training in a different country! The longest period I'd ever been away from my family was two weeks, when I was competing, and even then I'd feel homesick. Liverpool is my home and it always will be. It's the one place where I know I can always go back to and feel supported, no matter what. Even though it was ultimately what I wanted, the thought of living somewhere totally new, where I didn't know anyone and couldn't even speak the language, was daunting.

But complete change was exactly what I needed. It was the only way to break the cycle. As much as I would miss the people (and dogs) I loved so much, I knew I couldn't start another year on the same path yet again. Just the thought of it filled me with negative thoughts about myself and the sport that I loved.

Someone once said that 'nothing changes if nothing changes', and it's true. While I was in France, whenever things felt scary or my heart ached for home, that's what I told myself. Change

My mum, who has been by my side since day one.

Dad and me in the Bahamas.

My first Christmas. Probably still my best Christmas jumper.

 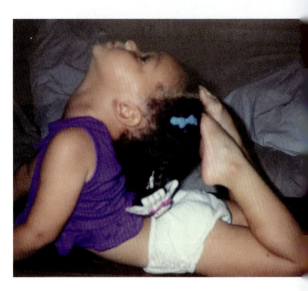

Above left: My mum has always been very stylish – I think she did a good job with my outfit here! *Above right*: Am I practising the high jump already?!

Enjoying that island lifestyle!

My short-lived stint as a dancer, following in my mum's footsteps.

Year Four, St Mark's – the obligatory first-day-of-school photo outside the front of the house.

My nan:
my protector, my hero.

In awe after meeting Daley Thompson (not my dad!) after winning at the National Youth League.

Competing against Jaz (*left*), who has become a friend for life.

'A bit new to this, so I'll just stand here while everyone else gets into a block start . . .'

Left to right: Barrie, me and Mike in 2012, after I had just scored 6,248 points and qualified for the London Olympics. 'Happy' is an understatement!

Mum and me trying to take a serious picture ahead of London 2012. We were a little too excited! These pictures really sum up our relationship – she feels whatever emotion I'm feeling in the moment.

In action at London 2012, where I was just loving life the entire time.

At Götzis, the Mecca for multi-eventers. Enjoying a great 100m hurdles!

Beijing, 2015.
I maintain that
this was NOT a
foul jump!!!

Beijing was devastating.
My dreams had been crushed
and it was all being played
out for the world to see.

Unbroken

was necessary. It was the only way to move forwards, away from Beijing, away from Rio, and towards what I hoped would be a better next chapter.

After the heptathlon, there was still another week or so left of the Rio Olympics, and I was more than happy to hang around. The thought of getting home and being forced to confront reality wasn't a comfortable one. For the first time in my senior career, I was on my own, faced with the daunting task of needing to find a new coach. I had no idea how that worked, or how to even start the process. A lot of people assumed that I'd just move to Jess's coach, Toni, but I knew that wasn't what I wanted.

The flight home from Rio felt brutally long. Everyone competing for GB travelled home as a team but, as we boarded the plane, we were divided into those who had won medals and those who hadn't; the first group were ushered left into business class while the rest of us turned right, into economy to cry our eyes out and pine for 'next time . . .' After eleven hours of travelling, all the medallists were asked to leave the plane first so that the press waiting outside could take pictures, while the remainder sat there waiting to be allowed off.

I went back to my little house in Liverpool, to my mum and my dogs. I was home, surrounded by comfort and love, but at the same time I was completely lost.

In that same period, Denise had called Barrie, wanting to offer her help. She mentioned the name Charles van Commenee, the Dutch coach who had led her to an Olympic gold in the heptathlon in 2000 and was head coach of British Athletics from 2008 until after London 2012.

The next thing I knew, Denise was calling me to say she'd

set up a meeting with Charles in Holland and was coming with me to meet him.

Denise had first come into my life in 2012, when we met at the athletes' parade that was held after the Olympics and Paralympics. It was an incredible, memorable day, spent riding on a float around London in front of huge crowds all cheering and celebrating what the British athletes had achieved that summer. But perhaps most important for me was the moment when I got introduced to Denise.

She's the kind of person who makes everyone feel heard, special and like they're worthy of her time, no matter who they are. And I felt that instantly. Even now, just being in her presence immediately improves my mood. It's hard to explain, but I think it's similar to what people say about David Beckham (or James Bond, who the quote was originally about): men want to be with her, and women want to be her! She's magnetic. That day, we posed for a picture, together with Jess, which the media used as a visual representation of the past, present and future of the British heptathlon. For me, it was just the perfect opportunity to connect with someone who had experienced so much within the sport.

We swapped numbers that day and, from then on, she was always on the end of the phone when I needed to talk, and would always send me thoughtful messages before a comp. After Rio, she saw a lost soul and took it upon herself to step in and help. We spoke for some time when she called to tell me about the meeting with Charles and I'll always remember two of the things she said. Firstly, that finding a new coach wouldn't be an 'easy fix' and that it had to be my decision, and mine alone. Secondly, she said that while some people's lives are nice and steady, others seem to be hurled over waves in a storm, leaving them to hold on for dear life.

Maybe I just wasn't destined to sail on calm waters.

Denise, Barrie and I flew to Holland to visit the Papendal Olympic Training Centre on the outskirts of Arnhem. It's an incredible training facility where a lot of the Dutch athletes (including some of my direct rivals in the heptathlon) were based. I hadn't had much interaction with Charles while he was at British Athletics, so it was interesting to spend some one-on-one time with him. He always had a reputation for being super strict and straight-talking to the extreme, and I definitely got a glimpse of that during the two days we spent in Papendal.

He was just as you'd expect – exactly as everything that's been written about him suggests. He's an intimidating man who really listens you say. You can't bullshit anything. You can see in his face when you're talking that he listens to every single word. You have to ensure those words have meaning, especially when you're talking about anything technical. Being around him makes you level up in terms of professionalism; everything he does has a purpose. Doing a session with him was the most mentally intense thing I'd been through, because you had to be on it all. The. Time. Even now, years later, nothing has changed; he's been helping me with my shot put for the past few years, and sessions with Charles are always mentally tough more than anything else.

On that first visit to Papendal, we did some running, shot put and javelin together and it was really positive. But during our sit-down discussions with Denise and Barrie, Charles said he wasn't keen on the idea of going back to one-to-one coaching. At that time, he was the head coach of the Dutch Athletics

Federation, meaning it was basically his job to make sure that Dutch athletes win medals, so him training me would have been a conflict of interest, and it was clear he didn't want to give up that role.

We discussed potential alternative coaches based in Papendal: by 2016, Dafne Schippers had switched from the heptathlon to sprinting, but her old coach was still based there. So too was the coach (and father) of Anouk Vetter, who had won the European heptathlon title earlier that year. Overall, there was a lot of talk, but in the end the Dutch decided it wouldn't work for them. As well as Anouk, they also had Nadine Visser and Nadine Broersen competing in the heptathlon at that time; three big Dutch athletes who were direct competitors of mine. It was a shame because I felt like the environment there would have been a really good option for me.

It was back to the drawing board in my search for a new coach. But Denise already had someone in mind: Jean-Yves Cochand, who she knew from her time competing against one of his athletes, Eunice Barber. And so, our European tour took us to Montpellier next, and to that memorable lunch date with Jean-Yves, Bertrand and Bruno which helped to cement the feeling that I had found the right place (and people) for me.

There was just one potential problem: Nana, the French heptathlete who was one of the senior athletes in Jean-Yves's training group. Given my experience with the Dutch team, I wasn't taking it for granted that the French would just accept a British rival into their ranks; I knew she would need to be consulted first.

This time, though, the potential problem wasn't a problem at all. I was Nana's direct competitor too, just as I was with the Dutch, but while they said, 'No, you can't train here,' she said, 'Come! It will be great to train together.' There aren't many athletes who would do that.

Nana was my saviour, not just because of her humility in agreeing to train with me. I moved to France speaking zero French, knowing nobody and still very much a mummy's girl. I'd been living on my own (well, with my two best mates, Bronx and Chorizo) for two years, but Mum was nearby and would come over every week to bring me meals, help with the cleaning and sometimes even stock the fridge. In Montpellier, I was going to be completely alone, without the comfort blankets that I had wrapped around me in Liverpool.

My first few weeks in France were saved by Nana. She invited me to stay with her while I found my feet and sorted out more long-term accommodation. She spoke fluent English and basically played Mum for my immature twenty-three-year-old self who had never been away from home. She was my translator too. Down at the track when the coaches were reeling off our target times in French, she was the one translating them all into English for me. She selflessly took me under her wing and I will forever be grateful to her for that, as well as for saying yes to my joining the training group.

After a few weeks with Nana, I moved into an apartment owned by another French athlete who lived abroad. It was small (Mum called it The Hatch, a reference to the underground portal in the TV show *Lost*), but somehow squeezed in two bedrooms, a tiny kitchen, a sauna (which became my storage room) and a jacuzzi. Even the oven doubled as extra storage space – it never got used for its intended purpose, so I thought I'd make it useful in other ways. Denise was one of the first people to come and visit me and she stayed in the second bedroom, which can only be described as what an estate agent would generously call 'cosy'. When Mum came to stay a little while later (bringing a stack of Tupperware so she could batch-cook meals for me and leave them in the freezer), I showed her to the same room and she was mortified.

'Please tell me you didn't put Denise in this room . . . ?'

'Yeah, what's wrong with it?'

'You feel like you're in a coffin. There's no window and the ceiling is so low you can't sit up in bed without whacking your head. Even when you lie down, you feel like your nose is touching the ceiling. Why didn't you sleep on the sofa and let Denise sleep in your bed?!'

Life in Montpellier was vastly different to life in Liverpool. It moved slower. People were more relaxed. In many ways it felt less stressful. Initially, although I was trying to find my feet in a new country, I was excited by my new life and loved being away from everything. It was only a year or so later, after my dad died in November 2017, that I started to feel the impact of being so far away from home – particularly from my family.

I enjoyed the anonymity I had in Montpellier when I was at the track. I was just another athlete. I could blend in and get my work done without being the centre of attention. I didn't even need to engage in too much 'small talk' because most of the time people were speaking in French and I couldn't understand what they were saying so I could just stay quiet. That also meant I didn't get dragged down by the subconscious negative moaning people do day to day. People had to really think about what they were going to say when they spoke to me, because they'd have to do it in English – so it was always something positive. For me, that was perfect.

Unbroken

Away from the track, I had fewer media obligations than when I was in the UK, because I couldn't fly back whenever something cropped up. So in France, my time was spent focusing on training and enjoying life, without having to fit media work in as well. And when I wasn't at the track, no one spoke to me about the sport; I could completely switch off from it, which was so different from being at home.

It took time, but I did adjust to a quieter life. I even learned to love it, and I crave that quiet time now when I don't get enough of it. Sitting on a park bench in Montpellier with a good book (and occasionally an almond croissant) became my happy place. I'd always leaned towards non-fiction books before; ones that I felt might give me some help or guidance as an athlete. But in France I developed a love for fiction; books I could lose myself in. A few years ago, when Mum came to Montpellier to help me pack up the flat and move back to Liverpool, she couldn't believe the number of books we had to pile into boxes. But these were more than books to me. They helped form part of the new comfort blanket that I needed during that first year in France.

On the track, there was also some adjusting to do. Not long after I moved to Montpellier, Jean-Yves told me I had been nicknamed 'Droopy' by the coaches there, because whenever they saw me compete my head was hung low and my shoulders hunched over. They wanted me to smile more; to be able to compete free from that feeling of huge pressure. I wanted that too! So badly. And I believed I was in the right place and with the right people to help me get to that point. But a few months into my time there, Jean-Yves dropped the bombshell on me that he was retiring early in 2017.

As usual, my face gave away my exact emotions as he delivered the news.

'Don't worry, Katarina,' he said, seeing my panicked expression. 'Bertrand [Valcin, his number two] is a fantastic coach and I trust him to do the best job. You are in excellent hands.'

I had no other choice but to trust his words and go with it.

Looking back, I think maybe it was meant to be. As it turned out, Bertrand's personality fitted perfectly with mine. He's a really measured, thoughtful and calm person, and he always has an answer to everything. He's Mr Reliable. He would endeavour to take all the stress away from you, so you wouldn't have to think about anything aside from getting yourself to the track, ready to train. Alongside all of that, he was an excellent coach who was working with one of the best decathletes in the world, Kevin Mayer.

Bertrand was basically the polar opposite of Mike. He was always so unaffected by what happened on the day. He never seemed sad or disappointed in me. It took time for me to adjust to the experience of not being told off after a shit performance. Mike did have a kind side, and he was always empathetic when things were out of my control, like injuries, but otherwise there was very little give. He expected you to turn up and give your absolute best all the time.

When it came to competing, Mike's philosophy was that we would only get on the start line if we were in shape to pull out a big performance – to do something special, like attempting British records or setting PBs. I'd gotten into the mindset that competitions were very high-pressure environments, and that was something that I had to change under Bertrand's guidance. I had to relearn what competitions were all about. I began to see them as opportunities to practise events and see where I was at, not caring what other people might think of the results. That approach took a lot of the pressure out of competing and, in its place, I started to find and re-recognize my love of the sport: I finally started to enjoy it again.

When I was coming back from my Achilles rupture in 2021, I remember Mum coming out to Montpellier and the three of us having a chat. I told her that I was going to be doing a comp in a few weeks' time and Mum replied: 'Oh great, that'll be a test . . .' 'No,' said Bertrand firmly, 'it's not a test.' He didn't want me thinking of it that way. It was just another opportunity to put things into practice and see what areas we needed to work on.

Bertrand's winters were also totally different from what I'd been used to. Mike was big on heavy winter work. Big on plyometrics. Big on rest and tapers as well. Whereas Bertrand was more of a 'little and often' guy. I went into doing double days (two training sessions in one day), which I'd never done before. So we'd do two double days at the start of the week and then training every day for the rest of the week, with just Sundays off – it was quite intense. But it meant that I was practising all the events constantly, whereas before, I wouldn't high jump or long jump all the time. With Bertrand we were breaking down each event and then building up and refining the technique. The sessions were shorter and sharper than I was used to, with a lot of focus on technical fine tuning. Their frequency meant I was also getting more used to putting my body through a load on the track, in the hope it would help build up my resilience against the muscle injuries I'd struggled with in the lead-up to Rio.

Katarina Johnson-Thompson

That first winter, I was a bit nervous. I knew how my body responded to Mike's winters. This was a totally new approach with an unknown result. Sometimes I'd go to the track and do one of the rowing conditioning sessions I used to do with Mike, just to check if I still had it. I was nervous because I wasn't dying on the floor after every session. But it was something that I just had to trust – and eventually I learned that, with Bertrand, it was more the accumulation of consistent training that got me fit. That's something I do have within me: the ability to make a decision and then trust in it. In this case, that meant trusting in the person and the process. A few years later, when I changed coaches again in 2022, that trust worked against me – but every other time, it has worked in my favour.

The message from everyone around me was, 'Don't look for too much in your first year with a new coach.' But to be honest, I wanted instant results. My mindset at the start of 2017 was the same as it had been when I left the UK. I'd spent the previous few years competing for medals and I didn't want to step back from that. That summer, the World Championships were taking place at the Olympic Stadium in London, and my full focus was on challenging for gold in the stadium where my journey as a senior athlete had really started.

Life after Rio didn't change only for me – like I said, there's always a lot of movement after an Olympic Games and, while I had been scouring Europe for a new coach, Jess had announced her retirement. That was swiftly followed by news of Brianne Theisen-Eaton's retirement too. Neither was a great surprise. Jess had basically told us in Rio that she was going to retire, so we knew it was coming, but with two big contenders out of the picture, it suddenly felt like the door to medals was more open than ever.

I quickly discovered that the worst thing you can do in sport is to think exactly that, because you have to realize that everyone else will see it the same way. At Götzis that year, I got a PB of 6,691 points – a highest score just six months into a new coaching setup, my first in a heptathlon since 2014 and, most importantly, a turning point, showing that I was capable of completing a heptathlon without disaster or injury. But that was only enough to put me in fourth place. Nafi Thiam won it with an incredible score of 7,013, and the two athletes between us both scored over 6,800. It was one of the highest-scoring Götzis competitions on record. I learned then that it didn't really matter that Jess and Brianne had gone, because the next batch of athletes were already there, ready to take their places.

It sounds like a wild thing to say, especially given my experience in Rio, but that competition was the first time I thought that, separate to my own demons, I might not be good enough. I'd experienced failures before, but I'd always been able to separate those from my ability as an athlete. I'd always been able to blame losses on an injury (Götzis 2016), or on what I could perceive as a sketchy judgement call (Beijing), or even on the state of my mental health (Rio). But at Götzis in 2017, I did better than I ever had before, and those three people were just better than me. I remember thinking to myself, *How the hell am I going to beat them?!* Losing when I felt like I was at my best was a big reality check for me, and it swiftly put to bed any thoughts I had of 'easy' medal opportunities without Jess in the picture.

Bertrand's response to Götzis was typically Bertrand: measured;

calm. He wasn't worried in the slightest. He reminded me that, with the type of training we'd been doing, we weren't peaking for Götzis; we were peaking for the World Championships a few months later. He knew exactly what to say to still my racing mind's response to a PB only being good enough for fourth place.

Returning to London's Olympic Stadium for the World Championships, five years after those two special days in 2012, was something I was really looking forward to. In the weeks beforehand I watched old videos from the London Games and felt all the emotions come flooding back; the pure excitement at hearing a crowd cheer my name so loudly, the joy of holding my own among the best in the world, and the spark of inspiration that was illuminated within me during that victory lap with Jess.

I felt like a different person compared to that excitable kid who made her senior debut in 2012. So much had happened since then. I'd experienced what I believed was every imaginable low an athlete can experience. And in terms of life, I had become what most people would say was pretty much a proper adult, doing my own cleaning and learning to cook (albeit with Mum directing me on FaceTime). I'd even fixed my own internet in the apartment when it had gone down – a particularly proud moment, I won't lie.

One thing that did connect the Kat from 2012 with the one returning five years later was my excitement about doing a heptathlon. For the first time in years, I wasn't scared of my quad getting hurt, or of feeling any pain in my knee. I went in with the mentality that I was just excited to see what I could do at a home championship, with the crowd on my side. And, boy, was that crowd loud! I remember walking out for the 100m hurdles on the first morning and being taken aback by the noise. The Worlds always feel different to the Olympics in lots of ways, but the energy I got from the crowd that weekend wasn't far removed from the huge buzz I'd felt in 2012. And that energy didn't drop throughout the entire competition – every warm-up jump or throw, the crowd was going wild! It really was quite special.

After the way Götzis had gone, I wasn't expecting to come away from London with a gold medal. I just wanted to finish on the podium, with a medal of any colour hanging around my neck. But by the time most people in the crowd were tucking into their packed lunches on the first day of the heptathlon, that podium place had become more of a dream than an expectation.

Mum can never eat anything on the day of a competition until after the hurdles and high jump are over and, at the 2017 World Championships, it turned out her nerves were warranted. In the bright morning sunshine, I made it safely through the hurdles and ran close to my PB (13.33 seconds) in a fast heat. But by the time the high jump started, the temperature had dropped and the heavens had opened, leaving the track dotted with puddles. As I tried to stay warm, while the officials mopped up as much of the water on the run-up as they could, my mind went straight to one place.

I hate jumping in the rain.

Nafi and I both entered the event at 1.80 metres, then chose to skip 1.83 metres and go straight to 1.86 metres, which meant a ninety-minute wait, in the cold, while the other athletes went through their heights. Eventually, my time came. I'd already jumped heights of 1.93 metres and 1.95 metres that season so 1.86 metres should have been a breeze. But as I approached the bar for my first attempt, it looked higher than I expected. I clattered into it, knocking the bar straight off.

Nafi, of course, cleared it first time.

On my second go, I clipped the bar with my ankles; another fail. Ahead of my third and final attempt, I felt a sense of panic. I don't know if that was the pressure, the rain or the crowd, who were shouting at my every move. My stomach felt like it was gripping onto itself, making my breaths short and shallow.

'Attack the bar,' I said to myself. But my body was unable to respond and this time I brought the bar down with my back. As I landed on the mat, I curled myself into a tight ball, desperate not to see the bar on the floor, the disappointment of thousands of people waving Union Jacks in the crowd or the faces of my coaches, Bertrand and Bruno.

In the stands, Mum's stomach lurched as her mind went back to Beijing and the broken daughter that she had to try to put back together in a lonely hotel room. But the message from Bertrand and Bruno was the same as always: keep calm and carry on. They weren't panicking. There were still five events left to go and anything can happen in a heptathlon. After the high jump, I was in fifth place, not completely out of medal contention (even if it felt that way with the shot put up next, where I knew I would probably drift further down the standings). But by the end of day one, I was back up into fourth place after running a 22.86 seconds in the 200m – one of my fastest ever.

I needed a really strong second day to stay in contention for a medal, and it started well in the long jump. With the sun once again gracing us with her presence in the Olympic Stadium, I jumped 6.56 metres, just 1 centimetre behind Nafi (who topped the long jump standings), elevating me to the bronze medal position. My javelin went pretty well too, with three of my throws going further than 40 metres for the first time ever, but I still dropped a couple of places to fifth ahead of the 800m, with Anouk Vetter up into third place – she went on to win the bronze medal, cementing the opinions of those in the Dutch setup who didn't like the idea of me moving in on their terrain. That meant I would need to run the 800m around 17 seconds faster than the girls above me to finish with a medal. It was the tallest of orders.

I crossed the line in 2:08.10, my fastest 800m since the Moscow World Championships in 2013 – four years earlier! Bruno's advice had played a huge role; he'd told me to stick close enough to the German athlete Claudia Rath (who had a PB of 2:05) that I could smell her hair, and also to see the crowd's immense noise as more of a boost than a pressure: 'Breathe in their noise,' he told me in his heavily accented English. 'Use it as energy.' I finished with 6,558 points; two places and 79 points away from a bronze medal. Compared to my high jump in Rio the previous year, I'd lost 233 points in that one event. Nafi had won gold with 6,784; a score of 228 points more than me.

In the immediate aftermath, I was gutted. I'd missed a huge opportunity at a home World Championship. But I was also proud of the way I had come back from disappointment. In my first championship heptathlon with Bertrand and Bruno, they had helped me take the first step towards becoming a true heptathlete instead of one who relies on one good high jump or long jump to put together a decent score.

Katarina Johnson-Thompson

In the past, I would have fallen apart after a bad high jump – would have wanted to sulk or throw it all away because my strong event hadn't gone well – but they helped me to see that one bad performance didn't have to make a bad heptathlon. They turned what could have been a negative experience into a positive one. Just a year on from 2016, I'd gone through another championship heptathlon and had a totally different experience – one that I knew would completely change the way I attacked a competition. Bertrand and Bruno were slowly turning me into a heptathlete; and, after our experience in London, I knew I could trust them to do that.

Four days later, I competed in the individual high jump competition. I was super nervous. What if the same thing happened again? What if I could only clear 1.80 metres? Bertrand and Bruno helped put my mind at rest and I qualified for the final with relative ease, clearing 1.92 metres. Two days later, I competed in my first ever global individual high jump final and jumped a season's best 1.95 metres to finish fifth overall.

Kevin ended up winning gold in the decathlon in London, which only confirmed to me that if I continued to trust in these people, I would be following the right path. But the best part of his win was probably the after-party. Kevin had chartered a boat on the River Thames for him and his family to live on during the championships; after he won, they hosted a really fun party on there that lasted until daylight!

I was delighted by the season's best. Normally, my experience in the heptathlon would have derailed me completely, but Bertrand and Bruno were changing my mentality. They were so influential in my being able to bounce back from that failure

Rio, 2016. 1.98m – a heptathlon world record, and at the Olympics to boot! That feeling was like no other.

Bertrand, my head coach, flew all the way to Australia – travelling for forty-eight hours – to be with me at the Commonwealth Games in 2018. This gold was definitely for him.

With Bruno, my running coach. He has the ability to dish out incredible pain when he's on that bike, but he always makes me smile. He's a ray of sunshine in my life.

Awww . . . Me and Pozz – we do scrub up nicely every now and then! The second pic is just us having a laugh, way before we knew what the future would hold for us.

Two of the most important parts of my life in one place . . . plus Pozz.

My managers, Greg (*left*) and Dan (*right*), who have been by my side through everything.

The girls, aka my 'Hoes in Different Area Codes'.

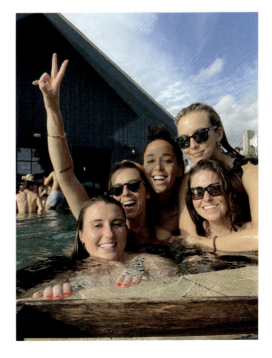

The legacy continues. I was so happy to share this full-circle moment with the heptathlon GOATs! Jess broke Denise's British heptathlon record and, in Doha 2019, I managed to break Jess's – en route to becoming world champion.

The light show in Doha! I typically shy away from the spotlight, but I loved everything about this moment.

Disbelief through the years! These three pictures are all me trying to process an incredible thing that's just happened. I'm not known for my poker face . . .

My family with their TEAM KJT hoodies straight after I won the European Indoors in 2019. This was the last comp my nan got to see me do in person.

Left to right: Bertrand, Andy, Cat, me, Helen and MJ (Derry was absent). The team that got me to the start line of the Tokyo Olympics. We were so happy to be there and ready to give it everything!

The lowest moment of my entire career. I left Tokyo not knowing – and, worse, not particularly caring – if I'd ever compete in athletics again.

Above: The agony of injury. It was such a long road to get myself back to fitness . . . twice! I've never been in a worse place, both physically and mentally, but now I tell myself that if I could get through that, I can get through anything. *Below:* Two-time world champ! This win meant everything to me. This one is for the underdogs – anybody who's ever been written off and told you can't do something!

In 2023, for the first time, World Athletics gave coaches a medal as well as the athlete. I'd just handed my coach Aston a gold medal, but he had no idea that it was his to keep! He's an amazing person.

There were so many moments on my journey, right until the very end, when it felt like the world was against me, so getting to the Paris Olympics was a real accomplishment. Bringing home a medal for my country made me prouder than I could have imagined.

in the high jump to compete so well in the same event a week later. That experience taught me a lot about mentality and how to approach a heptathlon. It changed me from someone who could put in a good performance in the high jump and then be hanging on and hoping for the best, into an athlete who was absolutely fighting for each point in every single event.

I used to dwell an awful lot on everything. But Bertrand and Bruno taught me that the best mode for me to be in is a working mode, where I'm just constantly trying to do better with each jump, each throw, so it doesn't really matter if you fail. It's more about how you fix it straight away, rather than dwelling on what's happened before. It reminds me of *Frozen 2*: even if you mess up, do the next right thing that you can possibly do, and things will start to get better.

At the World Championships, I'd finished fifth in the heptathlon, despite underperforming in my strongest event. If I'd competed in that championships earlier in my career, with less experience or with a coach who had the same mindset as me, maybe it would have ended differently. Mike was just too similar to me at the time: we wanted to win, we wanted gold and we were sad when we didn't do it. Whereas Bertrand was quite removed and could always see the bigger picture. He was never stressed in any situation.

If I replaced that failed 1.86-metre high jump with one I already knew I could do in my sleep, I could see that everything was there. In Rio, I'd lost my head and allowed everything to just spiral. I wasn't able to see what could have been, because I gave up. In London, I didn't give up on that score. Even though it was going to be very hard for me to make up the points, I was able to see what my potential was and ultimately that gave me confidence. I had the talent to win and I believed that, eventually, it would happen for me. I just didn't know when.

It had been less than a year since I'd changed everything – left my friends, family and boyfriend – to pursue my dream. Now, I know that moving to France was the start of something very special but, at the time, I was still adjusting to my new life, still struggling with the language and the distance from home and the loved ones I'd left behind. People said I was brave to do it, but I didn't feel that way. I just felt like I had no choice.

Change isn't something that I'm particularly scared of or reticent about. I love change. I think it's necessary. I get really shocked when people stay the same over long periods of time, even if we're just talking about coaching options. I feel like different people come into your life at different periods of time. That has certainly been the case for me, and I've needed all those different coaches for different reasons.

Even in 2024, I had to change a lot of things between the European Championships in Rome and the start of the Olympic Games in Paris, because it was necessary.

Nothing changes if nothing changes, remember.

2018 promised to be a huge year for competing: there was a World Indoor Championships, a Commonwealth Games and a European Outdoor Championships all happening in the same year. I was excited to see what I could do after another winter of training with Bertrand and Bruno.

But before I could reach that point, I was forced to deal with another huge change in my life. It's one that I was in no way prepared for. One that I am still dealing with now. One that will leave its mark on me for ever.

11
Grief

I WAS IN LONDON WHEN THE CALL CAME.

It was a few hours before I was due to board a flight back to Montpellier, and I was still asleep in my hotel room when my phone rang. I saw 'Mum' flash up on the screen and I felt an instant sense of panic. We always speak multiple times a day, but she knew I was heading to the airport that morning and so we'd arranged the previous day that I would call her when I was checked in and waiting to board.

'You OK?' I asked as soon as I answered the call.

'It's your dad,' she replied.

He'd had a heart attack, out of the blue. Mum had found out the night before from one of my aunties in the Bahamas. And just like that, he was gone.

At first, I didn't understand. He was only fifty-nine and he was getting ready to retire from his job at ZNS – the national broadcaster in the Bahamas. After that, he wanted to travel more;

he was excited to have the time to come and see me, and to watch me compete. The last time I'd seen him in person had been in 2012, after the Olympics.

It wasn't a long conversation with Mum. We spoke about what I should do and decided I should carry on as planned for the moment and go back to Montpellier. 'There's nothing we can really do for now,' said Mum.

I had a taxi coming to pick me up and take me to the airport so I said goodbye to Pozz; he was there and wanted to come back to France with me, but I was reluctant. I don't know why, but I wanted to go back by myself. I might make a different decision now.

The taxi driver who took me to the airport was going the longest way. I don't know if he was trying to get more money or what, but I was just sitting in the back feeling a mixture of anger and sadness, thinking to myself: *Not today. Don't you know what's just happened?!* Of course, he didn't. How could he? But also, I felt like, how could he not? My world had just come tumbling down; surely everyone else had to be feeling like I was feeling?

That's one of the things that's so strange and difficult about grief. There's a book called *Grief is the Thing with Feathers* by Max Porter, in which the mother of two little boys dies and there's this crow who helps them with the grieving process. At one point, the boys are talking about the moment when they heard that their mum had died and they're like: 'Where's the sirens? Where's the chaos? Where's everyone flipping out because this momentous thing has happened?'

That's how I felt that day. Everyone around me was just going about their days as normal. People at the airport were queuing up calmly for check-in and security. They were buying random stuff in the shops, magazines or new books for their journeys. Their world was still turning, but mine was collapsing. It was the same feeling those boys had: *Why isn't everybody crying?* It made no sense to me.

But that's how it works. You never know who is going through it. There's probably someone going through it right now. I could walk past them in the supermarket and not know. As I sat on the plane waiting for take-off, I looked at the faces of people around me. Tired people. Excited people. Anxious people. No one who looked like me. No one trying to understand how life had changed in the space of one brief phone call.

I closed my eyes and felt them dampen with tears.

It was November 2017 when I lost my dad, Ricardo, and I still don't know if I've grieved properly. It's one of the reasons I started therapy in 2022, but it's always something I'm putting off: 'Oh, we can talk about it after this,' or 'Let's wait until then . . .' Even in the writing of this book, I put off talking about it until it reached the point when I could put it off no more.

It all felt so strange, because something huge had happened, but it didn't change my day-to-day life because he was never there anyway. My life wasn't affected, because I wasn't in constant contact with him. It wasn't like he was in Liverpool with Mum, which would have made me feel I should go back home. Nothing had changed, but at the same time everything had changed. It was a very weird time. I was lost.

In my daily life, I couldn't find an outlet for that grief because we hadn't had regular contact. He was an island person; he wasn't big on mobile phones, and he didn't have social media.

It wasn't like we could WhatsApp or FaceTime every day. My relationship with him was a house phone call every now and again, and that was it.

When I think of him, I think of the Bahamas. And when I think of the Bahamas, I think of him – especially of that trip Mum and I took to see him after London 2012.

Money had always been tight at home. We had enough for the basics, and for me to train, but that was it really. So, when I got my first payment from a sponsor after the Olympics, which was about £3,000 (taking me out of my overdraft for the first time), I knew I wanted to do something special with it: go to see my dad. I spent every penny of it on that trip, and then went straight back to living in my overdraft afterwards (what teenager doesn't?), but it was more than worth it.

It had been around twelve years since I'd last seen him and, as our plane came into land over the sparkling turquoise sea and pristine white sands of Nassau, I felt my heartbeat start to quicken with a mixture of excitement and nerves. What would it be like to see him after so long? Would it be awkward? What if we had nothing to say?

I didn't have to wait long to find out. We walked into the airport, looking around for the signs to passport control, and suddenly there he was – standing right in front of us! I was so stunned I just said, 'How the hell did you get here?!' Security in the Bahamas was clearly very different to airports in the UK.

He looked at me and smiled his beaming, bright smile, while his eyes watered at the sight of his little girl (who was now as tall as him).

Then came one of the most memorable parts of the whole trip. Dad was driving us from the airport to the hotel where

Unbroken

Mum and I were staying and, as we drove off, he turned on the car stereo and Nicki Minaj's 'Did It On'em' started blasting out of the car's speakers.

'Shitted on 'em,' belted Dad, gleefully, looking at me and smiling as he sang. I didn't know what to do. I wanted to sing along but I never swear in front of Mum – ever. So I was like, *Can I sing? Am I allowed to sing along?* I looked at Mum, sitting in the back, to try to gauge her reaction. Normally, if I sing along in front of her, I beep out all the swear words, but there wasn't much point with Dad singing them loud and clear!

It was the first time I'd been in both of my parents' company as an adult and I had no idea how the three of us 'should' work. Could I be one person with my dad and a different person with my mum? I had so many different thoughts and emotions running through me. I felt like I'd had a momentary glimpse of what life with the two of them might have been like had things worked out differently; how we might have interacted, the things we might have laughed at or argued about.

It was surreal being there. I hadn't been on the island since I was a kid but, from the minute we arrived, I felt an overwhelming sense of familiarity; like the Bahamas was an old friend I'd grown up with but hadn't seen for some time. Every day we were there, Dad would come to pick us up from our hotel and he'd take us around the island, showing me where he and Mum lived when I was little, the beaches they used to take me to and even a track that was being built which is now used for the World Relay Championships.

We also went to see where he worked for ZNS, which is like the Bahamian BBC. He had all these videos of me competing at London 2012, but with the Bahamian commentary dubbed over, which was really cool. They were calling me 'Miss Thompson' and claiming me as their own – even now, every time I see an athlete from the Bahamian team, they say, 'Hi, Miss Thompson.'

I think 2012 was when Dad first realized that what I was doing was kind of a big deal, and he was so proud. The one thing he didn't show me in 2012 was his own house. I think he was a bit embarrassed by it, so we never went there. It was only when we went back for the funeral, in 2017, that we went there and all the memories of when I was younger came flooding back. The area was Kemp Road and there were three different houses packed together; one was dad's, one was his mum's and one belonged to his sister, my aunt Toni. It was a bit of a rough area, but when we were there in 2017, Toni told me not to worry – everyone knew I was Ricardo's daughter: 'He spoke about you all the time,' she said, smiling. 'You can walk here day or night, it's fine.'

It was on that same trip, in 2017, that Toni took us to a pub around the corner from Dad's house. As I looked around, I saw a wall plastered with newspaper cuttings. It was only when I got closer to it that I realized they were all about me. The whole wall was full of cuttings from the *Liverpool Echo* from when I was a kid, and from the national newspapers in the lead-up to 2012. Mum told me she had been sending him clippings for years as I was growing up, and he'd kept them all. We found the rest of them in his house, carefully wrapped in cellophane so they wouldn't fade.

I don't know how to grieve for Dad unless I go back to the Bahamas. My relationship with him only existed when I was there. The minute I go back, as I did again in 2021 after the Tokyo Olympics, emotions well up that don't appear anywhere else. I don't see him anywhere in my mind, but there. It was a very weird time when I got back to Montpellier after finding out he was gone. I was very lost. I drifted through training until the funeral got arranged, and that's when a whole new emotion appeared: guilt.

We booked our tickets to fly back to the Bahamas, I arranged to take three days off training, and it was all so easy – barely more effort than going to the supermarket to buy milk. My brain went into overdrive. *Had it always been that easy? How long had I been able to afford the flights there?* Before moving to France, I'd lived quite a sheltered life. I hadn't gone on any training camps abroad – my training camps involved getting from Liverpool to Loughborough. The only time I'd boarded a plane was to go and compete. My life had become very different the previous year; the French loved to do training camps all over the place, so I was always getting on flights.

When we flew back to the Bahamas for Dad's funeral, I was struck by an immense feeling of sadness and guilt that I hadn't gone there more often. It was so easy for me to do it. Why hadn't I done it all the time and cultivated a stronger relationship with him?

I grieved at the funeral. I grieved for him, for me, and for the relationship we missed out on. Life went on as normal once I got back to Montpellier but, before long, I grieved again. And then again years later. Then again and again and again.

Dad's death, and the way it happened, left me with an intense fear of bad things happening to people I loved – of losing them without the chance to say goodbye. Phone calls at unexpected times, or too long left between messages from Pozz or my mum, and I'd instantly fear the worst. I knew it was irrational but, for the longest time, I couldn't stop the thoughts from coming. There was no one I felt I could speak to about it, either. It was still relatively early in my relationship with Bertrand; we could have surface-level conversations and had a basic understanding of each other's thoughts and feelings, but it's hard to hit that deeper level with people when you can't speak the same language (and you don't know how to process grief, anyway). So, I tried to deal with it on my own, for years. At least until I started therapy.

That anxiety made the summer of 2022 particularly difficult for me. I was in America, competing in the World Championships in Eugene, while at home my nan was in hospital. Her dementia had left her very frail and weak, and I was terrified of losing her while I was so far from home – of not getting that chance to say goodbye.

I was constantly thinking about it, constantly looking at my phone, wondering if today was going to be the day. Even when I spoke to Mum and she reassured me that Nan was doing OK, I was worried that she was hiding the truth because I was away competing and couldn't do anything. 'Is she OK, really?' I'd ask repeatedly, never fully believing the response I heard. There was a lot of misplaced distrust, I guess.

Less than a week after I returned home from Eugene (where I'd finished eighth), Nan was gone. I'd seen her in the hospital as soon as I got back and then again when she came home briefly. I saw her on the same day that she passed. It's something I will always be grateful for.

The Commonwealth Games were due to start in Birmingham three days later, and I was supposed to be competing in the heptathlon five days after that. I couldn't see the point. I hadn't been in a good place in Eugene and now I was in an even worse one. Putting myself out there to compete was the last thing I wanted to do. I just wanted to call it there and then; put an end to the 2022 season and be done with what had been a terrible year (I'll come to that).

I told Mum I didn't know if I could do it, and she said to me that it was my choice completely. 'I do know one thing, though,' she said. 'Your nan would have wanted you to do it. You know how much she loved watching you compete.'

I had a few days to mull it over before I decided to go ahead. I could see that Mum was hurting and I thought it was something she wanted me to do; I thought maybe my competing could help bring some form of happiness back to my family, or at least a healthy distraction. I was really lucky that Pozz was competing in Birmingham too, and that they allowed us to share a room, which gave me the support I really needed.

To start with, I felt like I was doing OK. It was only on the second day, when it started to look like I was going to win the competition, that it suddenly hit me: Nan wasn't there.

We'd just finished the long jump, and I had a lead of over 100 points with just two events to go. But there were seven hours of waiting around before I was due back out into the stadium to compete in the javelin, which was an evening session. I went back to the rest room thinking I'd try to get some sleep but, out of nowhere, the tears started flowing. And they kept on flowing. I couldn't do anything to stop them. Up until that point, I don't think I had really allowed myself to grieve. I'd been so caught up with whether or not I should compete, and so worried about Mum, that I hadn't given myself the time to absorb what had happened.

But then it hit me. And all I could think was, *What the fuck is this? Why am I competing when she's not here? Why isn't she here?* Those thoughts circled endlessly around my head. I rang Mum from the rest room and bawled down the phone to her. Her immediate thought was that I was injured.

'No, Mum, I've just realized Nan's not here any more.'

It sounds strange, but it took that long for it to really sink in. Over a week for me to fully comprehend that Nan – my nan – somebody who had been so instrumental throughout my whole life – was now gone. It was the first home championships she'd missed.

Three years earlier, she'd come to the European Indoor Championships in Glasgow in 2019, which turned out to be her last one. By that time, she was in a wheelchair, but my aunties had arranged a minibus to drive the whole family up from Liverpool to watch. They even brought a little framed photo of my grandad Jimmy, so he was there too. All of them were wearing bright red hoodies with 'TEAM KJT' splashed across the middle and, somehow, they had seats right near the front so I could see and hear them the whole day. It's one of my favourite comps for that reason alone.

During that emotional phone call in Birmingham, Mum and I started talking about Nan, and how much she had loved boasting about me. Then Mum reminded me of some of our favourite moments: Nan saying, 'I don't want you going if you're going to finish last' when I qualified for London 2012. And the 'It's not the same when you don't win, is it?' comment that sent everyone into hysterics after I finished sixth at the European Juniors.

My tears were gradually joined by smiles at the happy

memories we had with Nan and laughter at the way she always said it exactly how it was.

'What would your nan say?' Mum asked. 'She'd want you to go out there and get that medal, so go and do it for your nan!'

I came out for the javelin a few hours later and threw a PB by 40 centimetres – my first PB in three years! I couldn't believe it. It was magical. Mum always says she felt like Nan was there that day. Honestly speaking, I don't know my full feelings on it, but I do reckon that when someone dies, they stay with you for a period of time to make sure you're OK before they really do cross over. I feel like the same thing happened when my dad died; the following year I went on to win a lot, especially in the first six months.

In the moments after I crossed the finish line of the 800m, to win the gold medal in the Commonwealth Games, I couldn't stop the tears from falling.

'This was for her,' I told the media, as I desperately tried to hold it together.

Nine days later, we said our final farewells to my nan, Mary Johnson. She was the most loving and generous woman I've ever known. It felt different to losing my dad. In a way, it was easier to understand, because I was used to seeing her all the time. She and my mum lived in the same house – the one Mum still lives in. After I ruptured my Achilles in 2021, I lived with them. Nan and I shared a sofa. Ate our meals off trays together. Shared a stairlift.

It was a very obvious reality when she was gone. Even the dogs felt it. They'd lived with Mum and Nan while I was in France, and even though I'd returned to the UK by 2022, they still spent most of their time there while I was training in

Loughborough. Bronx, the brown one, lost all his hair after Nan died. For a few months, he was completely bald; everyone reckons it was caused by grief, or just not understanding where she'd gone.

On the day of the funeral, we opened the front door of the house for Nan to get taken to the church and three or four white butterflies suddenly appeared around the doorway, as if they were there to accompany her. Ever since then, if anyone in our family sees a white butterfly, they feel it's my nan, popping back to say hello, or more likely to tell you to eat properly. That was her thing. When Pozz and I saw her the day before she died, she looked at Mum and said, 'Make them some toast.' It was one of the last things she said to me.

Nan was always trying to give to other people, whether that was buying extra shopping for my Mum when she was struggling to bring me up on her own, slipping a tenner in my hand for no good reason at all, or offering Greg a full-on cooked breakfast whenever he came to pick me up for an event or meeting. She was just that kind of person. I miss her.

When I think about losing my dad and my nan, I realize how many different ways grief can manifest, and how many different forms it can take. No way is 'easier' or 'better' than another; they're all just different.

I saw an interesting video on TikTok of someone talking about grief. They spoke about how, when someone dies, their version of the people they know dies with them. I know Pozz like nobody else knows him, so, if I was to die, my version of Pozz would die with me. By extension, his hypothetical grieving of me would then actually be grief for the person he was with me, which is why grief is such an individual experience. I'm grieving for relationships with my nan and my dad that nobody else had, and my mum is doing the same.

But I think if you know somebody really well, that person never really goes away. A lot of the time, if I want to ask Mum or Pozz something, I already know exactly what they're going to say. Those people don't need to be physically with you to always be with you – inside you, actively participating in conversations you can have with them inside your head. Maybe that's one reason I struggled so much with losing my dad. I didn't know him that well, so it was harder to feel his presence, or closeness to him, after he was gone.

It might sound silly to some people, but one of the things that made me really sad after my dad's – and my nan's – death was that my dad had never seen me win anything. The last championships he'd seen were the Rio Olympics in 2016, where I was sixth, and the World Championships in 2017, where I finished fifth. All he'd seen of me was explicitly *not* winning or, worse, public failure. I know he wouldn't have thought like that, and that he was proud of what I'd done regardless, but it was how I felt at the time, and it was a real wake-up call.

Going into 2018, all I wanted was to win medals. I didn't care about scores or setting new PBs. I just wanted to give my family that experience of me winning things, to create happy memories together that we could carry with us for the rest of our lives. I wouldn't think the same way now, because it can lead down a dangerous path. What if you don't win? Then you're left feeling ten times worse because you believe you've let your loved ones down, when all they really want is for you to be happy. Of course, I want happy moments along the way, but there's no need to make things as black and white as saying winning equals good and losing equals bad.

But at the time, I wanted it for Mum and Nan more than anything. They deserved it, and I was determined that I was going to deliver it for them.

12

Relationships II

'You shouldn't be here!' I said, looking across the table at Pozz as he took a sip of his pint. 'You need to get to bed.'

'It's fine,' he replied, smiling. 'This is going to help me relax and get motivated. I want to be celebrating like this twenty-four hours from now.'

We were sitting in my room at the team hotel, celebrating my first ever global gold medal at the World Indoor Championships in 2018. Outside, the city was covered in snow and ice; the streets eerily quiet as everyone took shelter from the freezing temperatures brought on by Storm Emma.

Some twenty-four hours had passed since I crossed the finish line of the 800m – the final event of the pentathlon – in first place, to finally secure the title of world champion, and I couldn't believe what a perfect weekend it had been so far. Just a few months after losing Dad, my family had finally seen me win something (the only downside being that Nan hadn't been able to leave the hotel to come to the arena because of the wintry conditions). The goal that I'd started the year with, of giving my family something to celebrate and enjoy, had been achieved, and I was so happy and relieved to finally be able to get one over the line.

After four of the five events (60m hurdles, high jump, shot put and long jump), I was in first place, 33 points ahead of Austrian athlete Ivona Dadic. Going into the 800m I had a 2-second lead on her; all I had to do was to not let her beat me, and the gold was mine.

After the first 200m lap, Dadic was leading and I'd found a comfortable spot in third, not far behind. I hadn't raced an 800m since the World Championships the previous summer, but the running sessions Bruno had me doing in Montpellier were pretty brutal and I was confident my body would be able to respond.

With 400m to go, I moved up into second place.

With 300m to go, I took the lead.

As the bell rang to signal that we were into the last lap, I felt someone close to my right shoulder, and I glanced over at the giant screen to see Dadic coming up fast.

By the time I looked back at the track, she was right next to me. I gritted my teeth and stretched out my legs, asking them for more speed, more power. Seconds later, I crossed the finish line, not knowing if I'd done enough. I sank down onto the track, gulping in air, and then I felt a hand on my back. I looked up to see Dadic looking down at me.

'Congratulations,' she said, smiling. 'Too good.'

Seconds later it was confirmed, and I went straight over to where Bertrand was sitting to celebrate with him. I'd finally learned how to win through sheer grit and determination, and he (and Bruno) had played a huge part in that.

I'd established so much belief and trust during our experience as a team during the World Championships in 2017, and the victory in Birmingham further cemented both of those things. I was competitive, dynamic, I fought for gold in every different aspect of the event, and then I actually crossed the line and made sure of the victory.

All that mattered to me was the win.

I didn't care about the score (4,750 points, which was 250 below my best) or who else I'd beaten, all I cared about was getting a championship win. That experience trumps everything else: even if you win one with a low score, it trumps a high score somewhere else, on another day, when the pressure is off. A championship win means the most. And that win in 2018 meant the most to me.

When it comes to competition, there's a popular understanding that you have to stop the young ones from winning, because once they win one, they know *how* to win, and that changes everything. That day in Birmingham was the first time I learned *how* to win, and it gave me a huge confidence boost ahead of a year that would include both a Commonwealth Games and European Championships.

My victory on the Friday night was followed by that of one of my training partners, Kevin Mayer. He won gold in the heptathlon (the indoor alternative to the decathlon for men) on the Saturday, and it was turning into the perfect weekend. All that was left was for Pozz to go for gold in the 60m hurdles the next day.

Yet here he was, sitting in the hotel bar without a care in the world. He fascinated me. I was a chronic worrier – someone who felt like I had to have control of everything in order to succeed – while he believed that around competitions, all stress was bad stress. He always says that being properly prepared is the most important thing, and in the final moments before you compete, the little things that bring you happiness are only going to add to your performance, not take anything away from it.

The next day, he proved it, winning his semi-final in the afternoon and going on to win the final a few hours later by a single hundredth of a second. We'd been on similar journeys up to that point; both seen as huge talents after breaking through as seniors at London 2012 but then struggling to get over the line for various reasons – he was six surgeries deep at this point, aged just twenty-five. And now we were both world champions, winning our first global titles, together, on the same weekend.

It was surreal. Especially when we woke up on Monday morning to see that the snow and ice had completely disappeared, as if it had never happened. The streets were filled with people again, and the roads were busy. Life was back to normal. It felt like a dream. Had we actually won gold medals? Were we really world champions? To confirm it for us, as much as anyone else, Pozz and I took a photo of our teardrop-shaped gold medals, side by side.

At this point, Pozz and I had been together romantically for quite a few months, but we'd kept it very low-key. No one outside of our immediate circle really knew. But it felt like the right time to change that. We both uploaded the picture of our medals to social media – a subtle relationship announcement, granted, but enough for those who knew us to understand what it meant!

Unbroken

The whole weekend had been that rarest of things in sport: a time when everything goes exactly to plan.

It's said that relationships and people come into your life when you most need them, and I believe that's true. Whether that's romantic relationships, coaches or guardian angels, I feel like there are always reasons you meet people at certain times in your life.

When I was younger, I didn't understand a lot of different emotions and maybe didn't need that close a connection in a relationship. But as I got older, I inevitably started to crave that deeper bond. I needed to share what I was going through with someone who really understood it. And, as it turns out, I didn't have to look very far to find him.

Pozz had always been there. Our Facebook messages go right back to 2008 (though both of us are a bit scared to actually look at them and cringe at ourselves, clearly liking each other but not making any moves). But we first properly bonded – or trauma-bonded, more accurately – a couple of years later in 2010, when we both got injured and missed out on competing at the World Junior Championships in Moncton, Canada.

It went something like . . .

'Well, this is pretty shit.'

'So shit.'

'Are you seeing all the pictures people are posting?'

'Yeah, it looks amazing. This is so unfair.'

'So unfair :('

Can't you feel the romantic chemistry just exploding off the page? It's hardly a script that's going to entice Hugh Grant to audition! From then on, we were pretty much on every GB or England team together, unless one of us was injured. And I can't really explain why, but I just always felt that he was going to be in my life.

Over the years, we were always push and pull. One of us would be single while the other one was in a relationship, and then it would flip around. Both of us probably always knew that we wanted it to happen, but neither of us acted on it because we were always with somebody else. The timing was just never quite right.

In 2017, that changed; neither of us was in a relationship and I realized that I was ready to give it a try, partly out of curiosity – we were such good friends, so could we make a relationship work? Despite the fact that I'm definitely the more indecisive one between us, I think it was probably me who made the first move to make it happen. In all honesty, the timing still could have been better, because I was away training in Montpellier and a year later Pozz moved to Italy. But I guess when you know that you've got something that's real and strong – something that you've been waiting for – you don't take any more chances. You just grab it. During the early summer of 2017, Pozz came out to Montpellier to visit me and that was it – we never looked back!

Everyone around us had been waiting for us to get together for years, so when we finally did, no one was surprised. They were just like: 'Finally, what took you so long?'

Pozz is the funniest person I know. Not many people get to see that side of him, because unless you really know him, he's quite reserved. Online, and in interviews, he comes across as pretty serious, but it's definitely a mask. He can make a joke out of anything. I love his opinion on things, too; I feel like it's always morally correct, so he's somebody who I always go to first, with anything. He's my gut-check person. That's the best way I can describe him.

Most of all, I just like being with him and spending time with him. He's like my best friend and boyfriend wrapped up in one. We have a proper laugh together, all the time. For one of our first dates in 2017, he hired a bouncy castle and got it put up in the back garden of my first house in Liverpool. He'd told me he was going to do it and I remember hearing him on the phone to the supplier asking some very specific questions: 'Would it be able to take two 70kg-plus adults who are both able to jump very high?!' But I still brushed it off as a bit of a joke, until one day it just appeared – a giant, Marvel-themed bouncy castle! We had so much fun. We ordered Domino's pizza and had it on there, and just had our own private bouncy castle party.

At a time when I was trying to rediscover joy and my playful side again, after so many years of having it beaten down by endless injuries and disappointments, it felt like the right time for Pozz to come into my life in such a big way.

I used to think that we were pretty similar in terms of personalities, but then we lived together for a few months during Covid. Pozz tells me I find it difficult to admit when I'm wrong. Well, Pozz, I was wrong about this! I'm not a planner, and Pozz definitely is. I'm more spontaneous; I'll think of something I want to do and just do it, whereas Pozz will think of something and then spend a month thinking about whether or not it's the right or wrong thing to do. He can't be rushed into anything; he thinks that when he rushes, he always makes the wrong decision – like with picking airport queues. I'm the one saying, 'Just pick that one, it looks like it's going fast.' When it turns out to be the slow one, he's the one saying, 'This is what happens when we rush . . .'

What we both are, though, is competitive and stubborn. In star sign terms, I'm a Capricorn and Pozz is Taurus, which are theoretically supposed to be really compatible, but it's said that the two (the goat and the bull) will inevitably 'lock horns', and that does happen to us quite often.

We argue a lot about little things. Before Paris this summer, we were playing a bit of Mario Kart and (unlike pre-Budapest, I'll add), this time he kept on beating me. In the end I decided to try to disrupt his rhythm; tap into his subconscious and throw him off track. 'You've ruined my confidence now,' I joked. 'The Olympics is going to go terribly because of you.' It was a sly tactic, but it worked! After an argument, he's more likely to be the first one to apologize. We're both as stubborn as bulls but, when push comes to shove, I think I out-stubborn him.

I don't think either of us are romantic, if your idea of romance is Hollywood-style grand gestures like baths filled with rose petals, or running through an airport to stop the other one from boarding a plane. To me, that's not stuff I like, so it's not romantic. I like the stuff Pozz does for me day to day, like making me coffee with proper latte art made into a heart, or always giving me the best seat on a plane or in a restaurant. That's my kind of romantic.

Out of everyone I know, Pozz is my biggest rock. Even in 2024, when he got hurt right before the Olympics, which meant that his dreams were over after he'd worked so hard to qualify, he put his own disappointment aside to come to Loughborough and help me when I needed it the most. I don't think I would

Unbroken

have achieved the results I did had he not been there for me in 2024, and in 2023 too, to be honest.

I guess that's the positive side of being in a relationship with someone who essentially does the same job as you; they understand what you're going through and what you need more than anyone else. He's been through so many of the same things as me, so Pozz instantly understands what I'm feeling more than anyone else. He's able to say the right things because he understands the pressure of the situation, the stakes, what performances mean, and every element of what I'm trying to work on. It's easier to have a conversation with him because of that, and I think I'm more receptive to hearing and fully appreciating his thoughts.

Over the years, we've realized that means we can help each other, even when one of us is injured. In 2023, Pozz was unfortunately injured for the whole year, but he was one of the most important voices behind the confidence I carried into the World Championships in Budapest, where I won my second world title. And he did it all in his own unique way, using Mario Kart and a board game called Catan. We play those two games all the time and who wins is usually pretty evenly split between us, but going into those champs I was beating Pozz every single day. Each time I won he would say, 'No way, you're on such a roll . . . You're unbeatable.'

I know it sounds ridiculous, but I went into Budapest feeling untouchable, and that gave me such an air of confidence. To this day, I still don't know whether he was letting me win (he denies it) or if I was just on the biggest roll of my life. Either way, I've got a lot to thank Pozz for. He's been a big part of my wins and a big support throughout my losses as well.

Katarina Johnson-Thompson

The hard part of us both being athletes is that our dreams have often collided at the same time, during the same events, and it's hard to support somebody else while also trying to focus on yourself. But that can also be a really cool thing when it works out for you both – as it did in Birmingham.

If Pozz is my rock, then Dame Denise Lewis is my guardian angel. We first met in that athletes' parade after London 2012 but our relationship really strengthened from 2016 onwards. Putting it kindly, I was drifting when she called me about going to meet Charles van Commenee. I'd lost my love for heptathlon a little bit and I was in no rush to sort out my future. I was going on holiday and just acting out, really – being a normal person. I wasn't actively looking for a new coach until Denise got hold of me. She was the one who saw that I was coasting and needed help before I floated too far away.

Since then, our relationship has developed from one where I was a young kid who didn't have a clue what she was doing and needed her to tell me what I should do, into one where I know I can go to her when I need to talk anything through – when I need advice. She's always there when I need the most help. It's weird; she just appears in places and I never really know how she gets there. At the European Championships in Rome in June 2024, she was just there of her own accord, not working for the BBC or anyone else, and in the moments after Aston decided I should pull out of the competition, she suddenly appeared in the rest room of the stadium – no accreditation, no media pass, nothing. I think she just has this aura about her of 'I'm supposed to be here', so no one really questions her when she walks in somewhere.

Unbroken

The day after I pulled out of the European Championships, she took me out for a drink and some food and we wrote down a plan of things that needed to change. We decided on no more media commitments before the Olympics, and that I'd spend more time with Charles (van Commenee, who had been helping me with my shot put). Lastly, the big one: we vowed to finally fix the Achilles tendon that was causing me issues.

She also took me back to the stadium to watch the end of the heptathlon later that day. It was something I didn't want to do; my normal reaction is to hide away and pretend it's not happening. But she convinced me to go and watch the javelin and the 800m. I think it shows my growth as a person that I was able to do that. As my competitors continued their fight, I sat in the stands and made some promises to myself that Paris would be different.

Denise didn't just give me a plan and then leave me; she checked in regularly from then on, to make sure I was doing OK. She was definitely a huge part of getting me to the start line in Paris in 2024.

She was also there at a pivotal moment in 2022, when I was in a terrible place mentally and on the verge of pulling out of a competition that I needed to finish to qualify for the Commonwealth Games that year. It was Götzis – one of my favourite heptathlons – but it wasn't going as well as I thought it should have been, and about halfway through the comp I decided I was done. I didn't care what that meant for the rest of the year.

Denise was there, watching and supporting, and I think she could sense that something was up. Again, the next thing I knew, she suddenly appeared in the rest room, gave me a hug and said, 'Come on, let's go for a walk.' We walked and talked all the way around the track, twice, and she made me see that I was about to embark on a pattern of behaviour that I didn't want to get caught in.

The heptathlon is so unique in that you can be doing badly in any given event and suddenly start to think: what's the point in finishing if I'm not going to get anything out of it? I've seen it happen and, a lot of the time, when people pull out, they end up never finishing another heptathlon ever again. I was getting into that same rut, where it wouldn't be going as well as I thought it should be and I was just pulling out – I'd already done it earlier that year when I'd pulled out after four events of the pentathlon at the World Indoor Championships in Belgrade and I wanted to do it again two months later, in Götzis. It's such a horrible habit to develop because sometimes the heptathlon can start badly and then go well, and by seeing it through you find out so much more about yourself.

Denise recognized that pattern of behaviour in me and she talked me through it, making me see that I had more to gain from finishing it than from pulling out. I ended up seventh overall with 6,174 points, but in the end I was happy I finished it because it gave me a reality check of where I was at, instead of just pulling out and saying 'I'm better than this.' By completing the heptathlon, I could see what I needed to work on, which was important with a World Championships and Commonwealth Games coming up that summer.

It was also good for me to be spoken to openly and honestly, because the team around me at the time (by then I was training with a group in Florida, after Bertrand had taken a job with the French Athletics Federation) weren't telling me what could happen. I was just bumbling through life. I think you need somebody on your team who's going to be real with you and tell you the truth, not just let you get away with doing whatever you want. At that moment, that was what I needed and, as usual, Denise was there for me to fill that need.

And her reality check ended up being more momentous than I could have known. I wasn't happy in Florida, and I wasn't reaching my full potential. I needed a new approach, a new direction. So, after finishing the Götzis heptathlon, and being shown in real numbers how far away I was from my own standard, I picked up the phone, and Aston Moore answered.

It's interesting to think about how my relationships with my coaches have changed as I've got older and more experienced as an athlete.

With Mike, I was so young and always needed to be told what to do. I didn't really have any autonomy over what I was doing; I just followed along with whatever Mike said.

When I started working with Bertrand, he definitely wanted more of a partnership, which I was initially really reluctant to accept. I still wanted to be told what to do; I felt like that was his job, and mine was just to listen. I didn't understand that he was operating from a place of trust; he trusted that I knew what was best for me because, ultimately, we were talking about my body. After the move to Montpellier, it took a couple of years for me to understand that I could make decisions for myself, and that the coach isn't always just *right*. I came to like that.

The whole vibe in Montpellier was different than what I had been used to with Mike. My running coach Bruno was all about 'the journey' and doing things for the feeling and for the pleasure of doing them. That was something that was repeated a lot: 'For the pleasure. We need to enjoy it. We need to actually have fun doing this otherwise what's the point?' That was chalk and cheese compared to Mike's approach, which had been more like: 'You don't have fun. This is a job. We're here to perform and we have fun if we do well.' It took me a long time to adjust from one approach to the other and to know which was right, because I knew that I had performed well with Mike, but I also knew that at times I hadn't. In the end, I figured if I went along with this new approach, then maybe it could work too, and be more enjoyable at the same time.

I remember one of the first times I had a bad competition with Bertrand. I walked over to him expecting him to be angry or disappointed or frustrated that I hadn't done what he had told me to do. I didn't get that feedback that I had done anything wrong, and that's when I started to grow in confidence.

This was Bertrand's superpower. He gave me so much as a person, which ultimately made me a better athlete, too. He wanted me to grow, so he chose to empower me and show me that my voice had value. His humility and genuine care for me allowed me to trust myself. With this in addition to his great abilities as a technical coach, I stopped seeing my weaknesses as negatives and instead began to see the opportunities I had to improve them; and, more importantly, that I was the type of person who was *able* to improve them.

The power dynamic between an athlete and a coach can vary so much depending on things like personality, age and experience. With Bertrand, I felt like we were pretty level, but with Aston, because of his frankly vast experience, I still see him as the boss. I give him that respect because of everything he's been through; he's sixty-eight years old and has been coaching since he was thirty! He's been around British athletics for so long, he's a legend in the coaching sphere. So we do have that dynamic where I just want him to be in control, but at the same time I want him to listen to me when I have something to say. (I'd never question his opinion on my technique, so this is just with regard to injuries.) And I think I've got that. If I say, 'I think this is too much,' he will listen to me (but most of the time I still just want him to tell me what to do!).

His training is probably closer to Mike's than Bertrand's was, but Aston's personality is more like Bertrand's. When you do something badly, he just laughs – this deep, belly laugh that takes over his entire body. Some other athletes don't like that; they're a bit like: *Why are you laughing at me? Do you find this funny?* But I'm that sardonic type of personality too, so I love it. Aston laughs at everything. If it's at something I do wrong, then I'll laugh too and say, 'I'll try again.' I'd much rather have it that way.

Aston loves Sudoku and Wordle and plays them religiously (he even covers his phone when he's doing the latter, even though none of us are really bothered about it any more!). I think he sees all his athletes as puzzles to try to solve, too. I can only imagine what type of puzzle he sees me as: maybe one of those huge 10,000-piece puzzles that drive you nuts! He's endlessly curious. If I ever don't understand something technically, he'll spend time with me to make sure I really know what's going on. Aston believes that, with enough time, everything can be figured out – for me, that's a real comfort to have in your corner.

I remember doing a shot put session with Charles in the first half of 2024 and after I did one throw, he came straight over to me and said: 'There were four things that could have gone wrong there and you did every single one of them.' *Shit*, I thought. I looked around and saw there was a biomechanist watching on one side, a physio on the other – all these people who'd come to help me and I was doing the worst session in the world. Then I saw Aston, his shoulders going up and down as he laughed at the situation – it reminded me of being in school and finding something funny, but not being able to laugh in case the teacher sees. It totally changed how I felt and responded to what could have been a really negative moment. And he does that with every single situation. He always builds you up; never tears you down. With him, everything feels nice, feels good and feels safe.

Just like Bertrand, Aston is also calm. He always has a plan. Always knows what to say, and has infinite wisdom. Whatever you need advice on, he's got it. He keeps it fun, too. If it's heavy all the time, you can't do it. It can be heavy for a period of time, like if you need some intensity in a session for something important, but day to day, especially in an event like the heptathlon, you have to have that lightness too.

I think it's also important to have a friendship with your coach – to know that they're not going to be angry with you for not executing your best performance. And to have someone with you in the rest room between events or in the lead-up to a competition who knows how you are as a person and can talk to you as that person, not just as a client or athlete.

In 2022, when I first called him up and moved to Loughborough, I needed consistency. I needed experience. I needed someone who believed in me and someone who I could trust. Around that time, a lot of people were telling me I was in good shape or I was ready to do this and that, and it was all lies. When I was just beginning sessions with him, he would take my track times and he wouldn't say anything. He wouldn't say anything bad, but he wouldn't say anything good either. I learned that that was him not wanting to lie to me by saying, 'You're in good shape,' but also not wanting to ruin my confidence by saying, 'That's a terrible time.'

I really respected that he didn't lie to me, or try to get me up for a comp that I wasn't ready for. He was just truthful, honest and dependable. And now, when I do something in training, he's got that trust from me, so when he says it's good, I know he's not just saying words out loud; his word is truth. I think that trust is the most important thing an athlete and coach can have.

Sometimes, I think people see the victory lap at the end of a heptathlon and think we're all mates as well as rivals or competitors. That's true, in the sense that it's genuine at the end. But it's less true in the sense that it doesn't happen until the very end, when the competition is over and people can swallow their pride and bond over how tough it was. We all know the heptathlon is a very hard event, and so we respect what every other heptathlete has done, because we're all trying our best. The victory lap is such a nice moment to share with them, even in defeat.

It's so different for athletes who are competing in individual events. With one-off races, people can think they were unlucky, or it's a split-second defeat where they made one wrong decision and should have won. Whereas I think the heptathlon is more decisive in that we've been going at it for two days and one person has come out on top, and the rest of us have to respect that.

During the actual competition, we are *not* on each other's side. Yes, I've got friends like Anouk Vetter, who I talk to throughout the competition; we have common interests outside of sport and I'll go for a coffee with her. I think there's a level of respect there from going up against her for so long and being of the same generation. I also used to have a good relationship with Brianne Theisen-Eaton, who retired in 2017. When we competed together, she was always someone I felt was going through it too, and we'd feel like we were in it together: 'Oh god, this is not going well, is it?' That kind of thing. While some athletes pretend that everything's going well, we would feed off each other in terms of being honest. It was refreshing to have someone to talk to like that. But I don't talk to just anyone and everyone.

Rivalries aren't something that I'll ever use as a motivating factor, aside from keeping an eye on what others are doing so that I know what I need to do to win – although I am very competitive, so it does stoke the fire if I see others doing well. With certain athletes, like Nafi Thiam and Anouk, they have very different strengths and weaknesses to mine, so a comp becomes like a chess game: if she's doing x in this event, then I need to do y in that one. What she throws in the shot put, I have to balance out in the 200m. It's quite exciting, and it doesn't put you into a negative headspace because it's driving you to be better in your strengths rather than comparing your weaknesses to somebody else's.

With others, like Anna Hall, it's hard to do that, because her strengths are also my strengths – so you're pitting yourselves directly against one another. It's something that I struggled with in 2023. I didn't know how to prepare for a battle with someone who shared my strengths, because I'd never had to do that in the past.

People always wanted a bigger rivalry between me and Jess, but I feel like our careers were in such different places that it never really materialized. To be totally honest, I've always had a genuine respect for her, and for what she's been able to do in her career. In 2012, she carried the weight of an entire nation on her shoulders and won gold, and in 2015, she came back from having a baby to win a world title at the first time of asking. I'm in awe of anyone who comes back after having a child!

Nafi is probably someone who is now seen as a rival to me, and I'd agree, but we're respectful of one another. I wouldn't call us friends. I really respect Nafi. In my opinion, she's one of the greatest heptathletes of all time, perhaps even *the* greatest. She's won everything, more than once. Scored over 7,000 points. Jumped 2.02 metres. She's won in so many different ways. She's overcome adversity. She's someone I'm always going to admire – and this admiration is what gets the best out of me when I'm competing against her. But we're not friends. Because we're rivals. We don't chat with each other. She keeps to herself and keeps her cards close to her chest.

I actually think Nafi doesn't get the respect she deserves for being one of the greatest heptathletes of all time. I feel like people are always writing her off, and I don't really know why.

I can't discuss relationships without talking about one that has been part of my career for longer than I can remember: my relationship with the media. As I've said before, I'm naturally an open and honest person, and I feel like that has been taken advantage of at times. At the very beginning, when I was talking about Jess, I think I paid the price of being young and not really understanding the game: what journalists were looking for and how they would use my words. I think, at that time, there should have been some grace given to a young kid who clearly didn't get it and was just innocently speaking her mind.

Other times, I've kicked myself for falling into traps. The one I pay for all the time is the 'imposter syndrome saga' of 2019, which I still get asked about now. It happened on the eve of Götzis, when Nafi wasn't competing because of injury and so I was the athlete being used as the 'poster girl' for the heptathlon. It came from a conversation that happened naturally when I was speaking to a journalist and Chari Hawkins, an American heptathlete, came over. It was the first time I'd met her and she came up to me and just blurted out, 'I love you,' then started crying and laughing at the same time because she'd wanted to say 'I'm such a big fan,' but that had just come out of her mouth instead.

The journalist overheard and started asking me if that was something I got a lot, and I explained that I didn't really understand her feelings or how she could be a fan while also being my competitor. Somehow that later came out as a headline that 'Katarina's got imposter syndrome,' and, in the years that followed, I got asked about that a lot. It's not a terrible thing – after all, it's true about certain points in my career – but I think it's something that most people deal with in some way, shape or form.

It felt similar to my experiences in 2015, when the media would latch on to any comment I made about Jess and blow it

Unbroken

up out of all proportion. In both cases, those comments usually form a tiny proportion of an interview that could be twenty or thirty minutes long, but everything else I've said gets completely overshadowed by one aspect that the media decides to hyper-fixate on.

It happens all too often in the media, and it's certainly been a theme in my career. Nuanced subjects, which require context in order to hold value for others who might see themselves in what's being said, are cheapened and, at times, weaponized through the nature of clickbait reporting and 'gotcha'-style headlines. Ultimately, it has made me – and other athletes – withdraw from sharing honest or vulnerable truths because we know it won't be reliably communicated.

One thing I *have* always wondered about during my dealings with the media is whether a male athlete in my position would be treated the same way, or asked the same questions. Before the Olympic Games in Tokyo in 2021, I was doing a press conference over Zoom (because of Covid) and it was a very intense experience. I'd ruptured my Achilles at the end of the previous year but had chosen not to really speak about it either on social media or to any journalists, so this press conference was the first time they'd had the opportunity to ask me about it.

There were so many questions, but then one of them asked me: 'Were there many tears during your injury?' Straight away, I thought, *They wouldn't ask a male athlete that*, and I stand by that today. I could see the picture they were trying to portray, that I was emotional and overly sensitive, and could just imagine all the headlines that would follow. That was why I had avoided speaking about it up to that point. And on the eve of an Olympic

Games, when you've worked so hard to put yourself into the strongest place mentally and physically, it's so tough to give interviews and then see that perception of yourself through someone else's eyes – that you're somehow weak. I had to be honest about my journey to that point, but I was clear with them that I wasn't in that place any more. I was about to compete at the Olympics. I was strong and I was ready.

I think that was the first time I noticed the gender difference. Journalists ask about and talk about our emotions a lot more, and that's not OK. Look at tennis: I don't think male players get called out for breaking their rackets as much as female players do. When men do it, the feeling is very much, 'He shouldn't do that, but look how much he wants to win!' When it's a female player it's, 'Oh no, she's letting her emotions get the better of her.' The narrative is completely different. And it's not fair.

After winning the World Indoors in 2018, I was on a real high. It was exciting to have the Commonwealth Games in Australia coming just five weeks later, though I remember getting back to France and talking to Bertrand and Bruno about it, and they didn't really understand the big deal.

'Is it important?' they asked me.

'Yeah.'

'It's in Australia. Do you have to do it?'

I told them I would really like to and they didn't have to come – I could go and do it by myself.

'No, if it's a heptathlon then it's practice, let's go.'

The caveat was that Bertrand needed to stay in France for a while longer so we decided to travel at the very last minute –

eight days before the heptathlon started. It was Easter weekend when I started packing and I realized I couldn't find my passport anywhere in the apartment. I went through everything I owned, tore the place up, and I couldn't find it. I was in hysterics because it was Good Friday, I was in Montpellier with no passport and my flight was on Easter Sunday (which that year was also April Fool's Day – I remember thinking it was ironic).

I phoned the British Embassy, which of course was closed because it was a bank holiday weekend, and I just got a recorded message: 'If you have been stabbed or you are in an emergency, please press one.' I pressed one, crying my eyes out. 'This is an emergency!' I spoke to a woman for ages who was really nice and tried to calm me down. Then I got my manager, Greg, involved as well, and he said he would try to get someone in Paris to go into the embassy on their day off, but that I would have to pay them their daily wage. I'd also have to pay for a security guard. She said there was no guarantee this would work, but that they'd do their best.

Looking back, this story makes me laugh, and sums up my relationship with Greg really well. He's been a part of my career since 2013, and his role and contributions to my career are constantly evolving. Over the past decade, I've come to rely on him in almost every situation for support that extends far beyond the predetermined confines of commercial and media management – including, but not limited to, opening and staffing an international embassy on a bank holiday! He's become an invaluable facilitator in my life and, more importantly, a friend.

I packed all my bags for a month in Australia and got the earliest train the next day to Paris, because I couldn't get a flight and I had to be there in case the embassy staff were only available in the morning. I then had to wait in an airport hotel and hope that someone had agreed to go in on the Saturday between Good Friday and Easter Sunday to sort out my emergency passport. Thankfully – and I'm still so grateful for this – they had. I filled out the necessary forms; they got the emergency documentation prepared, sent it off and said I'd have to go back and collect it. It was hectic.

Somehow, it all came together, and on the Sunday, I was at the airport with my passport, ready to fly to Australia. I remember thinking about calling Mum to say that I wasn't allowed on the plane as an April Fool's joke . . . then decided not to because we'd both already been through it the past few days. Then, when I got to check-in, they said I didn't have the visa I needed! I stood there for ages while people were making phone calls and talking, before eventually they decided to let me through. It was the most stressed I'd ever been before a comp.

(I found the original 'lost' passport when I was packing up to leave France in 2021, standing up straight and blended into a maroon cupboard.)

I had the minimum amount of time you can have in Australia to get over the jet lag and then compete but, somehow, I ended up winning the gold medal. I really shouldn't have. Halfway through the 200m on the first day I pulled my calf, so on day two I took two (out of three) jumps in the long jump and one throw in the javelin before pulling it even worse in the 800m. When you watch the race, you can see me at 350 metres in almost pulling up. I only continued for the rest of the race because in my head I was thinking that I'd come too far – I'd travelled too far, Bertrand had travelled, Mum had travelled, I'd vastly overpaid for an emergency passport and ruined the weekend of an employee of the British Embassy in Paris – I couldn't pull out of the comp when the end was literally in sight.

I blocked everything out and just concentrated on getting around the remaining 450 metres to the finish line, coming fourth with a time of 2:21.24; but it was enough to secure the gold medal, and I was proud of getting another one over the line, especially as I'd had to grit it out, again. But I wasn't fully in the moment; as I limped onto the medal podium, I was already counting down the weeks until the European Championships, which were due to take place that summer, hoping there was enough time for my body to recover so that I could have a crack at a third medal of the year.

In the end, I had six weeks of full training before travelling to Berlin for those European Championships. That's not a lot of time to prepare for a heptathlon; it's basically one block of training. It was one of the most nerve-wracking heptathlons I've ever had to start, because I didn't have a clue what performances were going to come out. I remember phoning up Steve Peters at the time, a performance psychologist who I'd started working with after Rio, and just saying, 'Help! I'm spiralling here. I don't know what's going to happen. I don't want to do it any more. I actually don't want to put myself out there.'

It was a really horrible position to be in, because it wasn't something that I felt ready to do. The injury was fine, but it was the lack of training and the lack of competition fitness. Ever since then I've tried to put myself in a position where I'm going into a heptathlon having done plenty of comps and knowing what to expect – if I can get anything else, it's a bonus.

Katarina Johnson-Thompson

Whereas in Berlin I just had no idea what was going to happen, and that's a position I don't like.

I was super nervous before the hurdles but, somehow, I managed to pull out a huge performance. I ran a season's best, and that immediately put me into a really good headspace. I remember thinking: *OK, maybe I am ready.* After what went on to become an epic battle with Nafi, I emerged from that comp with a silver medal, a new PB of 6,759 points, and the belief that I wasn't all that far away from Nafi (even though everyone else thought she was untouchable). The difference between us had been just 57 points. I'd pushed her right to the javelin, where she'd needed to throw a championship best to overtake me and go into the 800m with enough of a lead that I couldn't quite catch her.

The three different combined events in 2018 taught me so much. I'll never forget Birmingham, for being the first one I got over the line. I fought through bad circumstances and injuries to win in Australia. And then Berlin – it was about trusting my training, and my coach, and being reactive and competitive in my surroundings despite the chaos around me. I went from thinking about individual scores, like managing 1.90 metres in the high jump, to being completely present in and reactive to the competition at all times, grounding myself in every jump, every hurdle and every stride.

In Berlin, I finally found that sweet spot where I was in the zone *and* in the competition. I was thinking competitively: *If you clear that height, I'm going to clear it.* Or: *Another athlete is about to overtake me on the inside in the 200m; I've never been in this position before, but I'm not going to get startled, I'm going to respond and get a good time in.* I ended up pulling out my best jump in the third round of the long jump. Over those two days, I reacted to the competition and fought for the gold, pushing Nafi so close.

It gave me so much confidence. It had felt like everyone was just leaving it to Nafi to waltz home to victory, but that comp opened my eyes and showed me that there was a chance. All I needed was some consistent training. From then on, I was on a mission to *win*.

And I had the 2019 World Championships in my sights.

13

Acceptance

'KJT! KJT! KJT!'

The chant rang around the Emirates Arena in Glasgow. It had been started by a guy named Michael Inpong, who was marketing director of Müller. Müller was one of British Athletics' main sponsors and a brand I was an ambassador for, which included filming some TV adverts – there was a time when people would just shout 'Fat free?' at me when they saw me, mimicking the line I had to say in the ad. Even in the summer of 2023, when I rented a skip, the guy asked me: 'You got too many yoghurt pots?'

Michael was a really impressive character; a senior figure at such a big company, but no task was ever beneath him. For that comp in Glasgow, he'd produced a load of bright red hoodies with 'TEAM KJT' on both front and back. He was then on the ground handing them out – my family and friends snapped up a few – and starting chants, trying to take athletics into that fun space.

'SHE'S STRONG. SHE'S COOL, SHE COMES FROM LIVERPOOL!'

I was at the 2019 European Indoor Championships. It was being hosted at quite an intimate venue, so you could see a lot of the crowd; and, from the start of my long jump run-up, I was aware of the collection of red jumpers all standing up leading the chants, looking like they were having an absolute blast. It felt like I was at one of my old comps when I was a kid, where you knew most of the people watching and could see every smile (or grimace) on their face as they watched you compete.

I stepped up for my first jump and focused on my process.

Run . . . plant . . . oh, no. The dreaded red flag.

The prospect of putting out three no jumps is very real for every heptathlete, no matter what their history. Personally, I think about it for the long jump and sometimes for the high jump as well. With the hurdles I think about what could happen in terms of crashing into one and ruining my chances in a heptathlon before it has even got started, even though it hasn't ever happened to me. There's a moment where reality hits, and you realize that everything could be taken away in an instant. All your hopes and dreams for that particular event could be wiped out. I call it the Scary Moment, and it can be lethal.

Four years had passed, but whenever my first attempt in the long jump was a foul, my mind still defaulted back to Beijing (it still does – even in Paris in 2024). As soon as the red flag was raised, there it was: the little voice in the back of my head, reminding me, 'Remember that time you did three?' It immediately put me on edge. As I brushed the sand off my legs, I looked over at Bertrand and he beckoned me over to where he was sitting.

'KJT! KJT! KJT!'

My small army of supporters was still chanting, but my mind was racing too fast to take it in. I walked over to Bertrand expecting him to tell me that shouldn't have happened, but as soon as I got to him, he just said, 'Great, so what we do next is . . .'

There was no admonishment or negativity. He was just going about it as if everything was normal. 'That was a really good run but on the next one we're going to do this and just get your foot down . . .' He was happy. Chilled. And that immediately put me at ease, because I could see that he wasn't worried, so clearly there was nothing to worry about.

'It's my job to get you on the board,' he said before I went back onto the track. 'You just have to focus on driving off the take-off leg, keeping your chest high and accelerating into the board.'

OK, I thought. *The board isn't my problem, it's his problem.* Suddenly, all that weight was lifted off my shoulders and I could prepare for my next jump purely focused on the things Bertrand wanted me to do, and not on the plasticine line of pain. I stood on my mark at the end of the runway, inhaled deeply and breathed out hard, trying to expel any lingering anxiety.

Run . . . plant . . . safe. Thank god.

I think whether or not you spiral in the Scary Moment comes down to your coach and how they handle you as a person (neither Bertrand nor Aston ever look flustered or scared), as well as how effectively you can ground yourself and be process-driven. The Katarina of 2019 was a different athlete compared to the one from Beijing. I was able to stand on my mark for that second jump, go through my cues and not let the fear of fouling stop me from executing.

It was a decent jump of 6.53 metres, which was enough to keep me in the lead with one more event to go in the pentathlon, and ultimately enough to secure me a second European Indoor title (to go with the one I'd won in Prague in 2015). Doing it in front of my friends and family, who I could see (and hear) all going crazy in the stands, gave me one of the best feelings I've ever had in the sport, and getting to go over and give Mum and Nan a huge hug after the 800m only added to that. I had no idea at the time that it would end up being the last time Nan saw me compete, but I'm so glad I could share that experience with her.

Four years earlier I'd scored 5,000 points and won gold at the same competition but I'd been in tears because I'd missed out on the pentathlon world record. In Glasgow, I'd scored a little under that (though 4,983 points was still the fourth best pentathlon performance of all time), but this time there were no tears, just joy in the moment and pride in my overall performance. Bruno's message about doing things 'for the feeling' was taking hold. I was finding joy in my performances and learning how to stop fear and anxiety from taking that away. When I thought about what that could mean for the season ahead, I felt only one thing: excitement.

Pozz and I will never forget the off-season we had after 2018. After such a full-on season, with three major championships under our belts, we needed to get away. We decided on a New York city break followed by a trip to the Caribbean island of

St Lucia — where there lives a hotel owner who must be a huge athletics fan, because it seems as though any athlete who stays there gets their room automatically upgraded. Somehow, we managed to secure a room that was four times as expensive as the one we paid for, and it has ruined holidays for ever for us both! We can't ever go back there, because if we don't get the same upgrade then we'll know what we're missing, but at the same time we can't actually afford to pay for that room because it's so expensive! In any case, it was an incredible holiday where we were able to fully relax and celebrate the successes that the 2018 season had left us with, before rallying and trying to do it all over again — only better.

By 6 January 2019 I was already back competing, in a small meeting in Miramas, not too far from Montpellier. It was pretty unusual for me to be getting out so early in the year, but 2019 was going to have to be an atypical season, because the main event — the World Championships in Doha — wasn't taking place until October. We were concerned that I'd run out of steam by then, so we decided to split the season into two halves, competing in the indoor season, and at Götzis in May, before taking a mini off-season break and getting back into competition in late July.

From the very start of that year I had so much confidence that I could add more medals to the ones I'd won in 2018. Before then, I'd pretty much accepted that I could never challenge Nafi, because she was flying at the time: scoring 7,000 points and high jumping over 2 metres. But at the European Championships in Berlin, I'd pushed her right up to the finish line and was sure I had more in me, so I knew that I could win. I just needed the opportunity.

Unbroken

I had to wait for it, though. Nafi picked up an injury early in the year, which meant she didn't compete indoors and wasn't at Götzis. In her absence, I focused on performing, on improving. Bertrand was always drumming into me that we weren't going for scores, we were going after good performances. When you do that, the possibilities are endless. And this time, unlike in 2017, my performance was good enough to win.

He was right. After the first day in Götzis, I was in first place, 177 points ahead of the American Kendell Williams. After yet another first-round foul in the long jump on the morning of day two, I managed to pull out a 6.68-metre jump (equalling my best distance in a heptathlon) to stay well clear of everyone else. Then came a 76cm PB in the javelin, which put me well on course to break 6,800 points for the first time in my career; all I had to do was run quicker than 2:09 in the 800m.

That's when Bertrand decided it was time for a new approach to that event. Most of the time, the times I was running in training weren't translating across when it came to competing because I wouldn't commit to a faster pace in the actual race. In Götzis, Bertrand said, 'Let's just try to commit to it and see what happens, because we have nothing to lose.'

I committed too much, too hard, blasting through the first 400 metres in 59.41 seconds. Not long afterwards, my legs and lungs started to feel the after-effects and the finish line felt like it was getting further and further away. I finally fell over it, clocking in at 2:08.28 – enough to make it over 6,800 points, sure, but I was basically lying comatose on the track until I felt the bile start to rise in my throat and made it off to the side of the track to throw up.

Katarina Johnson-Thompson

I came away from Götzis with the victory and a new PB of 6,813 points – a score that would have been enough to win gold in four of the previous six Olympic Games. The best thing about that performance was that it wasn't perfect. I'd performed below my best in the shot put and the 200m and, despite the post-race vom, I knew from my training that I could squeeze more out in the 800m. Just over four months later, I'd have the chance to put that belief to the test on one of the sport's biggest stages: the World Championships.

Before then came the mid-season break. It came at a time of year when I wouldn't usually be free, so I grabbed the opportunity with both hands. I flew straight from Götzis to Las Vegas for a friend's hen do, from Vegas to Madrid for Liverpool's Champions League final against Tottenham (not a great game, but being there to see your team lift a trophy is always worth it), and then from Madrid to Rome to watch Pozz compete in the Diamond League.

When I got back to Montpellier, Bertrand took one look at me and said, 'You've literally not done anything, have you?' (Well, I wouldn't call Vegas, the Champions League final and Rome nothing, but training-wise? Eeek!) 'You've lost all your muscle . . . time to start again!'

I'd been in Montpellier for almost two and a half years by this point and, although I still had moments of loneliness, I was happy there. I'd moved out of The Hatch into a beautiful old apartment with high ceilings, double windows and vast bookshelves. I would ride my bike down to training, where my body had adapted to the six-day-week schedule set by Bertrand and Bruno. I'd spend my downtime in a local cafe, where the Polish barista, Kasia, became a friend (she speaks five languages, and really helped me find community in Montpellier) and made me laugh with her craziness. I'd even mastered cooking some meals – mostly poached eggs, avocado and tomatoes on toast. Dinner was a work in progress.

At the track, I was constantly learning, not only from my coaches but from the athletes around me, too. I loved the fact that I wasn't the number-one athlete there – I was maybe third, behind my training partners, Kevin Mayer and Nana. I really liked not being the centre of attention. I could just slide into the group, copy what they did, and try to learn from them. With Mike, it had been just the two of us and everything was on me, all the time. In France, that weight was lifted; I felt like everything was on Kevin – he needed to perform and I was just there for the ride.

At the end of 2018, he'd set a new world record in the decathlon, just a month after crashing out of the European Championships with three fouls in the long jump. Watching how he dealt with and came back from that was so inspiring for me, given what I'd been through in Beijing. More than that, one conversation that we had the following year helped change my entire mindset when it came to competing. I can't remember exactly how it started – it's possible I was telling him about the Scary Moment – but he told me that if you took away all his third attempts in the throwing and jumping events during his world record decathlon, he would have only scored 8,800 points, not the 9,200 that gave him the record.

As I sat there and listened to him speak, it felt like a switch had been flicked. If I'd been a cartoon character, a lightbulb would have been flashing over my head. So often, I'd been in the frame of mind where if I threw 11 metres twice in the shot put, I'd say, 'Oh well, that's just me for today; that's obviously all I've got. My warm-up was 11 metres, I've had two attempts at 11 metres. Realistically, am I going to get a PB here? Probably not.' You sell yourself a narrative and you believe that narrative so much that it becomes self-limiting. When Kevin shared his experiences, being in exactly the same position but reacting very differently to it, it was like a door that had previously been closed opened in my mind. He made me see that you can do anything at any time and, when you believe that, you develop a different mentality. Anything is possible if you can truly stay in the moment instead of dwelling on something that's already gone.

That one conversation didn't just change my mindset; it changed my entire approach to the heptathlon.

It might sound mad but, going into the World Championships in Doha that year, I felt the most relaxed I'd ever felt going into a competition. I wasn't scared to put myself out there; I was just totally at peace with whatever I was about to do. I knew I was in good physical shape, but I also knew that there was a chance I'd score really well and still come second, or third, or wherever. That didn't bother me. All I cared about was getting my performance out, because I accepted that the rest was beyond my control. I couldn't control what Nafi, or anyone else, did.

Maybe it was something to do with not being the favourite. Most people were expecting Nafi to win in Doha, and so I accepted there was a high chance that I'd get beaten. That opened up the space for me to think, *I just need to do the best I can.* Whereas when I'm the favourite, it feels different – like

I'm the one who has to set the pace. And that's much more stressful.

Doha was different from any champs I'd experienced beforehand, and that was for more reasons than just my mindset. It was the first time the World Championships had ever been held in the Middle East, and the heat was a huge factor in how it had been organized. I remember flying into the country on the day the women's marathon was being held; because of the high temperatures, around 30 per cent of the athletes didn't finish – despite the fact the race didn't start until after the sun had gone down.

It was so, so hot. SO hot. It wasn't great for the environment, but we were fortunate that the organizers had installed huge A/C units inside the stadium. The minute you stepped outside, though, the heat hit you hard and you were just desperate to get into a car or building again.

Even with the giant cooling units, it was decided that there would be no morning sessions at that World Championships. As heptathletes, we're used to getting to the stadium early in the morning and not leaving until late at night but, in Doha, nothing started until around 4 p.m. And those events that had to be outdoors – like the race walks and marathons – didn't start until midnight.

It was quite hard to know how to handle those long mornings and early afternoons at the hotel. Once I'd had breakfast, it wasn't like I could go out for a walk, because of the heat, so I ended up just spending a lot of time inside, not seeing daylight. I didn't really know what to do with myself; I just tried to relax and not overthink. I *did* like the extra sleep, though. On the first day of the heptathlon, there was no 5.30 a.m. alarm; I was able to lie in and have a leisurely breakfast. The nerves kicked in later, though, just as I had to eat lunch, so I forced it down before getting on the coach to the stadium. I was still far more relaxed than usual – I remember actually falling asleep on the way there, which shouldn't really happen before a big comp when you want the adrenaline to be pumping.

As I started my warm-up for the hurdles, I wasn't really feeling that fast. It was strange; as I moved over the hurdles it felt almost automatic. Easy. Like my legs were just going over the barriers without me really having to try. But I had no idea whether it was fast or slow.

'Tell me, is it good or is it bad, because it doesn't feel good,' I said to Bertrand, stressed-out.

'It's good,' he replied. 'Relax.'

I don't remember much about the actual hurdles race itself, aside from the fact that I was in the lane next to Nafi and that, as soon as I crossed the finish line, I looked at the clock and was in complete shock. I'd run 13.09 seconds, my fastest time ever. I couldn't believe I was capable of running that fast! It had felt so smooth and I wasn't used to the ease; I'd always believed that to be fast you have to *feel* it and put in effort, whereas that race felt almost effortless. I still don't know why or how I was able to do it – I've been fighting ever since to get back to that place and recreate that feeling!

It was the perfect start, and I went on to the high jump determined to capitalize on it; I felt like it would be a waste to do a bad jump after that. As the event progressed into the battle everyone expected, between myself and Nafi, I tried to stay in the moment and talk myself through it, repeating my cues to myself over and over again: 'Right leg needs to come through.

Unbroken

Right shoulder and right knee need to go up . . .' I reached 1.95 metres with just two failures along the way. Nafi was right there with me. But when the bar was raised to 1.98 metres, neither of us could press home an advantage and we went into the shot put separated by just 40 points. The narrow lead belonged to me and I felt like I was on a roll. I was just going to be responsive – whatever Nafi pulled out in the shot put, I was determined to react to it. There was no way I was going to give up the fight.

My first two throws were average: 12.33 metres; 12.38 metres. One throw left and I needed more – Nafi had pulled out a 15.22 metres with her very first throw. As I stepped into the circle for my final attempt, I remembered Kevin Mayer's words.

Anything can happen at any time.

I watched the shot put fly out of my hand and into the distance. When I saw it land close to the 14-metre line, I let out a small squeal of delight. Moments later the official distance flashed up: 13.86 metres, a PB by 71cm! I was in disbelief, for the second time that day! The only thing that had changed between my second and third throw was my approach. For the first two throws I'd just been trying to make sure that I had all the movements correct. For the third one, I knew I just had to respond – to be competitive. I was in the moment. In the zone. And it was paying off.

The only disappointment came in the final event of the day; the 200m. Although I ran the fastest time (23.08 seconds), it was a little way off my PB and, after the hurdles had gone so well, I'd thought I might have been able to get under the 23-second mark. Nevertheless, I was heading to bed on top of the leader board, with a 96-point gap over Nafi, although her score of 4,042 was her highest ever total at the end of the first day of a championship heptathlon. The level was so high, but the battle was on. And the best part was, I didn't have to wake up at the crack of dawn the next morning. Normally, you get zero sleep after day one; we have to get up early for the long jump and then wait around at the stadium for hours, trying to catch up on some sleep on a mat in the corner of a bright rest room. In Doha, I had my own room, a proper bed and the time to get a good night's sleep before the second day. Glorious!

The next day, I started the long jump with a clean jump: the first time in a major champs that year. Not only was it clean, it was a decent distance too. It was nothing spectacular, but it was a solid start (and 7cm further than Nafi's). With the pressure off, I felt like I could just run and jump with my second attempt, which is exactly what I did. As soon as I landed in the pit, I knew the gold medal was as good as mine. When the distance flashed up (6.77 metres!), I almost started celebrating there and then, but quickly caught myself before I got carried away.

I was right, though. Nafi's furthest jump was 6.40 metres, which put me 226 points clear of her. Now, even if she threw a PB in the javelin (which we thought was unlikely, as she was coming back from an elbow injury), it wouldn't be enough for her to build a big enough lead with just the 800m to go – historically a much stronger event for me than for Nafi.

The roll I was on continued into the javelin, where my first throw flirted with my PB and my second one surpassed it by almost 2 metres. I allowed myself a small smile but I tried to stay in the zone. Everything could still be blown to pieces by one giant throw from Nafi, which she is always capable of – just one of the reasons it had been more than three years since she'd last been beaten in a heptathlon. It seemed she was unflappable.

Except that day, she wasn't: her best throw was 48.04 metres, just over 4 metres better than mine. It was a great result for me, and I couldn't stop the excitement from starting to bubble in my stomach again as it sunk in that I was now just two laps away. Unless Nafi could beat me by 9 seconds in the 800m (an event in which her best ever time was 8 seconds slower than mine), I would be the world champion.

I wasn't taking anything for granted. With my history, it would be just my luck to get disqualified somehow – but I was very up for that race. I felt like I was running more for a big score at that point than for first place, which was far less scary than the situation I'd find myself in four years later in Budapest, or at the Olympics in Paris, where a medal depended on my performance in the race. I went into it feeling like I was in 2:05 shape, which would get me over the 7,000-point barrier.

It was just after midnight when I stood by my blocks and tried to focus purely on the two laps ahead of me. As I did so, the stadium was plunged into darkness. Giant screens replayed clips from the previous two days, bringing it all to the front of my mind: the magical hurdles, the high jump battle with Nafi, my shot put PB – it was a warm night but goose bumps covered my body. A light show followed, accompanied by some terrible house music, before, one by one, each of us was introduced to the (modest) crowd. Then, finally, the music stopped, replaced by the sound of a heartbeat played out across the entire stadium; the track transformed into an illuminated electrocardiogram.

I hated it. But at the same time, it was amazing and I think it should happen at the end of every World Championships heptathlon! It was something they did for quite a few of the finals in Doha, and I think they got that right; these are world finals. A world champion is about to be crowned. (As we ran around the track during the 800m, the words 'World Champion Pending' flashed up on the scoreboards. It's a big deal!) It multiplied the tension tenfold, and got the people who were in the stadium so geed up for what was about to come. If I had been one of them, or someone watching on TV at home, I'd have thought it was so cool but, as an athlete who was standing there waiting for the race to start, I just wanted to hear 'On your marks' straight away.

At last, the gun sounded, but I quickly found myself blocked in, running at a pace that I knew wasn't the right one. It took me about 30 metres to work my way out of it and move around the others to get to the front and, as soon as I did, I went for it. With around 500 metres to go, I was front-running, going as hard as I could to try to hit that 2:05 mark. I really wanted it. Before the race I'd been saying to everyone: 'If I don't run 2:05, I'm a shithouse; I've not done it properly. I know I'm capable of this.' I crossed the finish line and saw the time on the clock: 2:07.26. Ugh.

If you can believe it, for a moment I was actually sad. But then it hit me. *I was the world champion!* There's a time to be sad, and that wasn't the time. My emotions quickly bubbled up and over. After the deepest of lows in 2015, the fear and frustration of 2016, and the all-encompassing journey of change I'd been on since then, it felt so surreal to be in that position.

Everyone around me was raving about the score. I'd finished

on 6,981, a new British record, finally overtaking the incredible one that Jess had set in 2012. I'd set four new PBs and secured a 300-point margin of victory over Nafi, despite the fact that she'd had one of her highest-scoring first days ever. In her press conference afterwards, she told the media she had no excuses: 'I just got beaten.' At the time, though, I wasn't thinking too much about that; I was simply soaking in a moment that I had dreamed of for so long, one that felt like it might have moved beyond my reach in the aftermath of 2016.

I don't think it fully sank in until the medal ceremony. That was definitely the moment when my brain fully accepted what had happened. It's probably the only moment you get just to yourself after winning a medal, when you're not being dragged from one interview to the next and can't relax. That's why athletes get so emotional when they get up onto the podium – it's usually the only time you get to actually reflect, and that's when it all sinks in.

I had a grand total of around one hour's sleep that night – my brain and body were totally wired and refusing to come down from the high they'd been on for most of the day. Instead of sleeping, I lay in bed scrolling through all the different messages on my phone and looking at pictures from the most magical two days.

I actually thought I was hallucinating when I turned on my TV the next morning to see the Liverpool FC manager, Jürgen Klopp, answering questions about me in a press conference. 'What the . . . ?' He'd been watching the German athlete Niklas Kaul win the decathlon and knew that I was a huge Liverpool fan, so he was supporting us both throughout the competition.

He shouted us both out and talked about how much respect he had for the combined events, which was really cool – and completely crazy at the same time.

With the Tokyo Olympics only nine and a half months away, it felt like there wasn't much time to celebrate winning gold in Doha. I didn't mind that, either. Pozz and I had a short break on an island resort near Qatar straight after the champs, and a trip to the Greek island of Santorini a few weeks later, but after that I was eager to get back into training. Not only because I didn't want to lose all my muscle again, but because it felt like 2020 – an Olympic year – was already upon us, and I was in such a good place that the short turnaround between major championships felt like a real blessing. Winning in Doha was amazing but, from the moment I'd joined forces with Bertrand, Tokyo 2020 had always been my goal – it was those Olympic Games we'd always spoken about as the ones we were aiming for.

That was why, on 31 December 2019, Pozz and I found ourselves jumping over a fence to get onto the Wavertree track, for a training session of eight 300m reps. Everyone did it; Wavertree was never open regularly during holiday periods and, if we wanted to train, there weren't really any other options. So my New Year's Eve day was spent training and then toasting in the New Year at home with Pozz and a few glasses of wine. By 4 January I was back in France, competing in the shot put and high jump at Miramas, the same place I'd kicked my season off the previous year.

Bertrand liked to compete alongside training. We'd even do big sessions days before competitions, so they just became a regular part of my regime. He liked to not make a big deal out of it, especially with the shot put. When I first moved to France after Rio, he'd seen the fear I had about getting into the throwing circle and made a conscious effort to show me that getting into the circle and competing was no big thing. Bertrand and I had the first few months of 2020 carefully planned out: which comps I'd do, when and how much I'd travel, when we'd go into the holding camp for the Games . . . I was so excited; everything was coming together perfectly. But sometimes fate intervenes, and life takes a different path without you getting a say. For all our meticulous planning and plotting, I competed once more that indoor season before the entire world shut down.

I first remember Pozz talking about it. He was in Italy and told me how something called the coronavirus was spreading like wildfire around the country. People were terrified of catching it and parts of public life were being closed down. He talked about the risk of it spreading to other countries in Europe and I remember brushing him off: 'Oh, that's not going to happen . . .'

Within weeks, it did. France was further ahead of the UK, so everything in Montpellier started getting shut down before people back home in Liverpool had properly caught on to it. The first set of rules that the government brought in stated that people had to stay at home, unless they were going to the supermarket or outside to exercise. But there was a specific allowance for French athletes to be able to train at the track – and obviously, I'm not French, so that rule didn't include me.

'What am I supposed to do?' I asked Bertrand.

'I don't know.'

At that moment, I knew I was screwed. Bertrand always knew what to do in any situation, but this time he had no idea – it was the first time ever that he didn't know the answer to one of my questions, and to me that was almost as shocking as what was happening all around me.

France's reaction to the virus was more severe than the UK's. One rule mandated that you had to fill out a form every time you left the house, noting the time you left and your address. You could get stopped in the street at any time and had to have this (completed) form with you, otherwise you got into trouble. Even if you did have it, you could find yourself in trouble if you were too far away from home or had been out of your house for too long. It was really strict.

I did my final gym session with Bertrand on the day the lockdown was due to come into place – the last time I was allowed to train at the track – and after that I was on my own. I spent a week doing banded gym exercises in my house and hill runs right by where I lived, before Bertrand and I decided that it would be best for me to just go home, because the UK was mostly operating as normal and, with the Games just four months away, the IOC was adamant the Games were going ahead and encouraging all athletes to continue to prepare for them as best they could.

I flew into London from Montpellier feeling all this stress, but when I arrived everyone there was just going about their business as normal. It was so weird. It felt like I was the main character in a disaster film where no one else knew a meteor was heading straight for Earth and we only had weeks left to try to stop it; the UK felt just the same as France had about three weeks earlier, when I was telling Pozz not to be so dramatic (he was right – Italy had a particularly early, and deadly, introduction to the virus). I still had my priorities, though – I decided to make the most of the fact that everything was still open and got my hair done in London before heading back to Liverpool.

The track was open for use, but I was already preparing for what was inevitably to come. In 2018 I'd bought a beautiful Georgian townhouse, which I'd been slowly renovating ever since (with Mum's help as chief project manager). I'd always known I wanted to convert the basement into a home gym, but now I knew I had to get it done as fast as possible. Somehow, by the time lockdown came into place in the UK, I had enough equipment set up to at least do some weights training at home.

Before then, I was training at the track, getting more work done there than I could in France. In some ways it was nice to be back at a place that was so familiar, but it was also really stressful because I was so used to my usual schedule and weekly routine. Without Bertrand and Bruno there to guide me, I wasn't doing any of my actual, regular routine. I was basically free-styling, keeping fit and strong but not doing any technical work.

By the end of March, things had progressed; the UK announced a national lockdown on the 23rd. A day later, the Tokyo Olympics was postponed, and my immediate feeling was one of relief. It had been so stressful hearing the government telling us one thing ('don't go outside if you don't need to') and the IOC telling us another ('keep on training because the Games are only four months away'). Athletes were thinking, *Well, what the fuck should we do?* In some countries, they were training as normal with their coaches, so it felt unfair that the rest of us were doing burpees in our living room and operating in very different circumstances with the biggest competition of our lives just around the corner. When the IOC did finally postpone the Games, it weirdly felt like a weight had been lifted; now I didn't have to strain to try to put in this training that felt so pointless without the right guidance, at a time when the rest of the world was grinding to a halt.

In my head, it was just something that I (and everyone else) had to accept; the Olympics weren't going to happen that year. But I knew that, as soon as I possibly could, I wanted to get back to France and start again with Bertrand. Ultimately, I felt like one of the lucky ones; I had already qualified for the Games, I was healthy and I had good support around me, and I knew that wasn't the case for so many athletes.

It's only now, when I look back at pictures from that lockdown summer, that I can see the story within its wider context. I look back at this person who's finding so much joy in the simple life at home – I think it's potentially the last time I felt truly at peace. She seems like a different person to the one I am now.

For a long time, I saw my life as split into two halves: a time before my Achilles rupture and a time afterwards. Those moments of quiet during lockdown were my last truly happy times. They were filled with potential; I didn't know where life was going to take me, but I was excited to find out. The girl I see in pictures from that time has experienced setbacks, but she doesn't yet know true pain; when I think about that, I feel sad.

I feel sad that she didn't compete at the Olympics that summer, and that she never got the chance to build on all her momentum from the year before. And I feel sad thinking about what she's about to endure.

Because by the time 2020 was over, that athlete who had been the best in the world in Doha would be gone for ever, and no one will ever know what she might have been able to achieve.

14

Race

I FELT SICK TO MY STOMACH. HORRIFIED BY WHAT I'D JUST WATCHED. I threw my phone down on the sofa next to me and put my hands over my eyes. But nothing could block out what I'd just seen.

Nothing could take away the horrific, haunting sounds of a man begging for air as life was slowly squeezed out of him by a police officer's knee, pressed unrelentingly against his neck.

I don't like watching videos of horrible, violent things; if people post them on social media, I usually skip over them. But in the case of George Floyd, a Black American man murdered in cold blood by a white policeman on 25 May 2020, I realized that my aversion to those videos was, in effect, a reluctance to confront the real consequences of systemic racism, and it was making me ignorant. I was hearing more and more people talking about what had happened, so eventually I decided to sit down and watch the viral video that was sparking protests across America and, before long, internationally too.

Katarina Johnson-Thompson

I will never, ever forget it.

A few days after George Floyd's murder, there was a huge march in London, where thousands of people gathered outside the US Embassy to protest his death and, more generally, the treatment of Black citizens by police in America. More protests followed across the country, including in Liverpool, where I was living with Pozz while Covid kept the sports world on hold. Many of them were led by the Black Lives Matter (BLM) movement, sparking a wider discussion about institutional racism, and the treatment of people of colour closer to home.

As that happened, and conversations broadened to include racism in the UK, I felt an increasing connection to the cause. People were sharing their stories, highlighting that this wasn't just an American issue; racism was a problem here, too. When that happened, it created a space for me to look back on my own life, to add up all the experiences I'd been through, and to recognize the microaggressions I'd faced. The more people shared their stories, the more I realized how often racism is present in people's actions, and how deeply it can affect people's self-worth and how they see themselves. I had been impacted by systemic racism a lot more than I'd ever let on, or ever even admitted to myself.

I dealt with it the only way I knew how: I started writing. When I was a kid, I used to write in this big book everything that I wanted to happen – all my targets in sport. It's the same book where I noted down all the different ways that I could get to the score I needed to qualify for London 2012, and as that competition got closer, I would journal my thoughts on each event and how I felt. As I got older, I continued to use journalling as a way to get my thoughts in order. When I was in France and I didn't have that many people to talk to, using my journal was almost like speaking to an old friend – someone I could tell everything to without worrying what they might think of me.

In this instance, it started as a stream of consciousness. There was no structure to it; I just wrote down everything that was in my head. Everything that my heart was feeling. It was raw, and long. It included stuff from my childhood, the anxiety brought on by my dad's death and how those in the global majority have to deal with that fear about their loved ones daily, the impact of being one of a few people of colour in a majority white school (as I had been), and why it was time for people to recognize that racism comes in many forms; that it's not exclusive to outright murder or aggressive slurs shouted across a street, Tube carriage or playground.

I wrote and I wrote and I wrote. It felt good to get the thoughts out of my head; almost like therapy, in a way. I sent it to Mum and my long-time manager, Greg. He's from a mixed-race background, like me, so I knew that he would understand some of my thoughts and feelings. Greg's response terrified me. He thought it was something that I should share publicly; that a lot of people would be feeling the same things that I was and that, although he knew I didn't see it the way that he did, I was in a fortunate position to have a voice and a platform that could reach a lot of people.

I'd spent my entire career trying to keep my head below the parapet; not backing any particular corners, not showing the more opinionated parts of myself to anyone except for those closest to me. Now I was being presented with the opportunity to open up on a subject that millions of people all around the world felt deeply passionate about. It was petrifying, but it felt important.

I showed the piece to some friends whose opinions I really valued. 'Take half of that out because it's too raw,' was the overwhelming response. But they were positive about the idea of putting it out there and the impact that it could have. It was a really hard decision for me to make, but ultimately I asked myself one question: if you don't speak up on it, what are you really doing? I was just sitting at home in Liverpool not doing anything; taking in all this information and not adding to it in any way.

I followed their advice, took out the sections that I knew were probably too raw, and sent it back to Greg, giving him the go-ahead to see if anyone would be interested in publishing it (I wasn't convinced). He promised to find an outlet that would publish it in the correct way, in the tone and manner that I wanted, and said that ultimately, I'd have the final say on whether I was happy to proceed before it went out into the world.

After some back and forth over the edits, it ended up being published by *Vogue* at the end of August 2020. The night before it was going to come out, I felt completely sick. I didn't want to be in the spotlight. As I lay in bed trying to sleep, my body was filled with nerves and fear. How would people react? What would they think of me?

Being mixed-race has never been a straightforward process for me. I'd written about people who I'd grown up with, people who were close to me. It's scary to call out people who don't think that they've done anything wrong, especially when you hadn't made anything of it at the time because you didn't want to be seen as a 'problem' or like you were 'taking things too far'.

Unbroken

At the same time, I felt like speaking honestly about my experiences was something I just had to do. For the little girl growing up in Liverpool who knew she wasn't white (but wasn't quite sure what she was instead), who wanted to fit in so desperately that she chemically frazzled her own hair trying to turn it into something it wasn't, and who had grown up with a feeling of never being able to fully be herself, without ever stopping to ask why that was. It was for her, but also for anyone else who might have ever felt like that but been unable to express or voice the feeling.

If I was suddenly recognizing all these things in myself in the aftermath of George Floyd's murder, then I was sure that they were too. I hoped that reading my words might help them feel a little less alone as they tried to process them, just as I was.

Recently, in an interview, I was asked who my female role models were when I was growing up, and there was only one answer: it was 'Sporty Spice' (or Mel C) from the Spice Girls! She was a huge Liverpool fan, like me, and she always dressed in football kit or tracksuits, just as I did. In my mind, we were basically one and the same person. I idolized her.

It was weird to me, then, when others didn't see it the same way. At school, in Year 6, we had a special 'leavers' assembly'. Because our class was known for how beautifully we all sang hymns – though I wasn't a great singer, so I'd always mime the words – our performance was going to be all about music. The girls in the class decided to do a version of the Spice Girls song 'Wannabe' and, almost immediately, I was cast as 'Scary Spice' (Mel B), dressed in leopard-print trousers, and told to take the plaits out of my hair.

Katarina Johnson-Thompson

I was too young to really understand or recognize what was going on, but I knew that I wouldn't have had to change anything if I'd been Sporty Spice; I already had the clothes, and even the accent! I guess the teachers saw it differently. I was the only girl in that year who fitted 'the aesthetic' – the skin aesthetic, anyway.

Honestly, I don't think the school as a whole really knew how to deal with racism at that time. I think there were only two non-white students – me and a mixed-race Indian boy – and that was it. The first time I had a racial slur hurled at me, I was in Year 3. I was busy playing football in the playground, as I always did at recess, when a boy called me the N-word. I'm pretty sure it was because I'd either gone past him with the ball or had shown him up in some other physical way.

When the word came out of his mouth, I stopped dead. I didn't know what it meant, but I could tell from the way he'd said it that it wasn't anything good.

I spent the rest of the day going over it in my head. When Mum came to pick me up later that afternoon, she took one look at my face and immediately knew something was up. I usually came out of school laughing and joking with my friends, but not that day.

'What's wrong? What's the matter?' asked Mum.

'Nothing,' I replied, unsure about whether to tell her what had happened.

We always walked home from school through the park and Mum waited until it was just us and the trees before she tried again to uncover the reason behind the devastated look on my face.

Unbroken

'What's happened?' she asked, her own face overcome with concern.

'If I tell you,' I said, 'promise me you won't make a scene. Please, please don't go into the school.'

'OK, OK. I promise.'

When I admitted it and saw Mum's mortified look, I knew it was something even worse than I'd thought. I made her promise again not to do anything about it. But a few days later I was called into the head teacher's office, where he told me he knew what had happened and not to worry about it. Then he said, 'You're a Roman Catholic, aren't you? That's just like me; I'm Roman Catholic, too.'

I don't know what happened to the boy who said it, but I remember finding it strange that *I* was the one being called in to see the head teacher. I was also fuming with Mum, because I knew then that she'd come into school and told them what had happened. 'I'm sorry, love,' she told me later, 'but you can't let things like that go.'

But that was always my first instinct; brush it off, don't make a scene. A few years after that playground incident, I was walking down the street with my friends in an area of Liverpool called Halewood when someone brushed past and called me the N-word.

'She's not a (N-word), she's my friend!' shouted one of my mates. She was fuming. All I felt was red-hot embarrassment and I just wanted to move on. I wasn't angry; I just didn't like the feeling of being singled out. Other people were angrier on behalf of me. It's only now, when I look back, that I'm angry at myself for not doing anything. At the time, I had no idea how to respond.

Katarina Johnson-Thompson

As I got older, I became increasingly aware of how the colour of my skin could be used against me. I was fourteen when I went to a football match where the Black players on the pitch were getting shouted at – racially abused – and nobody said a word. A woman sitting on the same row as me turned around and stared at one of the people shouting, but that was the extent of it. No one told them to leave or even just to stop it.

I felt targeted and I slumped down in my seat, hoping no one would notice the Black girl sitting in the stands. For the rest of the match I was on high alert, hoping and praying that none of the Black players – no matter which side they were on – put in a bad tackle or played a dodgy pass, in the hope that it wouldn't happen again.

I felt the same as I had that day in Halewood, where I was the one left feeling embarrassed. Ashamed. I didn't want the people shouting those vile things to see me there and realize what they'd said. I didn't want to make a scene. I was always trying to cover up somebody else's mistake. Maybe it was all part of my desire to blend in and not always be the one who was 'different'; the one who didn't quite fit in.

Some thirteen years on from that day, I was putting my words – my heart and soul – out into the world in a way I never had before. Even before the *Vogue* article was published, I had a glimpse of the response I might get, when I posted a list of books on race and identity in the UK on my social media pages, thinking it might be useful to my followers.

'Stick to sport,' I was told – a comment most non-white sportspeople will have received at one time or another, when they have the audacity to speak about their own lived experiences.

Unbroken

Those types of comments used to affect me a lot, because they're basically what your inner critic is telling you anyway. In my own head, I was constantly questioning whether I should be talking about race and racism on my social media or in interviews. Was it the right thing for me to do? Was it even my place, given the privilege that I've enjoyed as a mixed-race, light-skinned person? When other people told me to stay in my lane, they were only amplifying the voice in my head that was telling me that kind of thing anyway – I really didn't need the extra encouragement to doubt myself.

Nowadays, I'm actively working on subduing those voices, and on being kinder to myself. If someone made a similar comment today, I think I'd just scroll past it, or maybe even have a little smile to myself. Those comments – people's opinions of me – can't affect me the way that they used to. I think that's because I'm more secure in myself, and strong enough to say, 'This is my opinion and you can take it or leave it – but what you think of it will not affect me.' That's not an arrogance on my part; rather, a recognition that we're all doing our best, and that I'm not trying to hurt anyone with my thoughts or opinions.

In the months after George Floyd's death, I started thinking about what I could do to create change in a more tangible way than words on paper (though I believe they can be powerful too). During that first wave of Covid, most of my days were spent at the Wavertree track where I'd spent so much of my youth, and it was bringing back so many memories; of walking through the park with Mum to the track, training in the pouring rain, and desperately trying to dry out my one pair of spikes after every soggy session.

Katarina Johnson-Thompson

Going back to Wavertree made me wonder how younger athletes were coping during lockdown, at a time when access to facilities was being severely limited – even for me, a recent world champion who was about to go and represent her country at the Olympics. I worried about the generation of athletes who were in the middle of their most important learning and developing years. If Covid had happened when I was in the midst of those early years as an athlete, I'm almost certain I wouldn't have made it this far, given the number of practical, logistical and financial challenges it created.

Athletics has given me so much – my whole life, my whole means of making a living – and I got really scared and sad that, with facilities closed and the increased cost of living, the same opportunity could be lost for a whole generation of potential future Olympians. On top of that, I wanted to do something that would help state-school educated athletes from diverse ethnic backgrounds have access to the facilities and guidance that could help them reach their sporting potential. I'd been so lucky to have Mum supporting me on my journey right from the start and Barrie helping me make it to London 2012, which kickstarted my career, but it hadn't been easy or straightforward. I knew there were so many kids from similar backgrounds who faced even more barriers to getting into sport. I wanted to try to open up the pathway for them.

After discussing my ideas with Greg and Dan, my management team, I was determined to help my community in any way I could – and thankfully, Liverpool FC Foundation was keen on the idea. And so, the KJT Academy was born. Being able to give back to a city and community that had supported me so much over the years was an incredibly proud moment. And it's working! More and more kids from Merseyside are receiving access to sport. I've already been semi-beaten by one of the athletes who's come through the Academy; her name is Success Eduan and, at the last Olympic trials in Manchester, she ran a faster 200m time than me (albeit in a different heat)! She's already *so sick* and has come on so well. But beyond joy on the track, it's just nice to be able to support the Academy athletes, full stop. It doesn't have to be a success story. It's just about giving people the chance – that's a success on its own.

When the *Vogue* article was published, and the feedback was largely supportive and kind, I breathed a huge sigh of relief. I didn't notice any change in the way people viewed me or treated me, but after it came out, I did receive a number of messages from people who said they appreciated the article and could resonate with a lot of what I wrote.

The year 2020 felt like a time when there was a real momentum behind the BLM movement and some really tough – necessary – conversations were being had right across society. But in the time since, I have often wondered how much has actually changed. I was terrified by the scenes across the UK just as the Paris Olympics were kicking off, when Islamophobia, racism and xenophobia fuelled riots across the country in the wake of a horrific mass stabbing at a kids' dance class in Southport, just 17 miles north of Liverpool. For anyone with Black or brown skin, the terror that rises in your stomach when you see people being attacked purely because of how they look is hard to describe. Any time you leave your home, it feels like stepping out into the unknown – imagine that you could be killed or severely injured, with absolutely no warning or provocation, simply while you're out buying milk for the tea. That's a genuine reality that people of colour across the country had to face in the summer of 2024.

These days, I'm so much more aware of my surroundings. After Paris, Pozz and I went on a short break to Madrid and, when we arrived there, three groups were stopped by security to have their bags checked; one was a sole Black man, one was a group of young Black and white girls all going on holiday together, and the last was me and Pozz. Countless white people strolled past freely while, in the space of just five minutes, the only people who got stopped were those three groups.

In the city itself, I noticed how few Black people there were and it made me a little bit nervous. It's possible that it was an after-effect of what had happened in the UK just weeks earlier but, even without the riots, I don't think things have really changed too much when it comes to racism. There are moments when something happens and it suddenly becomes newsworthy, but then the news cycle moves on and pretends the problems have disappeared. I spent a long time living by the motto 'anything for an easy life', trying to blend in with the crowd in any way I could. But I'm pleased – and proud – that I stepped out to write that essay in 2020, because I think it was very much what I needed at the time. As time has passed, though, I've found myself questioning it in some ways. Mainly, why did I have that amplified voice where a Black(er) woman mightn't have? Maybe I shouldn't have spoken up; maybe my mixed heritage is the only reason I was afforded that platform in the first place. It's one of the most common paradoxes of being who I am – even if, at the time, I knew it was the right thing to do, my inherent recognition of the inequality between people means that I'm in two minds about it now.

Like I said, being mixed-race is not a straightforward experience. I recognize that I have certain privileges and that, no matter what I've been through, those who are completely Black will have been discriminated against so much more. So while I accept and appreciate the platform that I have to speak up, it's never an easy decision for me to do so.

Maybe, outside of treating people as equally and respectfully as possible, there aren't any 'right' answers. Yes, I might be given a platform over a Black woman because I'm slightly whiter than her, but is that not better than a white person writing the piece? Does progress under an unequal or unfair set of conditions still count as progress? Or is it an appeasement to the status quo, the way things are? Should I even pay attention to what racists want, or should I focus on the young Black girl who might have seen my piece, and be thankful that at least she has a resource that I didn't?

Questions around race and identity are complicated, which is why I think I spent such a long part of my life avoiding them, focusing on my performances and my sport, and leaving them to the rest of the world to debate. And I'm still like that, to a certain degree. But the older I get, the more I recognize that not everybody has the experience or platform to change things. And yes, it's scary, especially because I can never be sure that I'm saying the right thing, I'm just speaking from my experiences.

But who knows what the right thing is? And when the situation comes down to literal life and death, is it not better to speak up and be honest, decorum be damned, than to stay completely silent and just hope that everything gets better?

15
Resilience

'Ahhhh, not again!'

I looked over at my training partner, Kevin, and threw the controller down in disgust as he smiled back at me, so happy with himself over what he'd just done. What had started out as a 'quick game of Mario Kart' had turned into an epic competition, not only between me and Kevin but also involving Nana and Jeremy Lelievre from our training group, going through every single course in the game to find out who was the ultimate racer across *all* the courses (one of Kevin's big personality traits is that he's all-encompassing; no wonder he ended up as a decathlete).

For what felt like the hundredth time that afternoon, I'd just been taken out by the dreaded Blue Shell. It's the great equalizer in the game that gets given to one of your opponents whenever you're too far ahead in first place. The moment they fire it, it tracks you down, hovers over your head and then

Unbroken

explodes on you, taking you out of the game. There's nothing you can do. It's brutal and cruel and inescapable, and frankly I almost question whether it's an appropriate addition to a game designed for innocent children.

Kevin thought it was hilarious. I was fuming. Only Mario Kart would be capable of raising my stress levels like that when we were in actual paradise. It's called Réunion. It's a beautiful French-governed 30-mile-wide island in the Indian Ocean, right by Mauritius, and a place favoured by the French for their training camps when the temperature drops too low in Montpellier.

I'd first been there in 2017, on one of my first ever training camps with my French training group. Three years later, we were staying on the other side of the island, which was a mixture of beautiful beaches and vast mountains. It was early December and, Mario Kart injustices aside, I was feeling totally at peace, grateful that travel had resumed that summer and loving being back with Bertrand, Bruno and my training partners as we started to build towards the Tokyo Olympics, which had been rescheduled to the following summer, in 2021.

The week had started with a couple of rest days to allow our bodies to adjust after the long flight – that was when the battle for the title of Mario Kart King/Queen had taken place. I'd also had to spend some time on the physio bed addressing a right calf and Achilles that had been feeling super tight and sore. The schedule for our first day of full training involved plyometrics and a big 800m session, and I wanted to try to loosen it up before that.

I woke up on the morning of that first session bathed in the warm sunlight that was flooding into my room through the blinds.

I opened them and looked out at the pristine white sand and calm, clear water of the Indian Ocean right outside. I took some deep breaths and walked back across the room. And, as I did so, my brain suddenly woke up enough to register the pain in my right Achilles.

Oh god, this isn't going away.

I tried to silence the voice of doom in my head, telling myself it would be fine. It was just morning stiffness; I'd stretch it out when I got to the track later. The French never rushed breakfast (I love that about them), so I had time to chill with my book before heading to the track. As I sat down with my then current read (*The Five: The Untold Lives of the Women Killed by Jack the Ripper*), I allowed my mind to be completely absorbed by the words on the page, the calming sound of the sea in the background gently soothing my soul.

Bertrand always schedules something before an 800m session in training because, in a heptathlon, the 800m is run at the end of two hard days of competition, so you're never running it fresh; you're always tired on that start line. That day, we had plyometrics first, starting with bounds on grass – an exercise designed to improve sprint power and help you jump higher off one leg. It sort of looks like you're running with strides that are twice as big and bouncy as normal.

I spent plenty of time warming up my right calf and stretching it out, then laced up my shoes and walked over to where Bruno had laid out a series of cones for us to bound between. I watched as other athletes in my group went through their first sets, then slotted in as the last to go, taking it relatively easy as I got my joints and muscles warmed up.

By the start of the third set, I was into it. I took my first steps towards the cone closest to me, planted my left foot and then heard a loud POP.

What the fuck was that!? Why am I on the floor?

I looked over to where Bertrand had been standing, 10 metres away from me, and saw him lying on the floor too. He'd fainted. His own athletics career had been ended by an Achilles rupture and, as soon as he'd seen it happen to me, he'd passed out.

As I lay there wondering what the hell had happened, people were running towards me. Clearly, it was something bad. I looked down at my left ankle and could see something white poking through just under the surface of the skin. Was that a bone?! I'd never broken a bone in my life, so I had no idea what it would feel like. I started hitting it, to test it out, but I felt nothing. No pain. Nothing. I tried to stand up, but I couldn't walk on it. I couldn't even set it down properly.

I think everyone around me knew instantly what I'd done. As I wobbled on my right foot, I saw Romain Barras – an ex-decathlete who had worked his way up to become Director of High Performance for the French Athletics Federation – coming towards me. He scooped me up into a fireman's lift and carried me across the grass, straight into the physio's room. From there, everything around me seemed to happen in fast forward, while I was frozen in stillness, unable to fully process what was happening.

From the physio bed, we were in the car, and then we were in the doctor's office where I first heard the words: 'Complete rupture.' I didn't understand, all he'd done was squeeze my left calf.

'Don't you need to scan it?' I asked, desperately hoping he'd got it wrong.

'Non, non,' he said, shaking his head. 'It is done.'

Your Achilles tendon connects the calf muscle to the heel bone, so if a squeeze of your calf doesn't create any movement in your foot – not even a twitch – then it's clear: your Achilles has ruptured. It's the simplest, most basic of tests, for one of the worst injuries you can suffer.

I was taken back to the hotel where I lay on the bed helplessly while a group of athletes helped pack my things. Bertrand had already set up a WhatsApp group (titled: EMERGENCY KAT) with my manager, Greg, and the head doctor of British Athletics. They arranged my flight back to Paris, where Greg was going to meet me, and from there to London.

While I waited, I picked up my phone and started googling: 'How long does an Achilles rupture take to heal? What's an Achilles rupture? Can athletes get back from an Achilles rupture?' You know when people have a headache and they google it and think they're going to die? That's what athletes do, but for injuries, and we always end up finding – and imagining ourselves in – the absolute worst-case scenario.

I called Mum, of course. It was early in the morning in the UK (Réunion is four hours ahead) but she answered almost instantly.

'Hi, Mum, I think I've done something really bad. It's really, really bad.'

It was 9 December 2020, twenty-two days before the start of an Olympic year, and 238 days before the start of the 2021 Olympic heptathlon in Tokyo. That meant I had eight months to get my Achilles back in one piece. More than that: it had to be strong enough to withstand sprinting, jumping and throwing, and powerful enough to propel me both vertically and horizontally. It was a big ask on either leg, but on my take-off leg? The leg that propels me upwards and forwards in both the high jump and long jump? It was humongous.

As I sat on the aeroplane waiting for take-off, I was in a state of shock. I had no idea what lay ahead; whether my Olympics was already over, or maybe even my whole career. I feel like, nowadays, Achilles ruptures are so much more common (although maybe it's like when you want a certain car and you start seeing it everywhere?), but at the time I didn't know anyone who had had one and been able to come back to the same level. What if that was it for me?

What if the Blue Shell had taken me out, and it was suddenly game over?

When the drinks trolley came around, I knew exactly what I needed: wine. Plenty of it. I just wanted to zone out; not think. Not feel. I put on the Beyoncé film *Black Is King*, muttered something to myself about how amazing she was and fell asleep before I'd even got halfway through. I've still not been able to go back to watch the rest of that film – it's the only Beyoncé thing I've not fully supported, but I think it will always just take me back to that long journey when all I wanted to do was shut myself down and block out reality.

Not long after the Tokyo Olympics were postponed at the end of March 2020, Pozz flew back to the UK from his training base in Italy, where he'd been quarantined inside a gated community that housed a training centre and accommodation for the athletes (basic rooms, tiny TVs and patchy Wi-Fi; not the best place to be stuck for weeks on end).

Initially, I struggled during lockdown. The Games had been cancelled, the European Championships that were due to take place in 2020 followed soon afterwards and, for the first time in my life, I felt like I had no purpose. Why would I train when I had nothing to train for? I was completely lost without a goal, without a date on the calendar to aim towards. That period proved to me something I probably already knew: I *need* goals and structure in my life, otherwise it's not good for me. It's mayhem.

My malaise didn't last that long. With no immediate goal, I quickly figured out that for the first time since I was a kid, I could afford to properly relax. And while it was a horrible time for the rest of the world, some of my favourite memories are from that first lockdown in 2020; Pozz and I would train at the track (part of our daily exercise allowance), come home and have a few drinks, and just enjoy each other's company. It was quite something – we even learned to perfect the French martini! I went on to enjoy a relatively chilled summer, barring a few Diamond League meetings to keep me in shape, before starting to ease myself back into 'proper' training; Bertrand wanted me back in early October to start preparing for the Olympics.

The Games had been rescheduled to July 2021, and I was excited. In my mind, there was no question that I would be able to get back to the same shape I had been in when winning the World Championships in 2019. Once I've hit a height with a coach, as I had with Bertrand the previous year, I have total trust in them. I know we have a clear path towards getting me into shape and that, as long as I'm dedicated and do everything asked of me, it'll just be down to me being able to produce on the day.

But then came the Blue Shell.

Unbroken

The flight from Réunion back to Paris was over eleven hours; that's a long time to spend considering your entire future, not to mention worrying about how to navigate an international airport in a wheelchair for the first time. And I was right to worry. After we landed in Paris, I only had a short amount of time to go and collect my case, meet Greg (who had come to help me get back to London) and board the next flight back to the UK. But wheelchair users don't get to rush; they're made to wait on the plane until everyone else has been allowed off, and then you're collected one by one. There were three or four of us on that flight, and, once they got us all off, they left us in a small, squared-off section of the airport to 'wait for further assistance'. Well, we waited and waited until eventually I could wait no longer, knowing that my next flight would be boarding soon. So I abandoned the chair, grabbed my crutches and made my way to baggage collection, where, thankfully, a kind-hearted person saw my struggle, helped get my bag off the belt and wheeled it through customs to where Greg was waiting. There's clearly a lot of work to be done when it comes to allowing wheelchair users to travel efficiently.

I'd never been more relieved to see Greg. I think we were both still in shock about what was happening but, as is my default way when things get dark, I veer directly into humour. Waiting to board our flight from Paris to London, I was alongside two other people in wheelchairs and, as the three of us waited to be taken on board, I let out a 'vroom, vroom', revving my 'engine' like I was on the start line of a Formula One race. I found it funny, anyway.

That night, Greg and I had a meeting with renowned foot and ankle surgeon James Calder, who immediately confirmed it was a full Achilles rupture (again, no scan needed, just the calf squeeze). I only had one question for him: 'How long does it take to heal?'

'Around eight to sixteen months.'

We looked at the calendar and counted up the weeks to the Olympic heptathlon in Tokyo: I had exactly eight months and one week.

'Good! That's enough time then,' I said, my brain latching onto the 'eight months' part of what James had said, and firmly blocking out the rest. In my head, that was it: I was still going to the Olympics. I don't know what possessed me to think like that, but I just decided it could be done. Today, I know that it takes closer to two years to get your force production fully back, but at the time I was only focused on one thing. It was theoretically possible to get back to competing by 4 August 2021; therefore, it was possible for Katarina Johnson-Thompson.

The earliest James could get me in for surgery was 14 December, four days after I got to London, so Pozz and I checked into a hotel around the corner from the hospital and got Mum a room next door. I think she was faring worse than me at that point; on the train down from Liverpool she'd been physically sick with nerves. The day before the operation I got my hair put into braids (they were green and reached all the way down to my bum), preparing for the weeks ahead, when a proper shower would be too much of a challenge. (Whenever I get coloured braids, it's a sign that I'm going through something – a bit like a 'tell' in poker. For those who knew that about me, the blue braids I got in the autumn of 2022 and the pink ones I got before the European Championships in Rome 2024 would have been real giveaways.)

I was alone going into and coming out of the operation because of Covid regulations, so I was grateful that it wasn't a completely unfamiliar experience to me, but I wasn't prepared for the knock-on effect of whatever drugs they give you to do the operation; for days afterwards, I was completely zombified. I'd had my surgery first thing in the morning and, when a nurse came round later in the afternoon to tell me the staff was about to change for the night shift, she asked whether I was staying for the night. They'd said I could go back to the hotel if I wanted, and I was adamant that was what I wanted to do, but every time I tried to send a message to Pozz and Mum to come and get me, I'd fall asleep. Then I'd wake up and say, 'I promise, I'm going to leave, I'm just getting my stuff . . .' And then it would happen again.

Eventually, I managed to make it out, but in hindsight I should have just stayed; I don't know what I was doing trying to leave on a rainy December night when I'd just had surgery and needed to rest. Thankfully the drugs meant I wasn't in too much pain that night, though they weren't without their side effects; I ordered some food from room service and promptly fell asleep in my plate. But when I woke up the next morning, the pain had really kicked in. Getting up to go to the toilet was torture, because the minute I stood up, all the blood rushed straight to my ankle and I could feel it expanding and pushing against the cast; it was the worst pain in the world. I'd pee as fast as I could so that I could get back to lying flat with my foot raised as soon as possible.

For the first two weeks after the operation, I was in a daze. My left leg was encased in a solid cast that was stopping my foot from dorsiflexing (where you bring your toes up towards your shin), I was in a lot of pain every time I stood up and I had zero independence. All I could think was that while I was losing more fitness and strength with every day that passed, my competitors were making more and more progress towards their goals. We were on directly opposing lines of the same graph, travelling in different directions.

It wasn't just my training goals that were in the bin – my life as a whole felt like it was one big mess. Coming off the back of a year in lockdown, everything was uncertain; the Olympics, my dreams, my day-to-day finances. I didn't even know how my life in France was going to work, with Brexit rules on travel to the EU about to kick in. It was all starting to fall apart.

On social media, I was still posting pictures pretending I was training, not wanting word to get out that I was unable to walk and making good use of my nan's stairlift. It's hard to explain exactly why I decided to do that. At the start I think it was partly to do with the fact that, when my Achilles ruptured, I was in the process of renegotiating my contract with Nike – I didn't know what impact it could have on things if they found out I was injured, especially because athletes' contracts normally run Olympics to Olympics, so mine had expired after the summer of 2020. In the end, they found out anyway, and everything was signed with them knowing full well what I was going through. I told them I'd be at the rescheduled Olympics and detailed all the things I was going to do to get there, adding more pressure to that which I'd already put on myself to make it.

I also didn't want my competitors to think I wasn't going to be there. I wanted them still to see me as strong, not as someone who needed sympathy or a fuss made of them. At the time, I didn't know the full extent of the rehab. For the first few weeks after my surgery, I closed myself off to anyone except Pozz. Everyone was going through him to contact me. That included British Athletics, who, in a bid not to overwhelm me, were only sending rehab plans going up to two weeks ahead. I remember thinking that when I came out of the cast, the hard bit would be over. Even once I realized that wasn't the case, I thought the same about coming out of the boot. Each time I moved forwards, I'd realize that the more you know, the more you understand just how far away you are. You think you're getting closer with time, but the more time you have, and the more progress you make, the further away you feel.

Looking back, I regret pretending life was going on as normal, because it was such a hard thing to keep hidden – it probably took more energy for me to hide the fact that I wasn't training than it would have for me to be open about what was going on. One of my close friends, Jazmin Sawyers, ruptured her Achilles in the spring of 2024, and she dealt with it publicly. She talked about it with friends on social media and did interviews about it, and she's had so much support in return. I look at her and realize her approach is the far healthier way, especially in the long term. It was such a dark time for me, and it took me *years* to get out of the injured mindset. I wish I'd handled it differently, but my method of shutting down was all I knew at the time; it was the only way I *could* handle it.

I was like a robot in that period; utterly convinced that the dream wasn't over and laser-focused on what I had to do to make sure that was the case. I had to convince myself that I could still get some happiness out of the situation – that was the only way I was going to be able to attack the rehab in the way I knew I needed to.

While I was in the cast, I barely felt any pain; it gave me a false sense of security because my foot was rigidly stuck in place. I thought that once the cast was off and I was in a boot instead, I'd get some independence back – but the worst bit was about to start.

After two weeks in the cast, I had to go back to the hospital for them to take it off and put my left foot in a protective boot that went up to just below my knee and would have to stay on 24/7 for the next five weeks. It was horrible – the worst pain of the whole experience for me. They basically have to force your foot in – it took two men to do it and, even then, they couldn't manage it with the first boot they tried. I was in so much pain afterwards that my mum had to stop off at the hospital on her way home to pick up some more meds because I felt dizzy with the pain.

The one plus side was that, once I was in the boot, I was going to be able to start the rehab process that I was determined would take me all the way to Tokyo. Although even that was uncertain. On the same day I got the boot, Liverpool was put into 'Tier 3' of the Covid restrictions pre-New Year's Eve, so I didn't really know what access to physios I would be allowed. Everything was up in the air.

I was lucky to have the best team of people around me coordinating my recovery, though. Michael Johnston (MJ), who's the Physical Preparation Lead for British Athletics, ended up becoming a very important part of my life over the next eight months or so. Without him, I wouldn't have made it to the Olympics. I also had Andy Walling, who's now a first team physio for Manchester United, and an excellent physio in Cat McCormick. They were all based at Loughborough, but I was adamant that I didn't want to be walking around the university campus on crutches; I'd stay in Liverpool, and go to them when I could walk.

With the gyms still closed, that left only one option: the basement gym in my house. MJ magically arranged for some additional rehab equipment to be sent across from all over the UK, no easy feat during lockdown; I had a leg extension machine, a leg curl, an elastic-based machine which basically offsets your bodyweight so you can start doing plyometrics really early, and a load of dumbbells and kettlebells. It was a decent rehab facility in the end!

Day One was New Year's Eve 2020. I was still at Mum's house and couldn't drive (I mean, I also couldn't walk, shower, carry anything, make my own food or drink, get up and down the stairs without being in pain or stay awake for longer than two hours at a time). Mum couldn't leave Nan on her own, so all of us (plus the dogs) piled into Mum's Nissan Juke that morning (and every morning for the next month or so) and did the thirty-minute drive to my house. That first day, it was MJ who drove the two hours up from Loughborough, put on full PPE (gloves, apron, mask) and hooked me up to something called a Compex machine, which basically stimulates your muscle, helping it to contract when you can't physically do it yourself. It was the start of the process of rebuilding the connection between my brain and the muscles in my calf – without that connection to the muscle, it's impossible to start building muscle mass, and we knew that there'd be a lot of muscle to rebuild once my left leg came out of that boot. From then on, I was training four times a week, with MJ making that journey to Liverpool twice a week, and Andy and Cat taking the other two.

They all had different approaches to getting me through the rehab, and each became part of it in their own way: MJ would do the upper-body stuff (because he's basically 'Arm Guy'); Cat would join in with everything, and do the aerobic circuits when I was able to do them safely; and Andy . . . well, Andy I'm convinced only came for all the amazing cakes my mum would make, but thankfully he was also an expert with my rehab, so he definitely earned his keep. We had our routine; Mum and Nan would stay upstairs, a safe distance away, with Mum always popping down to leave cups of tea and coffee, accompanied by homemade cakes and biscuits, outside the gym door.

It was good to feel useful again after being stuck at home and having everything done for me by Mum. I'd started to feel like my nan, the way that my mum was looking after us both; bringing out our meals together on a little couch table (I made her get rid of it a few years later – whenever I looked at it, I was just reminded of that bleak moment in time). I was still on some pretty strong pain pills (codeine and oxycodone, which are both opioids), so every day I'd get back from doing the bare minimum in a session, take the meds and sleep for the rest of the day. It was a nice break from reality. Mum would wake me up for dinner, then I'd take one again at night to try to stop the pain because it was so sore.

The challenge of making it back in time for Tokyo was immense. My Achilles needed to be back functioning but I also needed the fitness to be able to compete at an Olympic Games, so as soon as I was allowed to, I was using a pool and bike whenever I could, and doing arm circuits to keep my upper body strong. When I look back at the speed at which things happened, it's crazy.

Before the boot could come off, my foot had to go from a pointed position (similar to when you're wearing high heels) all the way down to 90 degrees. To do that gradually, there were four heel raises inside the boot that were each a few millimetres thick. Each week, I'd have to remove one of them to push my Achilles through more range; something that would usually be done by a doctor at the hospital, but during Covid, it was left to me. Every time one was removed, it was agony as my Achilles was stretched into a new position; but at the same time, each removal meant that I was edging closer to my goal.

When the boot finally came off on 1 February, I was still walking with two crutches, so barely putting any weight through my left foot – it was just over two weeks later, on 16 February, that I tried walking for the first time. Over the next few weeks I had to start learning how to push through both legs again: squatting, hinging, standing up from a bench, making the connection from the floor up again. After weeks of doing everything from a kneeling position – squats, kettlebell swings, overhead presses – it felt good to have two feet back on the ground, even if that was with additional support. A week later, we were adding small amounts of weight to those movements, and each week they went up. The programme from the team was meticulous and careful, but MJ wasn't scared to push things on.

By 18 February I was back at Loughborough and maxing

out seated single leg calf raises with 2kg (pre-injury I'd be doing this with 20–25kg), and Romanian deadlifts with 35kg. The following week, I was able to start walking 'freely' for the first time – no crutches! Although I couldn't walk further than about 20 metres before needing to stop, so it took me a while to get anywhere (though it still felt quicker than that 800m in Beijing!). Every session the weight I was lifting went up, and a few weeks later, I was using the underwater treadmill at St George's Park, focusing on my gait, particularly the heel-to-toe motion. From there, my plyometrics gradually progressed from using a special machine MJ had in Loughborough where I could hop using the equivalent of 5kg of my bodyweight, to using my bodyweight minus 40kg, and then 30kg. I'd be jumping off two feet to the sound of a metronome which dictated how long I'd be in the air, and therefore how high I was jumping.

By late March, I was jumping with my full body weight, then jumping forwards, backwards, sideways and onto a small box. Then we moved on to dribble runs, where you stay upright and take very short steps; they're a way of teaching your body how to hit the ground, and utilize it, without putting too much force through the foot and ankle. Fast dribbles went into strides (longer steps) and by 9 April I was running for the first time since my rupture. It felt . . . weird. I could feel the difference between the two legs. I could feel myself hobbling. And although I was so, so happy to be running again, I knew there was so much more work to do.

A week later, we ran again and this time it felt . . . normal! The progression in just that one week was so huge and really took me by surprise. I suddenly felt overcome by all the emotions of the past few months. If I could run properly, then I could train properly.

The progression had come so fast that, for the most part, I never for a second saw any reason why I wouldn't make it to Tokyo. When an injury is that bad, progress is a daily achievement, because there's so much that needs to recover. Even if it was just a tiny thing like the scar healing properly, I could still see that each day it was better than the last. There was never a time when I felt things were standing still or even going backwards; it was full steam ahead.

The one wobble I *did* have was more to do with other people's doubts than my own. It came around three months after my surgery, when I went back to see James Calder for one of our monthly check-ups. I updated him on everything I was doing in training – all the things that nobody at the three-month mark ever does – and on the progress I'd made since our last meeting, and he raised his eyebrows.

'Wow, you're actually really doing this,' he said, smiling. 'When you said you were going to do the Olympics three months ago, I thought it was a big ask . . .'

James is a magician, and I fully credit him with saving the second part of my career, but on this occasion he really pissed me off. As soon as he said that, my mind went into overdrive, immediately assuming that everyone was saying the same thing behind my back. For a couple of weeks after that I spiralled, thinking: *Is everyone believing I can do this or not? Is this doable? Because you all told me that it was and, now, I feel like I'm being laughed at, or having my dreams indulged just to keep me happy when in reality they're never going to come true.* I was so paranoid that I went up to the British Athletics doctor at the track one day and said to him: 'If this is not possible, don't not tell me. You have to tell me!'

A few months ago, I found out that that same doctor had been watching me at Loughborough during my rehab and had said to MJ at one point that he was going to tell me I wasn't going to make it to the Olympics: 'She told me to be honest with her, and I'm looking at her, and it's not gonna happen. I need to be honest. I need to keep my promise.'

'Don't you dare,' said MJ.

I'm not a confrontational person but, during that rehab period, I was basically willing to fight anyone who didn't believe in the plan (figuratively speaking – I am not a violent human). Early on, there was another physio around Loughborough who would work on me now and again, and, for whatever reason, he was saying to me that it wasn't possible. My belief was so strong that I immediately told MJ, 'He's off the team – he's done.' And he never touched me again. We can laugh about it three years on, but at the time I wasn't his biggest fan. I was so laser-focused on my goal that I wanted nothing to do with anyone who wasn't fully on board with the journey.

Right from the start, MJ had been contacting Bertrand a couple of times per week to share my progress, training videos and all the data that went with it. His view was always that once I was up to a certain speed and could do a certain number of reps at that speed, then it was time for him to hand me over to my coach because, at that point, the calf would be doing everything it needed to do. I feel so lucky that MJ was so committed to my goal and so scientifically driven. He believed in his plan and he believed in me. He had the data that proved I was ready to go back to France, and that helped me to overcome any niggling doubts I might have had in my mind. A few days after that second run, I couldn't have been happier to be on a plane back to Montpellier.

Despite the fact he'd been programming training sessions for me while I was in Loughborough (it's amazing how much you can actually do even when you're on crutches), and had seen the progress on paper and in snapshots on his phone, I think it was hard for Bertrand to pick up where MJ had left off. At first, he was very careful with me – too careful with me. For me, it was very frustrating. I'd already been through all of the stuff he wanted to do and had gone back to France ready to train.

It came to a head after I got to the track one day and Bertrand had arranged for me to spend time with this person who believed they could trick your mind into not feeling pain. He put me in a meditative state and was talking about moving pain around my body, then doing an exercise and coming back to it . . . I wasted a whole day with this guy and was absolutely livid about it. I'm not normally visibly angry, especially at my coaches, but after I was done with the Ghostbuster I just stormed out and went home, holding back angry tears.

Bertrand and Bruno pulled me in the next day to ask what was wrong.

'I came back here to train,' I said. 'That isn't training. Stop treating me like I'm injured.'

'Well, what do you want?' asked Bertrand.

'I want to go to the Olympics and finish a heptathlon.'

From then on, I was doing normal training every day. I

think it took that conversation for Bertrand to accept that was the goal and 'let's just go for it'. The next day, he had a plan and we were full steam ahead; I was with Bruno doing three 100m reps, two 150s, two 120s. Not too long after that, I remember having a particularly hard day and moaning to Bertrand how I deserved *one* easy ride into a championships. 'You don't *deserve* anything,' he replied. 'Look around this track now: everyone's working hard and they're not even going to get to represent their country. We're all just here, trying our best.'

That was a real moment for me in terms of my mentality. It brought me straight out of feeling like a victim to being grateful for the opportunity that I had ahead of me. I tried to hang onto it as much as I could over the next few months.

The highest percentage of people who re-rupture their Achilles do it in the first months of their first year of recovery. For me, that was hard not to think about. The horror stories I'd heard about athletes re-rupturing were hard to completely erase from my mind. On top of that, there had been no warning signs whatsoever before my Achilles ruptured. Sure, I'd had issues with the calf on my right leg, but the left one had been fine. People say that's the way it is with ruptures – you can't predict them – and I really struggled with that when I was coming back. I'd get into a fearful frame of mind: how could anyone train or live life normally when you could just be walking down the street and rupture your Achilles? What's the point?

I was most afraid of the long jump. I'd put my marker out (for the start of my run-up), sit down in the shade, and stare at the distance I'd have to run before planting my left foot.

It was terrifying. I had this voice in my head telling me, 'Please, stop doing it. You cannot do this. Why are you doing this?' I was having to override that voice a lot. A lot, a lot. It was a really hard thing to do and I think the only reason I was able to do it was because I knew there was no other choice; it had to be done in order to reach my goal, so I just had to get on with it. But I hated it.

I'd get really affected by the sound of things, too. If I was at the track and other athletes were doing the long jump or triple jump, or even just plyometrics, I would literally have to hum to myself, or stick my fingers in my ears, to not hear the noise caused by the impact of their feet hitting the ground. I remember going to watch a comp in Montpellier that summer and I couldn't watch the men's triple jump for the life of me – the slapping sound of their feet on the track was just too much. When I mentioned it to the doctor, he said it was almost a form of PTSD from when my foot had hit the ground followed by that *pop* sound that I now know was my Achilles breaking in half. Because it happened to me, my brain was expecting it to happen to everyone.

I couldn't listen to that sound for years afterwards.

By the end of June, Bertrand had decided it was time for me to get back into competing, so we entered a small comp in a town called Orange, about an hour away from Montpellier. It was a really low-key open meeting where I competed in the high jump.

I entered the comp at 1.70 metres. On my first two attempts, I knocked the bar down. I knew that after nobody had seen anything from me for months, it would look really bad to come back and no-height in the high jump, so I felt the pressure.

But on the third attempt I nailed it and, from then on, I was clearing every height first time. It was almost like I needed that moment of panic to break through the fear factor.

And it turned out to be a really good day! I jumped 1.84 metres, 1cm over my head height, and I'm 6 foot. Seven months post-Achilles rupture, it was a really big achievement. To this day, it has to be one of the most impressive physical performances I've ever pulled off, considering what my body had been through. We drove back to Montpellier feeling like we'd taken a huge step towards being able to compete in an Olympic heptathlon a month later. I know it wasn't my best height — I'd jumped 1.95 metres in Doha — but it didn't really matter, because my goal was to finish the heptathlon, and 1.84 metres was better than most.

Once I'd broken through that first comp, my fear became largely about fitness. Everything felt much more real — what I'd always believed *could* happen was actually happening, but that meant I now had to put everything else together. I wasn't going to Tokyo for a high jump competition, I had a whole heptathlon to get right. I needed to feel confident I could make it through two days of competition; that I could wake up on day two physically capable of competing in the long jump, javelin and 800m.

I didn't know it at the time, but Bertrand had concerns over the way my long jump was going in training. There was a Diamond League meeting in Gateshead in mid-July, which we had initially spoken about as being our penultimate comp before potentially heading into the holding camp in Japan, but in the weeks leading up to it, Bertrand wasn't sure he wanted me to compete. He told Greg that he didn't want me in the competition if I wasn't going to jump 6 metres, out of concern for the effect that might have on me and for the possible media reaction.

British Athletics wanted to make a big thing about the reigning world champion competing there, but even up to a few days before, Bertrand was still unsure – nothing in my training was giving him a firm grasp on what I might jump. But in the end, he decided to take the risk.

I had no idea that was the way Bertrand was thinking. The plan in Gateshead was just to do the long jump and see how my body coped with doing multiple jumps in one day, off a full approach for the first time since Doha. The fear was very much still there, but I had no choice other than to override it. Drown it out. It had to be done.

I think the anxiety manifested itself properly the day before, when I had to do a press conference – the first one I'd done since rupturing my Achilles. By this point, people knew what I'd done; it wasn't really possible to hide it once I was competing with a long scar down my left ankle. But I still wasn't really in a frame of mind to speak about it. I had a bit of an attitude, so when one of the journalists asked me: 'Can you run?' I just said, 'Well, I hope so, I'm doing long jump tomorrow.' I was really resistant to giving a straight answer.

When I landed my first jump in Gateshead I was so happy. I'd run as fast as I could for 38 metres, stuck my leg out and landed in the pit without any issues. It was only just over 6 metres but I was so, so happy. Overcome by a mix of immense joy and relief, I immediately bawled my eyes out. Jaz was also competing that day and it was a moment we shared together, her huge smile reflecting my happiness.

Katarina Johnson-Thompson

I took four more jumps that day (one of which was a foul) and came away with a best jump of 6.10 metres – ticking the box in Bertrand's head and sending us into our final comp before leaving France knowing that my body could handle five jumps in one day. We knew that the long jump still needed to be better, but it was also time to get competition practice in some of the other events, so we went straight from Gateshead to a heptathlon in Castres, back in France. The plan there was to do hurdles, high jump, shot put and javelin and then finish with an 800m training session – which was worse than running the actual race. It was two days of back-to-back competition, which would be a big test.

The comp went better than I could have hoped; particularly the hurdles, where I ran 13.55 seconds, which was faster than any of the times I'd ended up running in 2020. Everything else went smoothly, if not remarkably. Finishing that comp without any issues left us with no more obstacles to overcome. I went back to my apartment in Montpellier and started packing my bags for a flight to Tokyo the next day, not really stopping to process what that really meant, or what we had achieved over the previous months.

I knew my recovery had been extremely quick but, in the moment, my journey back to that point had felt like such a gradual process that I'd never really had that one instant where I went from believing it was going to happen to *knowing* it would happen. It wasn't until the plane was in the air that I started reflecting and taking it all in, and I had another big cry to myself as it sank in: *I'm actually on a plane to the Olympics. This is actually happening. We got there.*

* * *

Unbroken

When I made the decision in James Calder's office that I was going to make it to the Tokyo Olympics, it was because I wanted my dream to stay alive. The minute he said that eight months was achievable, I was locked in. I was never going to back away from it without a fight.

I've always hated the idea of giving up or not finishing something. It's one of my core values, and something I've had in me from a very young age. But as the weeks and months went by, I understood there was a wider motivation for me to get to the Olympics, too. I thought back to that horrible moment when I'd googled 'Achilles rupture time frame' and not seen a single positive outcome, and I wanted to prove Google wrong! I wanted to set an example. I didn't want anyone else to have to experience what I had. They would have hope.

I wanted to prove it wasn't the end of a career – which was largely what Google had shown me. That it was possible to come back.

I wasn't competing at the World Indoor Championships in Glasgow in March 2024, but a Spanish athlete who I've known for a long time – Maria Vicente – was competing in the pentathlon. We competed alongside one another in the same city back in 2019, when she was just eighteen, and I've always followed her career. She's super talented, so I was keeping an eye on her because I knew she was one to watch. She got a great start to the pentathlon, running the fastest time of everyone in the hurdles, but then in the high jump she pulled up when running the bend, and she grabbed her calf.

I saw the pictures and knew straight away that it was the same injury. I was devastated for her. I sent her a message on Instagram, wishing her all the best for her recovery and offering a chat if she ever needed it. She told me that so many people had mentioned my story to her and that she had already been thinking about it; that since the day we'd competed together in Glasgow, I'd always been a reference for her and an inspiration to move forward. She said she hoped she could recover and share the track with me again. I told her that, when she returned, we'd take a picture together on the track as comeback queens. I think that's what Gen Z does? If not, we could share a drink together after the comp – that's what nineties kids like me prefer.

'Your words keep me strong and hopeful,' she replied. 'I will fight to come back stronger and have that picture.'

It made me so happy that she'd seen my story and that she didn't have to be in a completely dark place in a moment that I know can feel so scary. I'd never refer to my time frame as a realistic one, because I don't feel like that's helpful or even necessary – but it's enough for people to just see that coming back from it is possible.

Although, thinking about it, it's possible that my story was a bit misleading for some. When I was back in France in June 2021, I came out of training to see three missed calls from my manager, Greg, who's based in London. I quickly called him back to find out what had happened . . . and he'd ruptured his Achilles! I couldn't believe it. He went to see James Calder and confidently proclaimed that he'd be 'like Kat, back running before the end of the year . . .'

. . . It took him a bit longer than me.

Towards the end of my rehab journey, I remember posting a quote on Instagram that really spoke to me. It was from a (fiction) book I was reading at the time called *Real Life* by Brandon Taylor.

Unbroken

'It feels impossible in the way only possible tasks can seem, when you know that despite the scale of what you must do, it's not really beyond the realm of possibility to do it, and so it feels impossible because you know you must.'

That was how I felt about making it to Tokyo: I knew it could be done, so I was going to do it.

I wouldn't ever do it again. I truly believe that getting to Tokyo was my biggest achievement, but I wouldn't do it again – it was just too hard. I could do it physically, but mentally I couldn't put myself through that again. It wasn't just about the injury itself, it was everything: the tight timeline I came back on; doing it with no one apart from those closest to me knowing; doing all the aerobic and technical work alone; doing it during Covid, with all the restrictions that entailed; doing it while living abroad, away from family and friends. It all amounted to the worst set of circumstances imaginable. I like the idea of doing something for a purpose, and I'm so happy that it gives athletes like Maria (and Greg) hope, but I would never ever come back so quickly again, because I put so much energy into it that it ruined me mentally, and it took a long time to recover from that. I couldn't do it again. I don't even know how I did it then.

Sitting on the plane to Japan, I felt so much pride at making it to my third Olympic Games, and eternally grateful to the team that had helped me to reach that point. Maybe that should have been enough.

Alas, once I knew I was going to make it to the start line, I wanted more. I wanted something to show for all the work we'd put in. I wanted to give something back to the people who'd worked so hard to help me, and to myself, too. Even

Katarina Johnson-Thompson

just finishing a full heptathlon and showing I could still compete with the best athletes in the world would be enough. Yeah. That might have been enough.

16
Despair

ALL I COULD SEE WAS THE FINISH LINE. ALL I COULD FEEL WAS the pain shooting up through my right leg every time I put my foot on the floor. But it was nothing I hadn't pushed past before, so I gritted my teeth, focused on the track in front of me and hobbled as fast as I possibly could towards that line. I just wanted to get out of that stadium – and out of view – as quickly as I could.

My heptathlon was over. My Olympics was done. My dream had been ripped to shreds.

I'd started the 200m in fifth place, which was amazing, because I'm normally way further back after the shot put. But I was worried; from the moment I stood on the start line for the final event on the first day of the Tokyo Olympic heptathlon, I knew that something wasn't right.

I first felt it during the high jump – a tightness in my right calf that was painfully familiar. It was the same feeling I'd had the day my (left) Achilles popped, in Réunion. It had never fully gone away. It had been manageable, especially in comparison to what I was experiencing with my left leg, but it was always there. When I went back to France, I constantly mentioned my right leg to the physios and doctor, but nobody could tell me what was wrong with it, and nothing showed up on the scans. Eventually, the doctor actually tried to refer me to a psychologist. They thought I was imagining it; like it was some sort of mental hangover from the Achilles rupture on my left side.

'I don't need a psychologist,' I told them. 'I need a physio to come and help me!'

During the high jump in Tokyo, it became a real problem. We did some work on it between jumps, trying to loosen it off as much as possible, then used the time gap between the high jump and the shot put (which started the evening session) to ice it, massage it, get painkillers – all the things you do when it's an Olympic Games and there's no turning back. Contrary to what I did at the European Championships in 2024, where I felt something and immediately pulled out of the comp, the Olympics isn't something you just quit. It only comes around once every four years (or five, in the case of Tokyo), and for most athletes, it's the absolute pinnacle of their sport. You don't have the option – I don't, anyway – to pull out.

It wasn't too much of an issue during the shot put, because of the movement pattern, but during the warm-up for the 200m it was getting worse and worse. After coming out of the call-up room, you always get a bit of time to get your blocks ready, practise your start (we call it a push-out) and do a little run before the start of the actual race. I did one push-out and felt my calf straight away. I tried to keep my face relaxed and not give anything away but all I could think was: *This is really bad, and I don't know if I'm going to get through it.*

'On your marks,' came the call.

'Fuck it.'

There was only one option. I had to commit. It's a horrible place to be in when you know something bad is going to happen, but you go ahead anyway.

I ran the best bend of my life, but as I came out of it: PAIN! Sharp pain soaring up my right calf. I stuttered to a stop before falling to the floor and curling myself up into a ball, closing my eyes tight to try to block out the reality of what was happening. As the emotions poured out of me, my whole body started to shake.

After a few seconds, I became aware of movement around me. I sat up and breathed deeply, trying to regain some composure as the medical team approached me. They wanted to help me off the track. I shook my head vigorously and stood up. Then I saw an empty wheelchair waiting just behind me.

Absolutely fucking not.

I shook my head again, and started hobbling away from them, towards the finish line.

I didn't want to be back in a situation where I couldn't do things for myself. I'd started the year that way and I couldn't deal with the thought of being there again. After everything I'd put myself through getting back to that start line, I was determined to finish the journey on my own two feet.

For a long time after Tokyo, I really struggled with people being overly sympathetic. Even though it came from a good place, I couldn't bear to see their faces feeling sorry for me as they offered their well-meaning best wishes. I hated that 'Oh God, wasn't it such a shame?' look. Some people saw me refusing the wheelchair and hobbling down the track as an instance of strength but, for me, I don't think that's strength. The strength, for me, came in the months before and the months after.

I had suffered yet another injury in front of the world, at a competition where I was seemingly destined for glory, but I didn't want that to be My Moment. I didn't want that 'Derek Redmond' moment, as memorable as it has been for *him*, to define my career. I didn't want it to represent a heartbreaking story, or what might have been, or to be associated with pity.

I wanted My Moment to be a moment of unquestionable strength.

With coronavirus cases still high in July 2021, every Team GB athlete felt extra anxiety heading out to the holding camp; catch Covid on the flight to Japan, and your Olympics could be over before they'd even started. There were lots of precautions in place before we boarded but, once we were on the plane, we could be sitting next to anyone. After everything I'd been through, I was so nervous about being exposed to Covid, being forced to isolate and missing the Olympics.

I was fortunate, but others weren't so lucky. After we landed in Tokyo, it emerged that six athletes had been deemed a 'close contact' of someone who had tested positive on the flight from Heathrow. One of them was the steeplechaser Zak Seddon, who was competing in his first Olympics. When we got to the holding camp, he had to isolate in his room for two weeks; all his meals were brought to his room every day. And because his event was one of the first ones on, he got taken straight from the holding camp to the call-up room in the stadium; he never even got to go into the Olympic Village. He competed, but didn't make it out of his heat, then got taken back to the holding camp to get his stuff and was back on the plane home. That was his whole Olympic experience. And there were a bunch of people like that. It was terrifying. Can you imagine putting all that blood, sweat and tears into one moment and then having it taken away from you because somebody near you had Covid?

It all made the atmosphere in that holding camp so tense and just *strange*. The first few days we were there, we were greeted by a load of Japanese people lining the walkway towards the shuttle bus, holding up boards saying 'Go Team GB!' They waved at us and gave us thumbs up as we passed. We thought it was so nice; it was incredible, how excited they were.

But once we'd settled in, we noticed that all of them were wearing earpieces. They weren't fans, they were security, making sure we didn't go anywhere we weren't supposed to. We quickly realized that we didn't have any freedom at all. Every single day saw us undergo a circuit: picking up a swab at one station, shoving it up your nose at the next, then dropping it into a bag with your name on it and depositing it at the final station. It was like being in *The Truman Show*, going through all these motions and not being in charge of anything at all.

Even once we reached the stadium and got off the coach inside the accredited area we were greeted by the same people: 'Yeah, go Team GB! We love you!' We knew they were only there to make sure we didn't run off into Japan. It was just mad.

While everyone else used that holding camp to apply the finishing touches to their Olympic preparation, I still had missed time to catch up on. I was training every day, and every session was super important, so the intensity was high and I was busting my gut getting through it. It wasn't ideal, especially because the track at the holding camp was (physically) really hard, which we knew could have an impact on my body. But I felt OK. I was so focused on my goal that there wasn't any space for fatigue – mental or physical – to affect me. I'd come so far; nothing was going to stop me from getting to that start line.

Throughout my whole rehab journey, one film had been stuck in my head: *Kill Bill* (stay with me here). It was actually one particular scene, which shows Uma Thurman's character lying in the back of a car she's stolen. She's just woken up from a coma that she's been in for four years after being attacked on her wedding day, and can't move her legs because she's been immobile for so long. But she has all these grand plans to find the people who attacked her and get her revenge, so she knows she needs to get herself moving. The camera closes in, first on her face and then on her feet, as she repeats to herself: 'Wiggle your big toe. Wiggle your big toe.' When she eventually manages to do just that, she smiles to herself and says, 'Hard part's over.' I'd first seen the film in 2018, and during my rehab journey I watched it over and over again. That scene resonated with me so much. I was stuck on my nan's couch as opposed to the back seat of a stolen car, but all I wanted to do was get from there to the start line in Tokyo – for me, that was the hard part. That was me 'wiggling my big toe'. Most people would think that doing the actual heptathlon would be the hardest part of my comeback, but in fact it was the journey to getting there in the first place.

During my time in Tokyo, in the holding camp and the Village, I watched *Kill Bill I* three times. It then became a bit of a ritual for me; before every heptathlon, I'd have to watch both *Kill Bill* films (because the best action is in the first one, but the best dialogue is in the second), which amounts to about seven hours. It was a big commitment!

I actually felt good when I woke up on the morning of the first day of the heptathlon. The day before, I'd called Steve Peters, the sports psychiatrist I'd started working with after Rio. He's been a big help in my career, especially come championships – if I'm mentally spiralling, he's always the person best able to put out that fire. But the day before the heptathlon in Tokyo, we didn't have much to talk about; I was all good. He told me to call him the next morning if I needed to and I did, just to tick every box. It was the shortest call we'd ever had. I didn't feel nervous, I was just ready to go.

The heat that day was something else. It was the kind of humid, suffocating heat that weighs heavy on your chest, making it feel hard to breathe. When we got to the stadium, there was a message playing on repeat out of the loudspeaker, saying: 'Hi everyone, today we'll reach 35 degrees. This is the hottest day of the year. Please drink water and let's survive this together.' Not exactly what you need on day one of a heptathlon: an automated voice saying 'let's survive this together'! But we had water, we had ice jackets and ice towels, and it wasn't exactly like there were many people in the stadium to add to the heat. Public spectators had been banned because of the pandemic, so for the first time ever Mum wouldn't be at a major comp to support me. Neither would Greg or Barrie. But their absence wasn't something I really noticed or thought about because the whole thing didn't feel real anyway. The stadium was largely empty, everyone who was there had their face covered by a mask. It didn't feel like this big thing was happening without them; it just felt like it was happening without anyone. It was a dead Olympics.

It was a strange feeling walking out into an empty stadium for the hurdles. Here was a venue built to stage the greatest show on earth; instead, it had become an uninhabited shell, dotted with athletes, officials and volunteers doing their best to bring some semblance of life to the bleakness. A stadium announcer shouted into the void. Random blasts of music broke up the endless silence. As I walked across the track to the start line, it all felt quite surreal. But as soon as I took my place in lane 7, right next to Nafi, my focus returned. This was it; all the work of the past seven months, all the pains, the struggles, the fears that had brought me to this point – a point that so many people hadn't believed would be possible. How much further could I go? I'd wiggled my big toe, and now it was time to see how many people I could take out – figuratively speaking, of course.

I'd been in the lane next to Nafi in Doha too and, as I settled into my blocks, I thought about that incredible race where I'd flown over the hurdles so effortlessly. I wanted that same start again. Even so, as I crossed the finish line and turned to look at the clock, I was stunned. I'd run my second fastest time ever! I couldn't believe it; it was actually happening. Pozz's coach, an eighty-year-old Cuban man called Santiago, had been trying to help me throughout the holding camp (mostly with feel-good stories and motivational talk), and was at the warm-up track that day. When he saw my hurdles race on the screens there, he ran around the track waving his arms in the air and shouting, 'It's over! It's over!' like I'd won the Olympics. I wasn't going to go that far, but the question definitely entered my head: What if we could actually pull this off and come away with a medal?

Then came the high jump, and the PAIN. At that stage, it was still manageable, though, and I somehow reached 1.86 metres – the second highest in the comp (behind Nafi), and the highest I'd jumped since my rupture. Although I still hadn't put anything official out about my Achilles injury, everyone knew about it, and I think there was some surprise (shock, even) among the other heptathletes at how well my first two events had gone.

That went up another notch after the shot put later that day, where I again pulled out the second-best performance of my career (13.31 metres!). I was in fifth place and very much in contention for a medal, with one of my strongest events, the 200m, coming up less than an hour later. All I needed was for my body to stay in one piece.

Everyone thought it was another Achilles rupture, obviously.

I knew straight away that this was something different. For a start, there was PAIN – actually, two separate, sharp pains. And, unlike that day in Réunion, I could walk on it. But, to be honest, as I slowly hobbled my way towards the finish line of the 200m, I couldn't have cared less what the injury was.

The dream was gone. The hep was done. I didn't care about my body, or if I was damaging it further by carrying on. I started hobbling faster, the adrenaline masking the pain just enough for me to break into a slow jog that took me all the way to the finish line, more than a minute after the other girls had crossed it.

I can see why some people saw it as 'bravery' to get up and

finish the race, but I don't see how I could have done anything differently. I don't see that scenario going any other way; for me, it was the obvious choice. I just wanted to get out of there as fast as I could, and I wanted to do it by myself.

It wasn't until much later that we found out three different things had actually happened in that moment when my 200m came to a sudden, agonizing halt: the sheath of my Achilles had completely detached, I'd torn my calf and the top of my soleus (the muscle at the bottom of the calf) as well. I don't fully know why it happened; maybe it was just one step too far. Maybe my right leg had been overcompensating for my left all summer. Maybe I was running faster than I had in years. Maybe it was the super-hard, super-fast track. Maybe it was the new spikes I was wearing. Maybe it was all of those things put together.

At the time, all I knew was that I had stopped running and my heptathlon was over. I had seen the other girls finish the race and start prepping themselves for day two of the competition and all I could think was: *That should be me. That future they are going into should be mine, too.* Life moves on so fast. For everyone else in that race, it was a split second in time. For me, it was life-defining. That moment, when I realized it was done – that it was too late to change anything – was the hardest thing to accept. How could it be over, after everything I'd done to make it happen?

The hours after it happened were incredibly tough. I was led off the track and into a small side room in the bowels of the stadium by the Head of Media for British Athletics, a small (but mighty) woman called Liz Birchall. She's about 5ft 1in, but she protected that room like a 6ft-plus 20-stone bodyguard.

Nobody could enter, aside from Bertrand. When he arrived, I collapsed into him and allowed myself to have a big belly-cry as the reality of what had occurred fully hit me. I finally had the answer to all those questions I'd had about my future. After wondering – and hoping – for so long, I finally knew.

It was late by the time I got back to the Village, on crutches, with my right leg bandaged up and placed into a protective boot. Pozz had stayed up waiting for me, wanting to be there for me; it was utterly selfless of him, but I was absolutely livid, because his 110m hurdles final was early the next morning. I told him to go to bed. 'You can't do anything. Please, just try to concentrate on yourself. Go and try to do well for us instead of being here. I understand completely.' Eventually, he listened.

The morning after, I was really sad; back in a boot, back on crutches, unable to go and get food because I couldn't carry anything for myself. I felt like I was back to square one. I had no immediate plans to leave my room but, when I got a message from Bertrand saying he really needed to talk to me, I knew something was up – because he's not a man of many words. He brought me down to one of the communal seating areas and basically told me that he was going to stop coaching at that point and was going to get a job. He had a young family and he needed consistency to support them, and coaching didn't really provide that. It was something he'd known for a while, but he hadn't wanted anything to get in the way of my preparation.

It was a really tough conversation. He hated having to tell me at that moment, when I was already so low, but it was the only option; he had to do it before I flew home and started my off-season, when he knew we wouldn't see each other for a while. It was a complete shock. Bertrand was visibly emotional, but at that point I was just numb to it all and almost in a state of shock. It took me years to fully realize that as a team, he had all these emotions tied to our partnership, which made it a tough moment for him, too. We had both battled something horrible and all-consuming; but at the time, I felt like this was just another bad thing that was happening to me, so I shut off any emotion attached to it. 'It doesn't even really matter,' I told Bertrand, 'because I'm probably going to retire anyway. So it's fine.' As I hobbled back to my room, my head was a mess; my Olympics had ended disastrously and now, twenty-one hours later, I had no coach. No support system. I'd have to find a whole new set-up. I'd finally had somebody who I completely trusted, somebody I enjoyed working with, somebody who I knew could take me to the top – somebody who'd done that already in Doha – and now I was going to have to start all over again. It felt like everything had been taken away from me.

It was one of the worst mornings of my life.

And yet, remarkably, that evening was one of the best of my life, or at least one which has left me with truly special memories. It started when I mentioned to Pozz how beautiful the views were from Team GB House, and how much I really just wanted to be outside on the grass, chilling and watching the sunset on our last night in Tokyo; to feel like I still had some semblance of independence and freedom.

'OK, let's just do it,' came the response.

Together with some of his training friends from Italy, they carried a load of deckchairs over to a grassy area overlooking the water and we sat outside watching the sun go down.

Gradually, more and more people started to join us. We'd watched Holly Bradshaw, my roommate in Tokyo, win her bronze medal earlier that evening, and she came and joined us. People were getting food and drinks in, I didn't have to move (Pozz was giving me piggybacks to the toilet), and it turned into one of those organically special summer evenings – the ones that nobody plans, but end up seared into your memory for ever. Every person there had been through their own journey and we were all there together, either feeling sorry for ourselves or celebrating with Holly. I guess that's the power of sport; it brings people together whatever the occasion. By the time I made it back to my room, the sun was up and my time in Tokyo was at an end; later that morning I boarded the plane back to the UK with Pozz by my side.

Before I left, I put out a statement on social media, trying to explain how I felt. It was such a complex mix of emotions. I was proud that I'd made it back to compete at the Olympics, when it would have been very easy to pull out and say I wasn't ready, and even more so for being on the way to putting a decent score together before the injury. I knew that, together with MJ, Andy and the rest of the team, I'd done everything I could for that to be possible.

But I was heartbroken at the way that it ended, as much for that team as for myself, because they had put so much into it while facing an incredibly tight time frame and a global pandemic. I felt like we didn't have anything to show for our efforts because, when you see the pictures of me from Tokyo, it looks like more misery. It looks like we didn't achieve anything when, in reality, we'd pulled off something that no one had ever done in the history of heptathlon.

Katarina Johnson-Thompson

I wanted my story of Tokyo to be a positive one. I'd set a goal to show people what could be done, and I was really sad at the thought that people would look at what happened and continue to believe that an Achilles rupture means your career is probably over. It was frustrating, because my left leg was in great shape, but I couldn't be shouting about how fine I felt, because that wasn't what people saw. They just saw me grabbing my leg on the track, being in pain and not being able to finish the heptathlon – and assumed it was my left one.

I ended the statement saying: 'I've been knocked [down] so many times and gotten back up, but it will take a lot of time for me to process this reality.'

I had no idea just how much time, or how deep and dark a hole that process would put me in.

What happened in Tokyo destroyed my relationship with the sport. I hated it. I felt like I'd given it everything I could and it had basically thrown it all back in my face. I had no coach, no base, no next step, and I couldn't face going through the whole process of starting again.

I didn't want to try any more.

The more I thought about things, the more I realized that life actually isn't fair. You could be walking around thinking everything's going well and everything's fine and then BANG: Achilles rupture. No warning, and nothing to change it or stop it from happening. If everything happens completely at random, totally out of your control, then what is the point in even trying? For one of the first times in my life, I realized that doing everything right doesn't always equal success. I'd tried with every ounce of my being, and I didn't even get the chance to lose honestly. I was deep in victim mentality mode and deeply sad about the sport. I was done with it.

I had lots of people around me – Mum, Pozz, my friends – all trying to help pull me out of it, but there wasn't really anything they could do. Shortly after Tokyo, I went away for a long weekend with my friends to Soho Farmhouse. Everyone was drinking and having a good time, but I was scared to drink too much in case I turned it into a *bad* time. In case it all came out. I didn't want to be *that* person, so I withheld it; locked it away. Even Mum couldn't bring it out of me.

Eventually, we spoke to James Calder to try to figure out what had happened in Tokyo. He advised me to go and see a specialist named Jarrod Antflick, who scanned my right side and said I needed surgery to remove the plantaris – a small muscle in the back of the leg that works with the Achilles tendon to flex the ankle and knee. I was fine with that; I wasn't bothered about timelines or getting back into training. I would have gone in for it the next day if I could, just so that I could waste some more time, do my rehab and not have to think about anything else. But Mum and I had flights booked to go to the Bahamas and Jarrod pointed out that it wasn't a great idea to be on the beach with a post-surgery wound. So, we delayed it, and then delayed it some more.

There's an episode of *The Last Dance* where Scottie Pippen talks about a period in his career when he needed surgery at the end of a season but he was so unmotivated (and unwilling to fuck his summer up) that he went on loads of holidays and then had surgery at the end, even though that meant he missed pre-season. That's exactly where I was; I didn't care how late the surgery was or if it would interrupt winter training. I wasn't even sure I was going back to training, full stop. I had two holidays, then went back to Montpellier to pack up my house. I eventually had the surgery at the end of September, when most athletes were getting back to work. And credit to Jarrod; after that surgery, I was pain-free in my right Achilles for the first time in years. He did an incredible job.

That summer was the first time Mum and I had been back to the Bahamas since Dad's funeral, and it was soothing to be there. Every time, the minute the plane lands I feel so connected to the island. It's as if my soul is tethered to that place. It was lovely to spend some time with my Dad's side of the family again and just be left to ourselves to enjoy the sounds of the sea. I did feel at peace, but I remember not being fully present. I felt like I was there physically, but I was just in my head the whole time.

Each morning, Mum and I would go on a sunrise walk along the beach. Well, she'd walk – I'd be hobbling along right beside her. At this point, I'd started to talk a little about what had happened in Tokyo, but it was always very definitive and emotional – not real opening up. I'd just say that I was finished with the sport, and go on about how it was a bad time, but I wasn't truly trying to get to the bottom of my feelings. It was so tough for Mum, because I don't think she wanted me to be finished, but she didn't really know how to talk to me at that time (it was the same for Pozz). I'd say things like, 'If you can promise me that I won't get injured again, then I'll consider giving it another go,' but of course, they couldn't promise that. The medical team couldn't. No one could. She was trying everything she could to give me hope, to convince me not to walk away and end my career in a way she thought I'd always regret. One of her attempts involved taking me to see a fortune teller in Southport, who told me that I wasn't finished yet and that she saw America and London in my future. Fortune telling wasn't something that I bought into, but I could see how much it meant to Mum, so I did it to keep her happy.

I hadn't given any thought to my future – both in terms of a new coach and a new set-up – until I went back to Montpellier to pack up all my stuff and say a proper goodbye to everyone. It was a very emotional trip. Bertrand and Bruno really wanted to help me; Bruno still wanted to be part of my team, as part of a hybrid set-up with another coach, but I couldn't really see it working. I rejected it straight away, maybe because I was still in my feelings a little bit and I didn't want to put any wheels in motion that would lead me back to training and competing. But it's something I really regret because it's basically the set-up I have now, and it's been great for me. Having people around you who really care about you is vital. If I'd been open to it back then I might not have wasted the next eight months of my career.

It was my agents, Greg and Dan, who really started the process of looking for a new coach. They were enquiring with different people and putting together a list of potential options. I knew they were doing it and I went along with things, agreeing to have meetings with people or chats, but I was a bit hands-off with everything. I just didn't have the capacity at the time to really look for something that would work for me, and I guess I was still keeping the sport at arm's length.

When they mentioned the name Petros Kyprianou, my ears pricked up. I didn't know him personally, but I knew of his athletes – he had a couple of good ones, including Kendell

Williams (one of the most talented heptathletes I've ever trained with) and decathlete Maicel Uibo, who won silver at the 2019 World Championships. Petros was based in America, and worked within the US college system, so I was impressed when he turned up in person to pitch to us. I was even more impressed when he pulled out a thirty-page booklet outlining what his approach would be, and how I was going to get back to the top, score 7,000 points, and break the world record. He'd detailed the weaknesses he'd seen in me over the years and explained exactly how he was going to fix me. I'd never seen anything like it before – he was very, very convincing.

My preference was to stay in the UK this time, so that I would be close to family and not have to move again. Originally Petros had said that he would come to London but, as talks progressed, we couldn't find the money it would have taken for his move. By this point, I think I'd accepted that I was going to carry on. I hadn't truly dealt with the feelings and emotions I'd had since Tokyo, but it was almost easier to get carried along with the tide than to make any real decisions about my future. So, I agreed to go over to Jacksonville, Florida, where Petros was based, for a trial two-week training camp. It was mid-November by the time that happened. I'd taken a couple more holidays with Pozz, just to delay things a little bit further, which meant that I'd had more than three months off – an eternity for me, or any professional athlete.

When I got there, Petros picked me up from the airport and dropped me off at the hotel, where he'd arranged loads of refreshments for me in the fridge. It was a totally different vibe to France, where I was looked after, but in a more relaxed, family-style type of way. In America, everything was thought out, prepared and put in place for you. They trained in a high school but it had amazing facilities: a 50-metre swimming pool, a track, manicured grass fields, recovery rooms and a quality gym. And they let us train there for free! One of my training partners had just bought a puppy and the puppy was at the track, which was obviously a huge win. And Petros took us all to a football game together.

I had a really nice time over those two weeks. I was training in the sun – unheard of in late November! – and I was so wonderfully detached from the rest of my life. I don't think it felt like reality, even. Unfortunately, what *was* real was that, mentally, I was not in a good place. I was in the worst place in my life, in fact, and I was just fumbling through, going through the motions of training, of life in general. But I was just sad. I was really, really sad.

By the end of 2021 I was on antidepressants; something I've not really wanted to speak about before now for various reasons, which I'll come to. It was actually when I was training in France pre-Tokyo that they were first presented to me as an option. Remember the doctor who suggested I needed to speak to a psychologist when I kept mentioning the pain in my right calf? Well, I took his advice and spoke to a psychologist in France, who suggested I could use some help. I completely rejected the idea. I was truly convinced that things were about to happen for me and couldn't see that I needed any help.

Looking back, I think people around me could probably see that wasn't the case; that I wasn't the real me. But the ones closest to me weren't there to tell me that – with me in France and Covid travel restrictions still in place, there was too much distance between me and those who knew me best.

But when I was in America, I knew things weren't right. Petros would pick me up to take me to training every day and, gradually, I'd push the time I got out of bed to meet him later and later. If I knew he was coming at 9.50 a.m., I'd look at the clock at 9.44 and think, *I've still got two minutes.* I just couldn't get myself out of bed. Steve Peters was someone I knew I could always speak to, and when I told him about how I was feeling, he said, 'Maybe it's time for a bit of help.' This time, I trusted that it was the right thing to do, because – unlike the psychologist in France – he knew me.

Initially, I felt like the antidepressants helped. I was more positive about life in general. But equally, I started taking them at a time when I was just starting to run again, and when you can do more things physically, you start to feel more like yourself. But when it came to competing, it felt like there was something missing. I didn't have the same intensity I normally would. When it came down to a third attempt throw or jump, when I'd usually back myself to pull one out, there was nothing there. No fire. No spark. I was just numb. When I look back now, I think it's impossible to know why I was really so bad competitively. Was it the pills? The training? Was it the fact that I was just over everything? Was it a long-term side effect of my Achilles issues? It's so hard to know, but at the time I did blame the pills a bit for me not being able to respond in competition.

That contributed to my decision to come off them just before the World Championships in Eugene in 2022, around six months after I'd started taking them. No one told me to stop, but I was worried that the medication was affecting my ability to compete, to feel, even just to care. All year, I'd felt like I was functioning,

Unbroken

I was present, I was competing, I was training, but I just wasn't *there* at all. So I stopped taking them of my own accord and have never gone back.

I know that, for some people, they really do work miracles; but for me, antidepressants weren't the answer. They were just another mask. For more than ten years, I'd been an athlete more than I'd been a person, and I'd done whatever I had to do to continue being that athlete, whether that was taking painkillers or speaking to a sports psychologist. Everything I did, or took, was just a way to bandage myself up. To mask something else. This time, the issue was my happiness, and the mask was the antidepressants. But they didn't work, because I didn't need a mask; I needed to change it all. I needed to find myself as a person, not just as an athlete. It was only months later, when I started therapy, that I recognized that.

Only those closest to me knew about the antidepressants. It wasn't something I felt anyone else needed to know about, and I thought long and hard before deciding to talk about it here. That was partly because I was worried that people might look at me differently. I felt like I'd finally erased that image of me from Tokyo, and I didn't want it to be replaced by another one that elicited those same expressions of sympathy. I also didn't want it to become the new 'imposter syndrome'; the only thing I'm asked about or the thing that people use to define who I am. I don't want it to become my whole story.

But I also know that there's an important conversation to be had here, because so many athletes still feel like they can't talk about mental health, which blocks significant progress in that area. The silence around the subject scares me. I only know of one athlete who's spoken openly about it, and that's Noah Lyles.

Katarina Johnson-Thompson

Athletes – and sportspeople in general – are constantly pushing themselves to the limit. A lot of athletes do things that shouldn't actually be humanly possible – particularly at the Olympics – and that requires you to push yourself to places that humans shouldn't, whether that's physically or mentally. I don't know what it is in our brains that makes us want to keep doing it.

We almost make it routine to push their limits week in, week out, because you know that everyone else is doing the exact same thing. Winning or losing often comes down to who can handle that the best. But a lot of the time, in athletics, your mental health isn't often considered; you frequently have to go against how you feel, otherwise it's seen as a weakness. In the years leading up to Beijing, I definitely felt that way. Looking back at myself in those World Championships in 2015, I see an athlete who was dealing with her mental health for the first time. I'd had small injuries before, which felt like the end of the world at the time, but what happened in Beijing was different; I was literally crying out for help and it was being ignored. Having to go out and run the 800m and do that shameful interview afterwards left a deep scar. You can have disappointments in life and then you can have things that really affect you; that was the first time that something really, deeply affected me, and did so for years afterwards.

In France, I discovered that they see the world differently. I think that's why I loved it so much there, because they did care about me as a person – they still do. And they try to find different values in life beyond just pushing yourself to the limit every day. But in 2021, I decided to do that. I decided to push myself to try to achieve my dream. Even then, they asked me if that was really what I wanted before helping me to achieve it.

It was my decision, but it broke me as a human. I was pushing every single boundary physically and mentally, and I found my limit. It took me years to fully get back to myself.

It's possible that my despair during that period made me somewhat uncoachable, but I don't remember and, at the time, I didn't really care. In any case, the beginning of the end for me and Petros came in Belgrade, at the World Indoor Championships in March 2022. It wasn't a comp that had really been on my radar, because I hadn't even started running properly until mid-December 2021 but, when I went back to Jacksonville in the New Year after spending Christmas at home, things started to feel good. I was pain-free in (both) my Achilles for the first time, I was back running properly and we could start building on Petros's actual training.

Right from the off, though, I'd had a nagging feeling that his coaching style was not the right fit for me. His type of training is based on dynamic, powerful bursts of energy, whereas I need that slow aerobic base; I build all my strength in the gym, and then focus on building power. He was expecting that power instantly, asking me to run drills like 600m time trials, even though I hadn't done anything in three months. It continued in much the same way. The more I was around it, the more I lost faith in it. And once you haven't got an athlete's trust, then it's just not going to work.

That said, in the New Year, I thought training was going really well. I'd do stuff and then get a load of positive feedback from Petros. I still don't know whether he was just building my confidence back up, but I believed it when he said I was in good shape. I started to add things up in my mind, and believe that I could perform well enough in my next comp to be in contention for a medal. As soon as I got to that point, it made sense to start the competitive process and see if Petros and I could build a proper coaching rapport in that environment. As the previous Indoor World Champion, I got invited to compete in the pentathlon at the 2022 World Indoor Championships in Belgrade on a World Athletics wildcard; we decided that would be a good place to open my season.

In hindsight, that was a big mistake. I wasn't ready, physically or mentally, to compete again.

After four of the five events in Belgrade, I was in sixth place and, with just the 800m left to go, I was done. I was done with putting myself out there. I'd put myself out there the previous year and it had gone horribly wrong, so in my head I was thinking: *Why am I still here, doing this?* With the right team around me, that would never have happened – maybe I wouldn't have even been in Belgrade in the first place – but at that time, I was in the wrong space mentally, with the wrong person in my corner.

The 800m was the only event I'd had real questions over before the comp. I'd done none of the prep work that I was used to; all we'd done was the odd time trial over 500m and, in the holding camp before the comp, I'd run the slowest time I had in years. It was the only event in that pentathlon that I knew I was going to be bad at, it was the only one I didn't have confidence in and it was the only one left after I felt I'd already done rubbish at the other four. It was going to be horrendous.

'I'm not doing it, and you can't change my mind.'

Unbroken

When you find yourself able to say that to a coach, you know you've got a problem. I could never have said that to Bertrand or Aston, because we were always in it together. I hadn't yet felt that connection with Petros, but I didn't see that as the problem at that point. I was still blaming myself and my own attitude.

What *actually* ruined the relationship was what happened during a meeting Petros called after one of my opening outdoor competitions the month after Belgrade. Things were continuing to go badly, and so I thought he might want to speak about why, or what changes we could make. But it felt altogether more personal than that. It felt like he wanted me to be the athlete that I had been before my Achilles rupture. I guess he thought me hearing that would be motivational somehow, but it really just felt like a massive punch in the gut.

My biggest fear at that time was that, post-Achilles rupture, I wasn't the same athlete; and it felt like he was saying that out loud, to my face. *I wish you were different.* What could I say to that? 'Well, this is me. I'm here, trying to change, with your help!' That one comment took years for me to undo, and marked the end of any possibility that Petros and I would build a lasting partnership. A month or so later, I found myself facing the exact same problems as I had in Belgrade. When we were getting crappy results at the start of the season in America, I could dismiss it based on the fact it was still early in the season, or maybe that a smaller comp wouldn't bring out the best in me, but when I got to Götzis and started the heptathlon in the worst way I could (I jumped 1.77 metres there!), I was like, *Wow, this is not a me problem. This is a training problem.*

I knew that I had to finish the heptathlon if I wanted to

qualify for the Commonwealth Games in Birmingham later that year, and that was a big goal of mine. There had already been a bit of a debate as to whether I should be picked for the team or not. I was still the reigning world and Commonwealth champion, which would usually be sufficient to qualify automatically, but there were a lot of girls hovering around the qualification score at that time, so I was told I needed to finish a heptathlon and get the qualifying score to get picked for Birmingham. That meant I had to finish at Götzis.

But halfway through, I was done. Checked out. Petros didn't have my ear at that point. Luckily, like the true guardian angel that she is, Denise was there to swoop in, stop my spiral and make sure that I finished the race. She refused to let me make a habit out of pulling out.

After the 800m, Petros told the press, 'When you support a champion, you have to support her in the good, the bad and the ugly. And right now, we're between bad and ugly . . .' He also said that he'd given me target numbers for each event, and that I'd fallen short in all of them except the 200m. It was really hard to hear, and I started to feel like maybe this partnership wasn't working out.

When I returned to Liverpool, I started writing down all the reasons I was going to leave Petros's coaching set-up and stay in the UK. I prepared this whole page of material, including counter-arguments and rebuttals and everything – I had it all written down on a big spiral map.

In the end, the phone call only lasted about two minutes. I wasn't prepared for that! It was a jarring, sudden end to our time together.

More jarring was this: with under two months to go before

the World Championships in Oregon, which would be closely followed by a home Commonwealth Games, I was without a coach again. And I was *full* of uncertainty; about who to trust, about my own form, about my mental state and the impact that it was having on my performance. It was a horrible place to be.

I felt like I'd reached my lowest point in the months post-Tokyo, when I hated the sport and wanted nothing more to do with it. But in 2022, I had to live through the consequences of that reality; I actually had to go *through* the low moment.

And honestly? I really don't know which one is worse: when you hit rock bottom, or when you realize how difficult it is to crawl back up.

17

Unbroken

I couldn't sleep.

It wasn't the rest room; between events at the 2023 World Championships in Budapest, we had our own little private rooms, blow-up beds to sleep on, pillows. They'd even turned the lights off for us. It was one of the best ones I'd been in.

It was my mind. I couldn't switch it off. Couldn't stop it from racing ahead.

I tried everything; deep sleep music at 528Hz (the best for reducing stress and helping you to relax), meditations on YouTube, but nothing was working. I just lay there with my eyes closed, worrying about what was to come.

'I'm scared I'm gonna fuck this up,' I told Aston, when I eventually gave up trying to sleep and called him in for a chat. With just the 800m to go, I was in first place, but Anna Hall, the pre-event favourite, was just 43 points behind, and was faster over two laps than me (she'd run 2:02.97 in Götzis earlier that year!). If I stayed within 3 seconds of her, I would become the world champion.

I knew that I was capable of doing that, and I wasn't nervous about the pain (I never am any more). I was scared that I wasn't going to commit to it – that I wouldn't commit to the pace. I was really scared.

When I said the same to Pozz, he reminded me of the many, many hours we'd spent playing Mario Kart and other games, and all the different times I'd done well in competitions. 'You're a killer,' he said, somehow keeping a straight face as he looked at me. 'When you get to that start line, that instinct is going to come in, so don't even worry about it.'

He was right. The minute I stood on that start line, I wasn't scared at all. I was ready. Aston's final instructions to me had been crystal clear: just keep to The Plan, which was to stay within 20 metres of Anna at all times (easier for me to stick to than the 3 seconds, because it was something visual). Between me and her, I had the easier job. It was much harder to be her and have to run as fast as possible, knowing that you can't control someone just sticking to you like glue. All I had to do was follow.

Aston had complete confidence in my ability to execute it. Nike had given me some headbands to wear, a silver one and a gold one, and I had both in my bag as part of the kit. I had a thought that it would be a cool thing to do to put them both on and then take one off at the finish line when I knew what medal I'd won. But Aston wasn't having it: 'Absolutely not,' he said. 'Put them back in your bag. There's no chance you're getting silver here.' I was a bit gutted about that; I thought it might have been a nice moment. But Aston was adamant: 'Don't even entertain the idea that you're gonna get silver.'

Katarina Johnson-Thompson

As we waited in our blocks for the starter's orders, a video played on the big screens around the stadiums, showing clips of previous heptathlon world champions. A decade on from my first senior World Championships in Moscow, it was a real trip down memory lane. I saw Jess winning in Beijing (something I hadn't seen or ever wanted to revisit), and both my successes and failures over the years. But when I caught a glimpse of the 2019 me competing in Doha, it reminded me: despite everything I'd been through the previous few years, that person was still me. She seemed so far away from the person who I was on that day in Budapest, but I knew that person was still in there.

She was different, though. In Doha, I'd been so confident in my ability to do well, whereas in Budapest I was still feeling things out. I was getting closer to who I knew I could be; a better version of myself. In Doha I was like a machine, and not in a good way. I'd experienced pain, but it wasn't anything like pre-Tokyo, at Tokyo and during the year after – the kind of pain that changed me as a person. Other injuries felt like setbacks by comparison.

The Katarina standing on that start line in Budapest had come back from two Achilles surgeries. She'd lost trust in everyone and learned how to regain it in the right people. She'd fallen out of love with the sport that had been her life since she was a kid, and she had gradually found a way back to it. She'd experienced deep grief and profound sadness and emerged the other side as a different version of herself; a whole one. No longer 'just' an athlete, but a rounded individual with emotions that weren't only connected to winning or losing. She had created space to be able to care about *herself* instead of just her performances.

Unbroken

I still wanted to succeed in athletics, and I still desperately wanted that gold medal in Budapest, but it wasn't all or nothing any more. If it didn't happen, it wouldn't make me any less of a person. I'd discovered who I was as a whole human, not just an athlete, and ultimately that had made me a stronger version of both.

Two more laps of the track, and everyone else would see that, too.

A year before Budapest, I'd been in a completely different place.

Around six weeks after splitting with Petros off the back of Götzis in May, where I felt and performed well below my best, I'd gone to Eugene in Oregon in the US for the 2022 World Championships full of uncertainty. I didn't know whether I was out of shape or whether my poor performances were down to my mental state, and I didn't trust anyone around me to tell me the truth. At the same time, Nan's health had really deteriorated, and I was worried about being so far from home and not knowing what was going on; I didn't even trust Mum when she'd call and tell me everything was OK.

I had all these questions and no idea what the right answers were.

I'd tried to find some during that six-week period between Götzis and the World Championships. Part of that involved approaching Aston about being my coach, via Christian Malcolm, who was head coach of UK Athletics (UKA). After Christian had spoken to him, I had a call with Aston and he was immediately suspicious: 'They're not making you come to me, are they?' he said, referring to UKA, who he thought were forcing me to have him as my coach just to get some order back. I couldn't help laughing: 'No, this was my decision!' He'd been wanting to retire for a few years, so he almost said no, but thankfully he decided to take it on (and he's just delayed his retirement again for another Olympic cycle!). Now, he claims that our partnership was always 'meant to be' because, back at London 2012, when he was coaching Louise Hazel, a cameraman mistook him for my coach, and panned to him after one of my javelin throws. Aston says that the cameraman knew, and foreshadowed the future.

With just six weeks to prepare for Eugene, I wanted to go back to something I knew, so I went to Montpellier where Bruno said he would help improve my fitness. We were smashing out 200m and 800m sessions (sessions that he knew I liked and that worked), hoping it would make a difference, and Aston would fly over every now and again to do a long jump or a plyometrics session. We were just getting to know each other really; we both still needed to learn how the other one ticked, while he needed to understand where I was at and, more importantly, what I needed to do to get back to some decent form.

It was during this period that I decided to come off the antidepressants. Pozz thought I should wean myself off them, but I'd already made up my mind that I was stopping. There was a period of adjustment, for sure, and I think I finally started feeling feelings again around the time of the Commonwealth Games – two weeks after Eugene, and days after my Nan passed away. It would probably explain the big breakdown I had in the middle of the Commies, when it first really hit me that she was gone.

The following September is when I started therapy, something I think I did need.

Neither Pozz nor I were in a good place in Eugene. There's

always a lot of change the year after an Olympic Games, and it just felt like we didn't know anyone on the team any more. Those joining the team were full of enthusiasm, happy to be there for the ride, and we just didn't feel that sort of stuff now. We became aware of it and isolated ourselves within a group of people who were talking about retirement. Not great motivation before trying to go out and compete.

Pozz spotted it. Instead of embracing the positives, we were finding faults and manifesting negativity. When we got home from Eugene, we really tried to focus on changing our attitudes, changing the way we saw our place in the team and trying to get our enthusiasm back. In that short gap between the World Championships and the Commonwealth Games – it was about two weeks – we held each other to account, promised each other we weren't going to be negative and if one of us slipped up, the other would call them out. We thrived off the back of that and we found big turnarounds in performance in just those two weeks, both of us winning medals in Birmingham after being well off the pace in Eugene.

I'd gone into the World Champs as the defending champion (from Doha, the 2021 event having been delayed a year), but came away from Eugene having finished eighth. My feeling throughout the whole comp had just been the same as it had all year; I'm here, I'm competing, but I'm really just in my head. I felt like I was in the competition but not really competing for anything, just making up the numbers. I'd never experienced that before, especially on an athletics track; I'd always competed to try to win a medal. Now I was there feeling like an NPC (a non-player character in a game), and it was one of the worst feelings I'd ever had in my life.

The one positive from it was that Aston was there. We'd done some sessions in the holding camp and he'd started to rebuild the trust that had been eroded over the prior six months. A lot of the time, Petros would react to things overly positively. If I was doing a 150m, he'd say: '16.9, that's so fast!' Whereas when I'd do a 150m with Aston in the holding camp, he'd be noting down the time quietly. He wouldn't say whether it was good or bad, he was just silent. I preferred that; I understood that it meant it was probably bad but appreciated that he wasn't trying to lie to me by saying it was good. That gained my trust in a big way.

During the competition, I could see how he wanted me to do well. I could see how he was thinking of ways to get me better, and how he wasn't even that angry that I was doing badly. I felt like he was on my side instantly. I came away from Eugene compelled to do well for him. It was the turning point in my motivation.

Even more than that; it was the turning point in how I felt about the sport.

It was Aston who helped me through the Commonwealth Games while I was dealing with Nan's death. I barely trained between the World Championships and the Commies because of everything that happened, but he still added 200 points to my score, just by being him.

I felt like I overcame so much to win the Commonwealth in Birmingham. It was a victory that was bittersweet, combining my happiness at winning with the sadness of Nan not being there to see it. Dad had never seen me come out the other side of Rio and I felt the same about Nan, whose last knowledge of me competing would have been in Eugene, and that broke my heart.

The girls I was up against at those Commies could quite easily have beaten me. Another British heptathlete, Holly Mills, had already done that in Götzis earlier that year, when my lowest moment had coincided with her best. She was ready for blood at that Commonwealth Games. It was a big battle at the time, so overcoming that made me realize I still had it in me to compete.

For so much of that year, I'd become used to hearing commentators talk about my age and how many champs I'd been to. And it's not just me – I can't watch an athletics meet without hearing a commentator talk about someone's age in a negative way. I remember watching the Olympics coverage on TV in Paris and hearing one commentator talk about an athlete who was twenty-nine – twenty-nine! – saying, 'Let's see if they've got eleven more seconds of their career left in them.' I don't know why they do it. It's as if they don't have any real insight to offer into an athlete's performance, training or background other than to say, 'Here's Katarina, who's thirty-one now . . . You have to wonder how many more seasons she's got left in her.' It's always something like that. In 2022, they'd see my performance and talk about the number of injuries I'd had and say, 'Oh, she's had a terrible time of it.'

When I look back now, I know that none of those things were anything to do with it – 2022 was probably the year I suffered the fewest injuries. But you take on that stuff and start to believe it, and then you start to *feel* it. It's the same as my Whoop band (a health/fitness tracker); if it tells me I'm feeling like crap today, I'll believe it and act accordingly. If I don't look at it, I might recognize I'm not feeling that great, but I'm still able to get on with my day and my training anyway.

If you've got people telling you you're past it and you're probably not going to PB any more, it takes an awful lot of either ignorance or belief in yourself to put out a good performance anyway. It's easy to believe other people's stories of you, even to start repeating them, losing your own opinion. Because when things go wrong and you don't know why they're going wrong, if those people are liars, at least they're providing an explanation.

It probably took me a year after the first half of 2022 to understand that, actually, the whole past-it thing isn't my story at all. I don't care what you say, it's not my story. I have Aston (and my therapist) to thank for helping me to figure that out. When no one else was expecting anything from me at all, Aston was one of the people who told me a positive story about myself. He had patience. He had a vision that nobody else could see, including me! And he stuck with that. He was also the one who told me to see someone who wasn't a sports psychologist, so I probably have him to thank for that too.

Right from the start of training with him, Aston had told me that we wouldn't be doing an indoor season at all in 2023. He wanted all the winter months – from October through to May – to just be training, training, training, before I touched a track again. It was the complete opposite of what I'd had the year before, but he was adamant: 'We need work. That's all you need, work and training, so we can get you into a place where you can go out and compete.'

I trusted him, especially after what had happened in Belgrade. Petros had a thirty-page plan but, really, there was no strategy. We were doing a comp here, a comp there, whereas Aston's plan was clear: we're going to train until this point and then

Unbroken

we're going to compete. I knew what I was doing from the outset.

It was a tough winter, though. Aston's training had all the strength, power and heavy plyometrics work of Mike's sessions, but with *less* rest, plus the hard technical work of Bertrand's. It was intense! My body hadn't had hard, prolonged, high-intensity work for a few years, especially if you add in the year I spent recovering from the Achilles rupture, when I was just trying to get fit. I was basically a couple of years behind on my endurance base and my strength.

But Aston had so much patience with the process, and he helped me to become process-driven again. It wasn't just him; the team of training partners I gained from working with Aston were just as important. They're salt-of-the-earth people. Dependable. Good training. Good vibes. Jazmin Sawyers, Zak Skinner, Livvy Breen – they were everything to me on my journey. Being in and around them and Aston day in, day out was the change I needed. It helped me to see athletics through their eyes, which is to see something they absolutely love! (Ironically enough, in Zak's case, as he's visually impaired – but when it comes to the sport, his eyesight is often so much clearer than mine.) That helped me to see the joy in it again. They're the ones who brought that back to me.

As the months ticked by, Aston was always trying to convince me that I could come back better than ever. I'd just nod. 'Yeah, I hope that too.' He was always talking about Paris, and I was just like, 'Yeah, that's a nice dream. We'll see. I'm just here enjoying it for now. I just hope to be competitive, that's all.'

I'd get glimmers of hope every now and then in training. And

I knew for sure that I was working very hard, especially with the 800m sessions where I was pushing myself to the limit every single week. But while I was building on 'glimmers of hope', I was seeing my competitors excelling. The 2023 indoor season saw Nafi, Anna Hall and Adrianna Sulek all score over 5,000 points in the pentathlon. Meanwhile, my occasional good training run off the back of scoring 6,377 at the Commonwealth Games felt a million miles away from where I needed to be in order to compete with these athletes in a few months' time. That's why the goal was always the Paris Olympics in a year's time and not the 2023 World Championships coming up that summer in Budapest.

Once we got into competing in 2023, we were pretty much straight into the main events. I started with Götzis at the end of May. I remember I was so nervous for that comp. I'd done a lot of training, I trusted the people around me, and our group had got off to an amazing start that year, with Jaz setting the tone when she won the European Indoors with an iconic jump of 7 metres. That gave me confidence, because I knew that Aston's training was definitely working. But it also meant if I didn't do well in Götzis, it would be solely down to me. Putting yourself out there when you've done everything you can is one of the hardest things to do as an athlete, because that's when you find out who you really are.

I didn't have any more excuses. I'd done the work; I was in a good place. The only question was: what have you got? Are other people right, or am I? I was so scared to get the answer.

Naturally, I got off to a terrible start, whacking one of the first hurdles, almost falling and bruising my take-off foot in the process. But weirdly, I think that actually helped to ease the tension I'd been feeling. Initially, I was gutted and had all those thoughts of 'Oh god, not again,' but five minutes later I'd switched into a different mindset. I knew my score was going to be below my best anyway, so I stopped worrying – I had nothing to lose.

It allowed me to relax into the heptathlon and just attack everything with freedom – something that really showed over the next two events. I threw a PB of almost 14 metres in the shot put, but it was the high jump that was a real breakthrough moment. Ever since my Achilles rupture I'd harboured a belief that I was never going to jump as high again – a belief Aston had constantly told me was not true. In Götzis, I got over 1.89 metres (and had a good attempt at 1.92 metres), which gave me a glimmer of hope about what I could still achieve.

Anna had a great overall comp and won with a really good score (6,988), but I was second with 6,556, and I finished knowing that I'd left points out there in both the hurdles and the 800m (which I'd really messed up). Add both of those things together and it equated to around 200 points. If you added those to my total, then I could be right back in the mix for the medals. That was all I wanted for that year – a little bit of competitiveness that we could build on going into the Olympic year.

Aston gave me a week off after Götzis and it just happened to coincide with Beyoncé's tour dates in the UK, so I used my week off in the best way I knew how: I went to see her twice! Both times I was in the standing section, dancing the entire night. The first was with one Dame Denise Lewis, the day after I got back from Götzis, so I wasn't exactly resting; but I did have an excellent time, especially as Beyoncé looked right at me and waved. (OK, I doubt she waved to me, but I'm manifesting positive things and it's my story, so nobody can tell me different!)

No one (aside from Aston and Pozz) was really expecting much from me in 2023. I wasn't being spoken about at all in terms of being on the GB team going into the World Championships in Budapest – not from a heptathlon point of view or even a British Athletics one. I'd come eighth in Eugene, and a year later, I couldn't even get onto a poster showing who'd made the team.

I don't get motivation from negativity, but that kind of stuff did make me see the sport for what it is – and it's something I've realized a lot more since then. It's brutal (I mean, eighth best in the world at something isn't *that* bad!) and it moves on quickly. It ties in well with one of the things that therapy has confirmed: life isn't fair. The sport is very fast-paced and it's always going to get hyped by potential more than previous success. It's always about the Next . . . And I'm not angry at that any more. I just expect that to always be the case, because people get bored with the 'same old', don't they?

There was a moment though, just before the World Champs, when I started to think that maybe Aston was right; maybe I did have a chance of a medal in Budapest. It was after the London Diamond League meeting at the end of July, the final comp we did before going into the holding camp. We'd really been working on my long jump since Götzis, knowing it was one of the events that we wanted to score well in, and in London I jumped 6.60 metres, another big post-Achilles turning point: 23cm further than my post-injury best. Adding a jump like that to my heptathlon score would make me competitive, and that was when I started to believe we might have a chance – probably not at gold, but at a medal.

I knew I was in shape, too. The 800m sessions (designed by Bruno, who still helps me out) were tough, probably tougher than the race itself. In the holding camp before Budapest, just over a week before the heptathlon started, the session was: 400m (55.13), 300m (41.95), and then three lots of 200m (29.19, 30.51, 30.43). I felt ready.

After her performance in Götzis, Anna was undoubtedly the favourite for gold going into the comp. But during the second event (the high jump), we saw a door open. We saw that maybe it wasn't going to be as straightforward as everyone had assumed, that maybe Anna wasn't on top form, and the gold therefore was anyone's to try to grab.

And I think I was the only one who went for it.

When I was younger, I'm not sure I would have been able to see that door ajar; I'd have stepped into line with everyone else. That comes down to one thing: experience. I remember speaking to my therapist in 2022, at a time when I was struggling with being the older athlete, questioning if I could still compete. If I could still win. She asked me what I had now that I didn't have when I was younger. Experience, that was the answer. It was how Jess beat us all in 2015, when I was too young to realize that it doesn't matter how talented people are or what they can do; it's all about how you handle yourself on the day.

In Budapest, I handled myself really well. There was a moment early on in the high jump where I'd cleared my opening height and then needed three attempts to clear my second height. It's still scary to think how differently things could have gone. Luckily, it went the way I wanted it to (I ended up clearing 1.86 metres), because I was just so focused on not repeating the same mistakes again. I was able to stay in the moment and concentrate on what I needed to do to get over the bar (right leg coming through, right shoulder and right knee going up), instead of worrying about what would happen if I knocked the bar off again.

I knew how to deal with that situation because I'd been in it before, and I'd suffered the consequences of not taking an opportunity that's in front of you. I'd done it in Beijing with the third attempt in the long jump, when I could have run and jumped 6.70 metres, and who knows what might have happened. But I didn't take that opportunity. At the World Championships in London in 2017, I didn't take it again, with the high jump that went wrong. There had been so many different times when I could have won and didn't, and I didn't want that feeling ever again.

It wasn't even like I really got off to a good start in Budapest. If you compare what I did there to Eugene in the hurdles and high jump, they're really quite similar. The difference between the two competitions was my belief and my team. The belief that everyone on my team had put into me in the months before Budapest, the change in my attitude to one of believing that anything can happen, and my ability to stay in the moment and believe that you can be better than what you're putting out every single time you release a throw or attempt a jump.

You've got to keep turning the screw each event.

Overnight, it was Anna who was in the lead, with me 93

points behind. But the long jump went my way and put me 19 points ahead going into the javelin – when I knew I had to turn that screw to avoid her having any kind of lead in the 800m.

That second day of the heptathlon was disgustingly hot. Probably even hotter than Tokyo. And there was no shade at all for the javelin; we were squished like sardines onto this tiny bench covered by a sliver of shade. Some people were sitting behind a bin, desperately trying to find any cover they could from the burning sun. I had no motivation to get up and drill in my throwing technique; all I wanted to do was curl up into the minuscule bit of shade that was left. I decided I'd just run out of there when it was my turn to throw, and then get out of the sun as fast as I could. That's how hot it was.

But then my first throw went quite far, and it felt quite easy, and I thought, maybe I'll just grin and bear it and do some practice and see if I can get one out on this next one. To my complete shock, it flew over 46 metres! And I'm still not sure how, because it felt like my aim was to survive that event more than thrive in it. I just wanted to avoid getting sunburnt or heat exhaustion!

My job in the 800m was so clear. So simple. People talk about that race as if it was a really challenging task, but I saw it as straightforward. The whole thing was set up for me. It wasn't like the Olympics in Paris in 2024, where I had no real control over what was going on with Nafi behind me. In Budapest, I was in first place, and I had control over my performance; my destiny. There was no way I was going to let that escape me.

Katarina Johnson-Thompson

When I was warming up for the race, Bruno looked me in the eye and said: 'I am sure, I promise you, that last session you did – that hurt so much more than what you're about to do. This will be fine.' He said the same thing to me before the 800m in Paris, and he's been right both times. The training sessions for the 800m are so much harder than the race, and I know that for sure because I set PBs in both Budapest and Paris and neither of them touched the sides in terms of the pain I felt while running them. Don't get me wrong – when I crossed the finish line, I knew I was tired, but during the race my brain wasn't aware of the pain my legs were experiencing. It was totally focused on The Plan.

Right from the start gun in Budapest, I had Anna in my sights. She went out incredibly hard. When I look back, it was a little bit shaky towards 300m to go, but at the time, I felt in complete control. I remember seeing the camera that was on the inside of the track moving alongside me, and not Anna, despite the fact she was 20 metres ahead of me, and that only reaffirmed my feeling that I was still in control. At no point did I feel it had gone beyond my reach.

The crowd was so loud for that race because one of the Hungarian athletes, Xenia Krizsan, had a shot at the bronze medal; and with 300 metres to go, she was right up alongside me. I could hear the roars getting louder and louder, but at that point I was so focused on Anna that I had no idea why – I just prayed it was nothing that was going to impact me in a negative way! With 200 metres to go, I remembered that Bruno had told me to 'try and reel Anna in', and I'm glad that he did. Even though I didn't manage to do that, it definitely helped to keep the gap as small as I needed it to be. Anna crossed the finish line and turned to look back down the track, seeing me coming up right behind her. It had been an epic battle, and we'd both given absolutely everything we had to try and win.

As I lay on the track at the end of those two laps, my legs and lungs burning, I couldn't quite believe what was happening.

I was world champion again.

It was something I had thought was beyond me. Something I'd believed had been taken away from me by the triple whammy of Covid, an Achilles rupture and the calf injury in Tokyo. It was against all the odds; something that had been consigned to the history books. Nobody thought that an athlete who was so reliant on jumping to compile a big score would stand a chance of making it back to the very top. And I don't blame them – for a long time, I didn't see it myself, either. But our little team had a vision, and had worked hard day in, day out to make it happen. Pushed for it relentlessly. It was the most satisfying feeling to know that we'd done something that nobody else thought I could do any more.

What won it for me that day wasn't my performance, it was my experience. It was knowing how to use everything I'd been through to my advantage. It was understanding that, although sometimes you can't do anything about someone who's just on fire, most of the time the victory can be anyone's. It's just about how you handle yourself.

I'd known it on the start line of that 800m already, but as I lay on the track at the finish, I knew that the version of myself who'd won the World Championships in 2019 was truly gone. The new me was stronger as a person. More competitive. Able to find ways to win that weren't just reliant on putting out a big score. In Doha, it had felt like a relief. This time, I was absolutely buzzing.

I said then that it was the best day of my life, and I stand by that still.

I see my life now as almost split in two, between the Kat I was pre-Achilles rupture and post. That's how big of an impact that injury had on my life. It wasn't just about the physical trauma, or the challenge of getting back to being the best athlete I possibly could be, it was about the mental and emotional journey that it sent me on. It's one that has taken me years to understand.

Now, I know that sometimes really bad things happen and you don't know why. There's almost always a reason, but sometimes it takes time to understand what that is. It took me years to figure out that what happened in Tokyo, while horrendous to go through at the time, was actually the catalyst to me discovering who I was as a whole human, not just an athlete.

All my life I'd been: athlete, athlete, athlete. But when Tokyo happened, I didn't care about athletics any more. I hated the sport – the thing that, aside from Mum and Nan, had been the only constant in my life.

Losing it led me to the therapy that I did need, and that helped me to become a more rounded person – to care about me more, instead of just my performances. It helped me to process myself as a human first; one who has these emotions that can't always be ignored or suppressed. I wasn't able to use that in 2022, but I was in 2023. Alongside training well and maintaining my competitive desire to succeed in athletics, the lessons I've learned from therapy helped me enormously in my journey to becoming a world champion again.

Unbroken

I felt broken after Tokyo. But if I hadn't gone through that period, who knows what kind of athlete and person I would be now? So I say thank you to the Blue Shell (which I've since had tattooed over my Achilles scar as a constant reminder that anything can happen, at any time), for setting me on this path, and helping me to see that there's always a route back – one which sometimes takes you somewhere that's even better than where you started.

18

Paris

I woke up on the morning of 4 August absolutely buzzing to discover my period had arrived. It had been due to start on the 6th but the previous month it had been two days late, and I was beyond worried that was going to happen again – because that would mean it would be starting on day one of the Olympic heptathlon in Paris. I always suffer with crippling pain on the first day of my period (I'm fine by day two) and I have to take really strong painkillers to manage it, so I was desperate to avoid that clash.

I was so stressed about it! There's a medication you can take that blocks your period from coming (I actually took it in Budapest in 2023), but I hate doing that to my body, and it can make you a bit emotional. You have to take it two days before your period is meant to start too, so you need to make the decision to take it early. I was in the Team GB holding camp in Saint-Germain-en-Laye, not far from central Paris, where we were fine-tuning things before going into the Olympic Village, and from the minute we got there I'd been willing my period on. Every night I'd lie in bed and think about it coming on.

So when it actually happened, I was over the moon. But as I was getting ready to head down for some breakfast before our last shot put session, the pain hit me; and it was one of the most debilitating period pains I'd ever had in my life. I had my strong painkillers with me, but I wanted to get some food in my stomach before I took them. I tried to just carry on getting ready but every five minutes or so I'd have to stop to lie down and curl up on my side, until the cramps eased long enough for me to get up and try again.

Serves me right for being happy about my period coming.

I made it to the breakfast room, but I didn't feel like I wanted to eat at all. I got my usual plate of scrambled eggs and toast and sat there just pushing it around my plate and eating tiny, bird-sized mouthfuls. My physio, Sarah, suggested some porridge and a smoothie instead. I decided to give it a try and brought some back to our table where Aston had joined too. We were chatting away but I was feeling worse and worse and got up in the middle of a conversation, telling everyone I was going outside for some fresh air.

As I lay on a bench outside, Sarah came out with some coffee. She took one look at me and said: 'You look really sick. Go upstairs and I'll tell Aston that we're going to delay the session by an hour or so.' Weirdly, the dining hall was over the road from our hotel and as I was making my way across, I suddenly felt really faint. I rushed into the hotel reception and MJ was there, just coming down for breakfast. Apparently (I don't remember this, but he told me afterwards), I said to him, 'I'm just gonna lie down here for a sec,' and then proceeded to slowly sit down on the floor, then lie down and pass out.

Everyone always tells me that I control everything in my life; that I never just let go of the reins – and, apparently, that's true even when I faint. There was no dramatic fall to the floor, just a slow, controlled descent before I allowed myself to pass out. (I can only image it looked something like Gillian McKeith's 'episode' on *I'm a Celebrity . . . Get Me Out of Here!*)

I opened my eyes to see a doctor holding my wrist, trying to take my pulse and check my blood pressure. Then they closed again. The next time they opened there were some screens around me. Then they closed again. I opened them again to see more screens, as if someone had just died right there in the hotel reception. I was so embarrassed. 'I just need to go upstairs,' I said, dragging myself up and into the lift. I was shivering, suddenly freezing cold, but at the same time, my skin was soaked in sweat. I made it back to my room, vomited up the small amount of breakfast I'd forced down, and fell into bed.

By lunchtime, I was absolutely fine – back to normal. I'd never, ever experienced that around my period before, and I still can't believe it happened the weekend before the Olympic heptathlon started. When I saw Aston later that day, I asked him what he'd thought when he'd seen me passed out in reception (he'd walked in while I was lying there surrounded by screens).

'I just thought we were going home,' he chuckled. 'I thought we were just gonna pack our bags and go home.'

As world champion, I didn't feel any extra pressure going into an Olympic year. As someone going into their fourth Olympics, though, it was a different story. After three Games, I had a total of zero Olympic medals, and the idea that Paris might be my last chance to change that kept me up at night for months.

Underlying that was a burgeoning anxiety about getting injured again. I think I had a scan (of various things) every single month leading up to the Games – I'm now an expert at lying super still, and also low-key scared about the long-term effects of the radiation from a lifetime of injuries and scans. I had three in the three weeks leading up to the holding camp, and one more while I was in there. Basically all of them were precautionary. No one around me wanted to make any mistakes so even the slightest niggle was met with a decision to scan, just to be sure. That constant, low-level anxiety is horrible.

You wake up, you feel a twinge, so you go into training and you question if the session is actually necessary. If the answer is yes, then you go to the physio, to see whether or not they can do anything to release it. But once you tell a physio you're in pain they don't want the responsibility of releasing you back to training, in case you get injured. So then they take you to the doctor who wants to do an ultrasound, of course. Meanwhile, it's two hours later and you're *still* trying to get ready to train and warm up. All you wanted was to get a muscle loosened and now it's become this big thing, and the doctor wants to get an MRI 'just to be safe'.

It became a never-ending conversation of people escalating situations because they didn't want to make the wrong decision for me, especially given what had happened in Tokyo after I'd been talking about my right calf in the lead-up to the Games. And I knew that if I overrode them, then the responsibility would all be on me. It happened so many times. My alternative? To not mention the niggle, just because I couldn't be bothered with the constant physio or extra exercises – and that left me with equivalent, if not higher, levels of anxiety.

It was constant. I couldn't just go to training and *train*.

Heptathletes – and others who compete in athletics – are a different breed. It's not like we're footballers, competing week in, week out. We get our one big chance every four years. And that leads to a pressure that we don't highlight enough as professionals: the pressure to just *be* healthy, and show up at the starting line unencumbered. When people ask me if I'm going to do a fifth Olympics, I think, yeah, I'd love to. But I don't know if I can handle that pressure every single week – the constant anxiety of wondering whether my body is going to play ball. I've had a lifetime of it. And that's the thing that's the hardest to deal with day after day.

One of the things that was different in coming into an Olympic year as world champion was the amount of media and brand work that was coming my way. After winning in Doha, the turnaround to the Tokyo Olympics was so short that I didn't really do anything brand-wise. I turned down a lot of opportunities (and money!) because I wanted to focus on being as prepared as possible for the Games. Then Covid hit, the Olympics got postponed and I lost out financially again (various sponsorships depended on me competing at the Games).

So, coming into 2024, I had all these concerns in my head, because the only time that opportunities really get handed to athletes on a plate is leading up to an Olympics. I found it so difficult to get the balance right between taking the money now, not knowing for sure whether I would still be competing by the time the next Olympics comes around, or playing the long game like I did in 2019, which I regret. Who knows what's going to happen in life? Ultimately, I had to make a choice, but I was concerned that by not committing fully to one or the other I would end up damaging both.

Juggling those decisions with the aforementioned body anxiety started to feel seriously overwhelming so, when we left for a warm-weather training camp in Turkey in March, I told Greg I just needed to not be bothered with anything that wasn't training-related for those three weeks. I'd felt like I was experiencing interruption after interruption at home, and I needed the space to see if I could put together three weeks of solid training, so I could feel good about myself. Once I had that, maybe then I could start to think about doing some of the stuff he was offering me.

I didn't hear from him the whole time I was away, but the camp itself was a bit of a disaster. Within the first few days of us getting there, Jaz ruptured her Achilles. Thankfully, I wasn't physically there to see it happen (because I might have genuinely gotten sick), but it was so sad because she'd been jumping well and we were both getting so excited about being at the Olympics together; talking about when we'd go into the Village, who we'd room with and how we were going to celebrate if we won medals. We'd been rooming together for that camp too, so when I woke up the morning after she'd flown home and looked to my left to see her bed empty and all her stuff gone, it was an immediate reminder that someone's dream had just ended. Bang. Straight away. It resonated so much with what had happened to me.

It was hard to process at the time, because it strengthened the belief that anything can happen at any stage and sport isn't fair and life isn't fair, and what's going to happen to any of us and what's the point? I'm happy that I was there to help, and could offer Jaz my experience to make hers better, which is all I'd wanted when I was going through it. She was so strong about it, too. Apparently, the thing she was most worried about was me seeing her like that and the effect it might have on me, which is just about the most selfless thing I've ever heard.

The week after Jaz left, I pulled my quad. It was a very minor pull, but it had a sizeable impact on what I was doing at the track and where my energy and focus were placed. When you pick up these small injuries, you almost end up being busier than you would be if you weren't injured. You still have to find ways to train and stay fit, but you also have to add extra physio and rehab exercises into the mix. In the end, you're more drained than if you were doing your usual training, but without any of the benefits – and that's not only physically but mentally, too. I was immediately questioning whether I should or shouldn't push myself. Should I persevere anyway because Turkey was meant to be all about getting a steady flow of training in, or should I take my foot off the gas a little and then push again when I got back? But I knew that when I left Turkey, I'd have to start talking to Greg again, and he'd have a bunch of non-training stuff for me to address. I didn't know what the best thing was for me to do. It was a lot to deal with.

Everyone is nervous before their first heptathlon of the year. I don't care who you are; everyone gets self-conscious, nobody knows what to expect or how training has gone. It's always the same. That's why we normally open at Götzis, or a comp away from a major championships, but this time I decided to open up at the European Championships in 2024. It fell around the

Unbroken

same time as Götzis anyway so I thought, why not do it and try to add a European gold to my World gold and then try to complete the set in Paris? Doing something like that (a bit like the Serena Slam in tennis, where one player holds all four majors at the same time) had been a dream of mine for a long time. When I won the World Outdoor title in Doha in 2019, I was also the holder of the European and World Indoor titles, plus the Commonwealth Games crown from 2018. Coming away from Doha, I saw 2020 as a chance to potentially add European and Olympic titles to that haul, so I'd have them all at the same time. It was like an Ultimate Goal for my career. In 2024, five years on, I saw another opportunity to do something pretty special.

I guess sometimes you get a bit greedy.

By the time Rome came around in June, I was not in a good place. I was burnt out. Between media work, training and constantly trying to manage little injuries, it had started to feel as if I didn't have a moment to myself. And I need that downtime, especially when things are getting on top of me. Meditation is something I've been trying to do more of in my day-to-day life, because I overthink, and I can get carried away trying to control every single aspect of my life. Sometimes that involves listening to a guided meditation, other times it can just be a moment to yourself to look around and be completely in the moment. Leading up to Rome, I'd really started to struggle to find time for those things.

I'd been struggling physically too, with pain in my right Achilles, which I hadn't had in years. I was waking up with it every morning. Rome was absolutely the worst preparation I've ever had. Everyone who watched that comp has said the same thing to me: it looked like I didn't want to be there. Even Bruno said it when I met up with him afterwards: 'You know, you don't have to be here, if you don't want to. Because it looks like you don't want to do it. Do you want to do it? Because it's fine if you don't. Has anyone ever asked you that question? Because I think that's an important question to answer.' His words slapped me out of it a little bit. I did want to do it, I really did. But at the same time, I was struggling.

After three of the first four events on day one, Aston called it: my European Championships were over. 'I'm just going to make this decision for us,' he said, because he knew that I wouldn't. I think it's a hard thing to do as a coach; to make a decision for someone else. But he knew that my Achilles was bad and that even though I probably could finish the heptathlon, it would mean two weeks off afterwards to calm the injury down again – and we needed that time between Rome and Paris.

I'd wanted to do the next event, the 200m, because that had actually been going well in training at the time, but Aston wasn't having it. 'That's literally like Tokyo; the right side, going round the bend . . . what is the point in risking it? Let's just wait.' I knew he was right, but I was also hyper-aware that it meant the end of my dream of holding all the titles at once. I know I had no guarantee of Olympic success, but I'd so badly wanted the chance heading into Paris.

I have enough humility to admit that I mourned the end of that dream. Denise's input helped me through it – both in Rome, where she took me out the next day and came with me to watch the end of the heptathlon, and afterwards, when she (once again) helped me draw up a plan for the following two months. I knew I had to try to refocus, because ultimately the Olympics was what I wanted; an Olympic medal was what I really *really* wanted. And we only had eight weeks to avoid a repeat of what had happened in Rome.

Fixing my Achilles was job one. That involved getting an injection of something called Ostenil, which would help free up the tendon from the sheath, because they were sticking together. After that it was just about loading the tendon properly, multiple times a day. It wasn't a quick fix; I was still struggling with it for about a month after Rome, and then it gradually started going away.

That whole time, there was never any thought in my head that I wouldn't make it to the Olympics; I just didn't know in what form I'd make it there. The Achilles was always something that I could manage with painkillers and strapping but it didn't make sense to do that for Rome; I wanted to put that effort into the Olympics. For a Games, I would fight through the pain. I can do that easily; I've been doing it most of my life.

I knew I was better than the performances I put out in those three events in Rome. Going into it, I was aware I wasn't in a great place. I was saying out loud to Aston that I wasn't ready, but he just thought it was my confidence, like it had been the year before, and told me that training was going well. And it was going well – I was putting out good times – but that was masking the impact that media work and anxiety over my fitness were having on me. Looking back, I think all my effort and energy had gone into making sure that my training stayed strong despite that external stuff. So, by the time I got to the start line in Rome, I didn't have much left. Point being, we weren't starting from rock bottom after the Europeans, we just needed to make things right; make the right decisions around comps in the lead-up to Paris, the right decisions around injuries, and cut out as much media as possible.

We decided I wouldn't do any more hurdles comps until I was more confident in the event. My hurdles had been a bit of an issue all year, to the point that Pozz came in to help me with them after he broke his ankle in training for the Olympics; an injury that ultimately prompted his decision to retire from the sport. He became my hurdles coach, which actually really helped with the process of drilling in the right patterns of movement. He was dealing with huge life decisions at that time, calling time on his career when he'd been so close to competing at his fourth Olympic Games. I knew he was putting on a brave face for me; it felt like he was the strongest he'd ever been in that moment. He was taking control of his life and deciding his future himself. It was inspiring for me to see that, while he was obviously disguising his feelings about his situation so as not to worry me, he was completely at peace with every decision he'd made and the way that he had committed to both the 2024 Olympic campaign and his career.

Once we put the plan into practice, training started going really well. There were still various stresses around injuries (pretty much a different thing each week), but it was nothing that was stopping me completely, nor distracting me as had happened before Rome. When I did compete, I was competing tired because I was training hard, but I was still getting results, which made me feel like I was in a good place going into Paris. The Europeans had thrown me a little bit; they'd shown me that my mind was still capable of fucking things up.

All I wanted was to be competitive on the day and to be able to respond to the competition around me – and not be the person in Rome who looked (and performed) like she didn't want to be there.

The heptathlon was placed right at the end of the athletics schedule (which ran during the second week of the Olympics), so I sat at home watching the Paris opening ceremonies on TV, just like everyone else. I did my last comp in Birmingham on the Sunday after the Games started, which was a real full-circle moment for me. Birmingham used to be the place where everything was held when I was a kid, whether that was the English Schools or the Young Athlete League finals – I spent so many weekends in that stadium. And the comp itself was an England Athletics one, which I would definitely have done when I was a young teen, so it was all really familiar. A lot of athletes did their last comp before the Olympics at the London Diamond League a week earlier (I competed there, too), which is all glitz and glamour, in a stadium packed with thousands of people. This couldn't have been more different; I think the crowd in Birmingham might have amounted to about a hundred people. But it was a really nice way to be sent off to the Olympics; it felt like I was going back to the start before one of the biggest moments of my life.

After competing, I changed clothes in the car and drove straight from the track to the airport to catch a flight to Paris. After one day in the holding camp with all the other Team GB athletes, about 70 per cent of them went into the Village and there were just a handful of us left for the following week, so it was pretty quiet.

There were plenty of familiar faces, though, because MJ was

there, as were Aston and Sarah. Charles (van Commenee) came in and out to do some shot put with me, and Bruno came to do my last 600 session with me on the bike. It was like a Mount Rushmore of all the people who had played such an important role in getting me through the previous few years.

The Village was pretty much the polar opposite of the calm, safe vibe in the holding camp. In 2012, I loved the whole Village experience. At the time, I was living in my nan's box room, so rooming with all my mates in the Village was the best – and there was a twenty-four-hour McDonald's! But these days, I like my own space. I've also experienced Village life a few times now, and it's different for me now. In Paris, there weren't as many of the people I would usually hang out with. This was partly because my event was on at the very end of the Games, and they'd already competed; partly because some had retired; and partly because some were injured. It was more of a lonely experience in 2024. But also, there are a few things that just don't work for me: I don't like the cardboard beds. I don't like the thin walls. I don't like the mattresses. I don't like the Village food, but also I don't like how the food hall is so far away from where I've stayed every single time. I don't like being around people who have finished competing and haven't got that same vibe as you. And I just don't like how long it takes to get everywhere.

So, yeah, not a huge fan!

Aston gets itchy feet when he's somewhere for too long; I think he just gets bored. So when I asked him, the day before we were due to move into the Village, what he thought about just staying in the holding camp and commuting in for the hep, he looked at me, horrified. 'I'm going into the Village tomorrow,' he said. 'You can do what you want, but I'm going.' That was the decision made, then. Three nights before the heptathlon, we moved into the Village. It was obviously a nicer experience than in Tokyo, because not everyone was in masks, there were no plastic dividers at the dining tables and there were more people about – but it's still not ideal. You spend your whole year making sure you eat right, sleep right, and do all of this preparation, then you go into the Village and it's just like being in student halls during Freshers' Week. It's mad.

Despite the beds and the paper-thin walls, I did actually sleep well the night before the heptathlon started. I've learned how to switch off my mind when I'm going to bed the night before a big comp; it's something Steve Peters helped me with a few years ago, so I'm pretty well versed in it now. It's about understanding that there's actually no need for you to be nervous until that very moment of 'On your marks'. So, when I'm going to sleep the night before, I can just say to myself, 'Now is the time to sleep. There's no point in thinking about it right now. Just sleep and you can think about it during warm-up tomorrow.' It's a way of staying in the moment. I can only do it for a comp, though. When it comes to life issues, it's a different story!

By the time I got to the track the next morning, I wasn't nervous. When I stepped out into the Stade de France, I was just excited. It was incredible. All three tiers of the stadium were full of people (there were a lot of Team GB supporters), and that purple track was beautiful. It was just so aesthetic. It was crazy pretty.

The only thing I would have changed if I could was being in the first heat, which I don't love. It was the slowest one of the lot, which wasn't ideal, but I tried to change my feelings about it by reminding myself that I'd been training by myself in the hurdles all year, running my own race (not measuring myself against anyone else), so it was just the same as that.

I had a clear idea of what I needed to do in each of my events, particularly the hurdles. It was all about getting a good start, because I'd had a problem with hesitating about three steps into the race. So, on the start line, I was thinking about the rhythm going into that first hurdle. It was like a metronome sounding in my head: *de, de, de, de-de-de*. Then it was about trying to attack, lean forward with my shoulders, and sprint. I was happy with the result: 13.40 seconds was the best I'd run in a heptathlon for years. It wasn't the perfect start, but it was a really good one.

It was a big season's best, which meant that I was in a great headspace moving on to the high jump – I had been struggling so much all year with the hurdles. It's such an important event; not just because of its point score, but also because it's the first event of the heptathlon. It sets the tone for the next two days, and this performance confirmed that I was not the same athlete I was in Rome. I was my best self and I was there to compete! We had achieved the turnaround we'd needed.

The high jump was next, and that was where everything shifted. The high jump used to be My Event, but after my Achilles rupture, that had changed. I'd been stuck with people who were jumping 1.83 and 1.80 metres, sometimes 1.86 if I was lucky. I so badly wanted to get back into the 1.90s. In Paris, I entered the comp at a modest 1.77, clearing it first time and doing the same with the next two heights at 1.80 and 1.83. I watched as Nafi cleared the next height (1.86) with ease, and then it was my turn. I attacked the bar with good speed, planted, jumped and brushed the bar with the top of my back. Damn. On my next attempt, I executed it almost exactly the same, but this time I flew over with room to spare. There were just four of us left attempting the next height: 1.89. It was the one we knew I needed to get if I was going to be in the running for a medal. Nafi cleared it first time. I stood on my mark, closed my eyes and went through my cues.

Go time.

I ran at the bar, jumped and brushed the bar with the top of my back for a second time. It was almost a carbon copy of the previous height. No panic, though. I knew I had more in me. And I was right; on my second attempt, I cleared it! I was so happy – I even allowed myself a little celebratory shout on the mat. It felt amazing to be back in the later stages of a high jump as the number of competitors got whittled down.

1.92 metres next, and it was just me, Nafi and Anna Hall left. Nafi soared over it first time again. Time to respond.

I hit the bar heavily on my first go. On the second, it was more of a light brush, but it still followed me down to the crash mat. I put my hands over my mouth; I'd been so close. I had one chance left to match Nafi and jump the highest I had in five years.

One last shot.

Attack. The. Bar.

When I landed on the mat, the crowd let out a huge roar. I felt it and I reciprocated, releasing a huge shout and actually allowing myself to celebrate. 1.92! It was a HUGE moment – both for me personally, being back in the 1.90s, but also for me in the competition. It put me right in the picture for a medal, and that was something I had barely allowed myself to think about until that moment. I was absolutely buzzing. To come away from that event with an advantage – Anna hadn't cleared 1.92, so it was just me and Nafi who'd hit that height – meant I felt like I had *returned*, both as a medal hopeful and as a top-class high jumper.

I allowed myself to really enjoy it, too. That was another one of my goals for Paris; I had been working on being more uninhibited. My joyful reaction was a real one. I was overwhelmed by emotion – whatever came out, came out. But I was also consciously trying not to care what I looked like. I wasn't wearing make-up. I wasn't bothered about the noises I was making or my facial expressions. This heptathlon, I just wanted to be me.

It's something I'm trying to work on in general: to not care about being judged. To not put on a mask. Sometimes when you see me compete, you can see my lips are almost folded in on themselves, as if I'm trying to stop myself from speaking. A lot of my competition pictures are like that, where instead of my lips you can just see the line between them because I'm holding something back – a scream, a shout, some words. But I've been working on just being me. I've been thinking about why women believe they have to spend a lot more time getting ready in the morning and putting a 'presentable' face on. In the heptathlon, we have no time! I'm already waking up at 6.45 a.m.; why should I wake up at 5.30 a.m. to put on a full face of make-up? In Paris, I made a conscious choice not to do it. (Although, in the interests of full disclosure, I should say that I put a bit of concealer under my eyes before the 800m, because I was looking really tired, but that was the only make-up I had on for the entire comp.)

Unbroken

At the start of the evening session, I was 24 points ahead of Nafi, but with one of her strongest events up next: the shot put. I went into it feeling like there was the potential for something good to happen for me, though. At the warm-up track beforehand, we'd done a little activation session and I threw the shot really far. Aston and Charles were coaching out of their skins; I felt so positive, and found myself executing every cue they suggested with complete clarity. I could feel distance being added to my throw. After my big practice throw, everyone started packing up to go back to the stadium, but I was desperate for someone to measure how far it had gone; I was sure it was over 14 metres. But because we were at the Olympics and we were in a throws area where specialists warmed up, the first marker was way out at 18 metres – so I couldn't know for sure where mine were landing. I was desperate to ask Aston to get his tape measure to find out the distance but I bit my lip because I knew he'd just tell me to do the same thing in the comp.

As the event started, I knew that I had a big throw in me, or at least that things were going well. That was why after my first throw of 13.38 metres, which was actually a really good throw for me, I looked a bit disappointed. After my second throw, I sat and watched as Nafi threw big: 15.54 metres. She was in the other shot put pool to me, Group B, but I'd set up my bags facing theirs rather than my own Group A throwers. It's something I sometimes do when I'm feeling confident or feeling like I need to be pushed (I remember doing it in Budapest in 2023). But I think you need to be in a really good headspace to do that, because it could just send you the opposite way if you're not.

Patience. Load. Explode. I repeated those three words to

myself constantly throughout the shot put. They were the cues we'd been working on for months, drilling in what they meant for my technique; and by the time Paris came around, they were a really clear instruction for what I had to do. Instead of a list of instructions like 'turn your foot' or 'keep your head back', these were just three words that had meaning. It was really good coaching.

I think my third throw was a direct response to Nafi's. The moment it left my hand it felt like a big one. I watched it thinking, *14.00 metres, maybe, or 14.01?* When I saw it soar beyond the 14-metre line, I couldn't believe my eyes. It was incredible!

I was probably unreasonably happy with that moment. After all, it was a very modest throw in the grand scheme of things – but so much work went into that shot put. I threw 11.68 metres in Rio – it was such a big turnaround to hit 14.44 in Paris, and I was just so happy to nail a distance that measured up against my effort. A lot of the time I do high jump and I reach a good height but I know it's something I've always done. The shot put is so different; I enjoyed that throw more than I enjoyed my 1.98-metre high jump record in Rio, I really did. In my BBC interview afterwards, I dedicated it to Denise, because she and Charles have always said I could do it. She's been so invested in my shot put over the years, so it was a long time coming!

Day one was turning into one of the best days I'd had in a long time. The only disappointment came in the 200m, which is an important event for me, and one I was hoping to do well in, considering I'd run 23.20 seconds in Manchester at the end of June when it was cold and rainy. Training had been going well, too, so when I crossed the line in 23.44 seconds, I was a bit gutted. As I went through my cooldown rigmarole, I felt the frustration of not being able to continue the pattern of getting a season's best or PB as I'd done in the first three events. I felt I could have done better. But I tried to take the positives from it: I was the fastest out of the heptathletes, everyone was down on what they could do, and my heat was run into a headwind when the others all had a tailwind. Sometimes you just have to accept what you have and I knew that ultimately it hadn't been a bad day at all.

So much always depends on the long jump; that's what makes it such a nervy event.

I still don't really know what happened on my first jump, apart from the fact that my leg seemed to buckle about eight steps out from the board, and so I ended up just running through it. Straight away that threw me into a bit of a tailspin: *Oh god, what did you even do? Did my leg buckle? Was I in the right place on the board? Would I have been in the right place if that didn't happen? Is the wind a headwind? A tailwind?* I just didn't know any of the answers. So we thought, OK, we'll just try again and do the second jump the exact same, hoping that was a one-off error that's not going to happen again.

My second one, I stuttered really badly into the board. Maybe it was because of the wind, which was swirling that morning, or maybe it was because on the first one I actually should have moved my run-up back. Either way, it wasn't anywhere near what I needed to be in the race. If that had been my finishing jump, I would have been fighting for a bronze medal.

Katarina Johnson-Thompson

Throughout the whole long jump comp, I was keeping a close eye on what Nafi was doing. Every time she jumped and didn't get a 6.60 metres, I felt like I'd been let off the hook; like it was still in my hands even though I hadn't jumped further than 6.04. I still felt like I was in control because she wasn't shutting the door on me. In my head, I was still in it. And I still had my third jump to go.

Pozz was in the crowd watching and he's already said he'll never do it again because that long jump competition was so horrible to watch. I felt like I was mentally strong, though. I wasn't letting myself panic until it was actually done. I was just trying to get a proper jump together.

In my third attempt, I jumped 6.40 metres, just 1 centimetre behind Nafi. It wasn't the performance I wanted before the event began, but when I reflect on my journey now, I can see this was a full-circle moment. At every apparent impasse, I was a competitor, pulling out a big performance from the jaws of despair. I no longer shied away from these moments, I met them head on and came out on top. We'd both known that if I could have gained 20 centimetres on her there, that would have been the end, and vice versa. Similarly, if I had gained half a second on her in the 200m, that would have been the end, too. Funny how it wasn't the shot put, my traditional foil, nor the hurdles, which I'd come into the comp worried about. That's the beauty of the heptathlon, and sport in general; it ebbs and flows, and you never know what's going to happen. Unfortunately for me, I didn't get 20 centimetres on Nafi in the long jump or an extra 0.5 seconds in the 200m.

The javelin only added to my frustrations, because it felt unfair – the only thing I'd describe as unfair in the whole heptathlon. Normally, World Athletics seed the javelin based on heptathlon event standings. Those in the top twelve form Group B, while the bottom twelve in the overall standings form Group A. Group A get to throw first and Group B get to respond and compete against each other. Pretty simple stuff! But in Paris, despite the fact that I was in first position after the long jump, I was put into Group A and Nafi was in Group B. Why?

For those of us in Group A, it was a huge rush to get from the long jump pit to the javelin course. Even before we'd long-jumped, the officials were telling us: 'Group A: make sure you take your things. You won't be able to come back to the rest room. You have to take your javelin spikes out and we're going to go direct over to throw after the long jump.'

Most of the athletes around me in the overall standings who were going for medals were in Group B, so they got to go back into the rest room after the long jump and reset, see their coach and warm up properly. More importantly, they also got to see us throw first, and respond second – which means that every Group B athlete knew before she threw the javelin exactly what distance she'd need to put herself into a good position going into the 800m. Whereas in Group A, we had to get the sand off our legs, put our javelin shoes on, walk directly from the long jump to the javelin, not see our coaches, and throw instantly – all while blind as to our competitors' performances. The whole competition, I'd been in that competitive mode where I was actively responding to the performances around me; I wasn't able to do that in the javelin, and in any other heptathlon I would have been. And that upsets me, because I don't think it should be like that.

It was a horrible position to be in. I knew I needed to create the same intensity I had in the high jump and shot put, but I couldn't, because Nafi wasn't there.

I threw a season's best of 45.49 metres, then I just had to go back into the rest room and eat my lunch while Nafi went to throw, knowing exactly what she needed to do. I was constantly checking my phone between bites of my lunch to see what was happening in Group B, while Aston was having a laugh and a joke trying to distract and keep me busy. He never once asked me what the results were, even though he could see me checking my phone. After Nafi's first throw I finished my food, shovelling the last few bites in all at once, and went to try to get some sleep (the 800m wasn't until 8.15 p.m., so we had many hours to kill).

I'd been in there for about half an hour, and was just falling asleep, when Aston came running in with a huge smile on his face. 'Eight seconds, we've got a chance. It's on!' he said, celebrating the gap that I had to make up on Nafi in the 800m. While everyone else was framing eight seconds as a fairly impossible gap to build, he was celebrating it and making it a positive thing, which was really nice. I was crying when he was doing that; crying with sadness, but laughing at the same time, thinking: *I do have a chance. This is horrible, but I'm really enjoying it.* THIS IS WHAT I LIVE FOR! *It's all I've ever wanted, but at the same time, I've lost the gold.* BUT I STILL HAVE A CHANCE!

All these different emotions were going through my head at the same time. It was a trip.

For the next five hours, I tried to sleep. You know when I said I'd mastered the art of switching off? Yeah, no.

Eventually, Aston came back in and we just spent the remaining hours chatting about everything. He's not much of a talker,

Unbroken

really, but that day we just couldn't stop. We couldn't stop laughing; laughing out loud. We were like two little kids, just chatting and giggling. I had my feet up on a wall trying to recover my legs and he sat next to me and we just chatted about all sorts: the training group, the journey, funny moments, other competitors. We were saying that Nafi was like the big final level boss of the Olympic Games. The year before, at the World Championships, was a different level. The year before that, at the Commonwealth Games, was a different level again. Each year, the level of the game got harder, and the players became even harder to beat. We'd fought our way through each one and now we were at the final level, facing the toughest opponent yet with no more lives remaining. Honestly, we were a little delirious; we were writing our own story, and giggling so much that people must have been walking past thinking, *Are they all right?*

Bruno and Aston thought I could run a 2:02. I thought I could too, and if I could do that then I had a chance. I knew Anna would run the first lap in around 58.50; I just wanted to stick to her for the first lap, then push from 300m and see what I had left for the last stretch. I expected Nafi to step up and PB because she's that type of athlete. So I didn't think it likely that she was going to run as slow as 2:12 – her PB before Paris. So, when I crossed the line in 2:04, I knew it probably wasn't going to be enough for the gold.

I don't think I could have run that race any better than I did. At the end of a long two days, I think a PB was all I could ask for. I'd gone out swinging and I'm really proud of myself for that.

The first thing Aston said to me after the 800m? 'Game over.'

* * *

Immediately after the race, I was a bit gutted. I was annoyed by how close I was to gold. It was really hard to get my head around. There are always what-ifs, but they're so hard to rely on in sport – because if anything had happened differently, who knows how Nafi would have responded?

By the time the victory lap had finished, though, I was crying with happiness. Happiness for the moment, happiness for the occasion and then, as it sunk in that I'd won an Olympic silver medal, happiness for the journey. Each Olympic cycle, I've pretty much had to start again, and it's that ability to bounce back and keep trying that I think I'm most proud of.

I think that's why I was ultimately happy in the end, because mine is a success story. It's not like I lost gold, because from where I was at, it was a really, really big turnaround. Even when you look at where I came from after Rome, it's a big turnaround. What we did in the six weeks before Paris is something that has given me that 'no regrets' attitude towards the medal. I am proud of my comeback. I got my second-best-ever score in Paris. I didn't believe Aston when he first said I could be back better than ever – I didn't even believe him in 2023, to be honest – but now I've finally started to believe that I can still do this.

I still think I can PB my score. With a different set of circumstances in the long jump and 200m, I think I could add another 150 points to my score. So I feel like it's definitely there to be taken if I want. I've found a different way to put together my heptathlon, one which I'm really happy about. Sport is not for ever, so I'm really happy that I can keep it going and remain competitive.

I love that I pushed right until the end for gold. I wasn't

scrapping to get onto the podium, I was pushing for gold, which, a couple of years ago, I don't think anyone could ever see happening again.

Since Paris, I've been thinking a lot about the journey I went on. Truth be told, I *do* feel a little bit sad after the Olympics, even though I know that it was a really good result for me. And I don't know if that sadness is because I didn't win.

I think maybe instead it's because I enjoy the journey so much more than the result. For example, I feel like the last 800m session that I did before Paris, when everything was in the air and the anticipation of the Games was high and we knew that I was in good shape and we didn't know what was going to happen . . . I feel like that was a nicer experience than the actual race. And the gap in between the javelin and the 800m, when me and Aston were just absolutely chatting each other's heads off talking about everything and having a massive laugh? I live for those moments probably more than anything else. As much adversity as I've faced in the past three years, they've been amazing for those kinds of moments – moments that today are so much more precious to me than any actual comps.

I'm sad that my (latest) Olympic journey has stopped now, more than anything else. I'm really sad about that. After focusing on two days for the past two years, the comedown has been tricky. I'd been wanting to be back in Liverpool for so long but, when I finally got home, I just couldn't sit still. I've had that feeling after Olympics in the past, but I always thought it was because I hadn't done well. Now I've realized that, for all my mental anguish, it wasn't that at all; it was because the thing was over.

Katarina Johnson-Thompson

One thing I know for sure is that I'm not done with the sport. I can't give up now, given the way that silver medal was won. I can definitely look towards 2025, and to two home championships in 2026 (the European Championships in Birmingham and the Commonwealth Games in Glasgow); it would be incredible to try to do well there. Beyond that, who knows – but a Hollywood ending is not off the cards.

For now, I just hope people read my story and get something from it.

There will be days when you think you're at rock bottom, and then there will be days when it gets worse than that – and then worse again. But there's always a way out. Even if you've messed yourself up beyond recognition, there's a way back. I don't know that I was ever destined to be a world champion; in fact, when I think about all the things that had to go right, it sometimes feels like I trumped destiny to get here. But it doesn't matter. Screw fate – fortitude is better. And it's something we all have in us. Humans are pathetic, obnoxious, petty creatures, but they possess an innate willpower, a strength to survive increasingly difficult circumstances, and a determination to find happiness and hope in the most despairing of times. That's the club you were born into. It's pretty amazing, when you think about it.

And to all the young athletes out there, reading this: the idea that each championships feels like the end of the world is one of the most inspiring, romantic, backwards and essential contradictions of our sport. But try not to get too lost in it. Use it to fuel you, use it to push yourself and use it to learn – but never forget that there's always another chance. If you get injured, or completely screw up an event, or lose inspiration for months

Unbroken

at a time, that is not the end of you. Whatever you're struggling with, just remember: you're not the first person to face it, you will overcome it, and it doesn't have to hold you back for ever.

There's always hope, even in the darkest spaces. Sometimes, it just takes a little while to find it.

All about me:

Now that you know the story of my life, can I ask you a few things?

Would I prefer inner peace or Olympic gold? What brings me the most joy in life? Am I more comfortable at home in Liverpool or in a place where nobody knows who I am? Am I happier maintaining the status quo or changing things up? Would I rather have a large group of acquaintances or a small group of close companions?

What's more important to me: the outcome or the journey?

I went back and forth for a long time over whether or not to do this book. I've been approached a few times over the years, but I always said no. I'm uncomfortable being the centre of attention. I'm still getting used to the idea that letting stuff out can be better for me than keeping it all in. And I'm wary of how some sections of the media might use (or abuse) the truths I've shared.

But, ultimately, I did this because I wanted to help others.

Maybe I'm maturing; maybe I'm becoming a more rounded person; maybe I've been humbled by my experiences. But what motivates me now is helping others to find their path. Mine was rocky; it had twists and turns, dead ends, cliff edges, U-turns, blackouts and full-on car crashes, but I stayed behind the wheel – even if I *did* get out of the car every now and again.

Hopefully, sharing my route might help others to find a different one; one with more clear roads, signposts and street lights. If this book does that, even for one person, then my entire journey, from despair to glory, will have been more than worth it.

Acknowledgements

Thank you to my mum. My journey is your journey.

Pozz, I am grateful for every day since we found each other. My Mac Mittens!

Sarah Shephard and Ause Abdelhaq, thank you for your patience, understanding and late nights! I'm also grateful to Melissa Bond, Siân Chilvers, Josie Turner, Rosa Watmough and everyone else at Pan Macmillan for their hard work and support in writing this book.

I'm so indebted to Aston Moore for his belief in my resurrection, Michael Johnston for helping me to build my second chance, Bruno Gajer for his perspective on life – summertime baby! – Bertrand Valcin for sculpting this lost athlete into a champion heptathlete and Mike Holmes for lighting this fire and setting my wheels in motion.

Francesca, you understand me better than anyone and, in turn, you help me understand myself. Thank you.

Katarina Johnson-Thompson

To Steve Peters: thank you for helping me out of the well so. Many. Times!

Thanks also to Greg Kirkpatrick and Daniel Smith – you push me out of my comfort zone and you're always there to help and support me in all situations. You're the best.

Thank you to my family and friends, including but not limited to Lauren, Jodie, Liv, Charlotte, David, Celie, Leila, Marie, Colette, James, Kathleen, Margy, Toni, Kasia, Antoinette and Samantha; for always being there for me, no matter the result.

And finally, back to where it all started: to Mr Coakley, thank you for giving me the opportunity to fall in love with athletics.

Picture Credits

All pictures courtesy of the author's friends and family unless otherwise stated.

Page 5 (top and bottom) © *Athletics Weekly*.
Page 5 (middle) © David Ramos via Getty Images.
Page 7 (top) © GABRIEL BOUYS via Getty Images.
Page 7 (bottom) © *Athletics Weekly*.
Page 8 (top) © Ian Walton via Getty Images.
Page 8 (bottom) © Cameron Spencer via Getty Images.
Page 9 (top) © Ian Walton via Getty Images.
Page 10 (top) © Matt Lewis via Getty Images.
Page 10 (bottom left) © Mike Marsland via Getty Images.
Page 12 (top right) © Gabby Logan via X/Twitter.
Page 12 (bottom) © Matthias Hangst via Getty Images.
Page 13 (top middle) © GABRIEL BOUYS via Getty Images.
Page 13 (top right) © KARIM JAAFAR via Getty Images.

Katarina Johnson-Thompson

Page 14 (bottom) © Christian Petersen via Getty Images.
Page 15 (bottom) © KIRILL KUDRYAVTSEV via Getty Images.
Page 16 © (bottom) Christian Petersen via Getty Images.